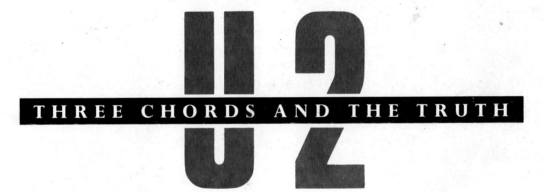

U2

THREE CHORDS AND THE TRUTH

NIALL STOKES

AND THE EDITORS

OF **HOT PRESS** MAGAZINE

HARMONY BOOKS

N E W Y O R K

Liam Mackey

Niall Stokes

Edited by NIALL STOKES
with Liam Mackey

Designed by Paul Wonderful

All photographs by Colm Henry
(except where otherwise indicated)

Cover Pic: Anton Corbijn

CONTRIBUTORS:
Liam Fay, Bill Graham, Graham Linehan, Liam Mackey, Neil
McCormick, Pat Singer, Sam Snort, Dermot Stokes,
Niall Stokes

PRODUCTION:
Jackie Hayden, Mairin Sheehy, Damian Corless, Pamela Burke,
Yasmina (Les Fleurs Du Mal)

Typesetting by Jack Broder
for Hot Off The Press Productions

Production Editor, Hot Press: Mairin Sheehy

Printed by Lithographic Universal, Bray, Ireland

Positives by Cosmon, Dublin 2, Ireland

Published by Harmony Books, a division of Crown Publishers, Inc.,
201 East 50th Street, New York, New York 10022.

Originally published in Ireland by Hot Press, 6 Wicklow St., Dublin 2.

Harmony and colophon are trademarks of Crown Publishers, Inc.

Manufactured in Ireland.

Library of Congress Cataloging-in-Publication Data.

U2: Three Chords and the Truth/by Hot Press Magazine:
edited by Niall Stokes.

1. U2 (musical group) 2. Rock musicians — Ireland — Biography.
I. Stokes, Niall. II.Hot Press.
ML421.U2U1 1989   89-20085
782.42166'092'2 — dc20

ISBN 0-517-57697-X
10 9 8 7 6 5 4 3 2 1

First American Edition.

SPECIAL THANKS: To Bono, Larry, Adam, The Edge, Paul McGuinness, Ann-Louise Kelly, Barbara Galavan and everyone in the
U2 organisation. To Rob, Regine, and the Island press corps. To Michael Pietsch in the US. To Ossie Kilkenny, Steve Averill, Alan Leamy
and Anton Corbijn. And especially to Liam Mackey, Jack Broder, Paul Wonderful, Colm Henry and all the staff at *Hot Press*.

For Duan and Rowan

INTRODUCTION

BY NIALL STOKES

"All I've got is a red guitar
Three chords and the truth... "

SOMETIMES THE simplest statements are the most powerful. There is of course a whole lot more that rock'n'roll can aspire to, musically and politically — but strip it back to the bare essentials and there they are, in that luminous couplet from "Rattle And Hum".

A red guitar, three chords... and the truth, not in any biblical or messianic meaning but in the sense of honesty that's implicit in the phrase. There is a nakedness to those lines that is brutally self-revealing, with Bono cast in the role of the Emperor With No Clothes — except

that in this instance the nakedness is self-imposed, a matter of choice. Forget about superstardom, and the money and pomp and circumstance and status it implies. Strip away all of that and the man in the spotlight still remains in possession of the only things that really matter.

All I've got is a red guitar, three chords and the truth? Yeah, well, sometimes even the President of the United States has to stand naked!

BUT THEN there always has been a nakedness about U2 and their music, a quality which has occasionally seemed like their greatest weakness — while remaining, in truth, their most crucial strength. From the outset it was their willingness to go out on a limb, to take risks, occasionally to make mistakes, but always to aim higher, and strive harder, to realise their full artistic potential, that differentiated them from the rest and gave their every new waxing a fascination and sense of excitement which is greatness' enduring hallmark.

A lot of bands are born great, emerging apparently out of nothing, coining a noise that's fresh, exciting, radical and challenging: rock'n'roll's magnetism centres to a large extent on that kind of instant access to immortality. But the majority burn like fireballs, blazing in the cauldron of their own creative intensity, only to fizzle out one, two or even three albums later. Very few in the turbulent history of rock'n'roll have really been in there for the long haul, growing, developing and maturing in the full unforgiving glare of the spotlight, and successfully producing music that reflects that growth in a constantly intensifying level of creative depth, imaginative scope and artistic assurance. But that is what U2 have achieved, as they battled their way from obscurity to a position on the rock'n'roll frontline, that's simultaneously right at the cutting edge of the music's artistic glory and close to the pinnacle of its commercial power — a rare combination indeed.

The first part of that epic, decade-long voyage was captured in "The U2 File", a collection of interviews, reviews, critiques, confessions and dissertations from the pages of *Hot Press*, which was published in 1985. The book you're now holding, "U2: Three Chords And The Truth" brings the epic saga up-to-date. It opens, however, with a long, lingering and detailed look back at the musical story so far with "The Making Of A Legend", a chapter which is dedicated to a complete musical retrospective, in which U2's total recorded output — from the first Ireland-only EP "U23" right up to and including the various b-sides which have provided a vital supplement to the band's album output from "The Unforgettable Fire" to "Rattle And Hum" — is exhaustively and critically reassessed. The U2 File itself opens with *Hot Press'* coverage of their historic performance at Live Aid, and proceeds chronologically chapter by chapter, through to the close of the decade.

That story brought up to date, "Three Chords And The Truth" also contains a fascinating and detailed account of the increasing range of musical explorations which members of the band have become involved in, away from U2, reflecting the poise and assurance with which they now, individually and collectively, occupy a centre-stage position in the rock'n'roll pantheon...

I suspect I may be accused of tribalism, in suggesting that U2 have occupied that exalted position with greater dignity, and integrity, than almost any other band in the star-crossed history of rock'n'roll, since Elvis Presley's genius was first captured on tape by Sam Philips in Sun Studios in Memphis in 1955. Worse still, it will almost certainly be argued that I'm contributing to the insidious process of deification which has crept up on and around the band, as their collective star has continued in the ascendant. But what the hell! As will be perfectly clear from the various close-ups of the band that follow, on a day to day level Bono, Adam, Larry and The Edge are just four ordinary blokes doing their best to get on with their lives in extraordinary circumstances. Indeed, if and when the band ceases to exist as an

entity, there is no guarantee whatsoever that the individuals involved will continue to make artistic statements which will merit the acclaim to which this book frequently treats them. But that story will be written another time, another place — and right now, the answer is in the grooves. Ordinary blokes they may well be — but together U2 make the most magnificently transcendant noise, of a power and potency that's more capable than ever of, at once, transfixing me and touching me to the core.

From rock'n'roll, I ask for nothing more.

CONTENTS

PART ONE

THE MAKING OF A LEGEND

PART TWO

THE U2 FILE 1985 – 1990

PART THREE

AND NOW FOR SOMETHING

COMPLETELY DIFFERENT

U2

From "Out Of Control" to

THE MAKING OF A LEGEND

"All I Want Is You", Neil McCormick presents a major critical retrospective on the complete recorded works of U2, the band who went from being one of the world's worst cover groups to become a leading force in modern Rock'n'Roll

I WAS looking over an old school photograph the other day. Sixth year, Mount Temple, 1978. Blurred young faces staring earnestly out of the past in grainy black and white. This one here became skateboard and laser sailing champion of Ireland. This one here wound up in prison for rape. This guy here played football for Leeds United. And these two are in one of the most successful, critically-lauded and essential rock bands of our time.

Superstars aren't born, they arrive fully-formed, usually from America. I have laboured under this delusion for years. People often ask me who, on my travels as a journalist, is the most famous person I have ever met. The question throws me; I am not in the habit of consorting with superstars. Celebrities, perhaps. But is Carole King more famous than Paul Weller? Is Ray Davies more famous than Chrissie Hynde? I usually claim Bob Dylan, a certifiable 24-carat superstar, though I actually only stood next to him once, something not generally construed as a meeting.

The most famous people I have ever met were smiling up at me from the photograph.

I feel like sparks are about to suddenly erupt from my fingers every time I try to write about U2. I fear I could go down in a burst of electrical activity. This isn't just history, it's memory. This is my life. Look at the youthful Bono and Edge. Who knew what lay in store for them, for any of us, back then? Eleven years later they've been, along with schoolfriends Adam and Larry, on the cover of *Time* magazine. They're in the papers, they're in the charts, on TV and the silver screen. Sometimes, I walk into a stranger's room to be confronted by their picture, pinned to a wall. I always have to stop myself asking, "How do you know them?". Everybody knows them.

The last time I saw U2 live they were onstage at Wembley and I was standing so close it might as well have been the old school gymnasium. They were extraordinary at Wembley but they were extraordinary at the first performance in the gym, back in '76, too. It seems to me they have always been extraordinary, even when, realistically, they must have been, well, shit. That gig was my first live rock'n'roll and it changed my life. I told Bono so some years later and he could only agree. It changed his life too.

The gap between Wembley Stadium and Mount Temple Gym

is, of course, immeasurable. The distance between the same four individuals in Feedback in 1976 and U2 in 1987 is beyond comprehension. What *is* the same is the spark. "We built ourselves around that spark," said Bono in 1980. It still fires inside them today, spitting white heat at the heart of the matter, connecting them, in some indefinable way, with rock'n'roll greatness. You could feel it, recognise it, believe in it long before it actually exploded the group to life. Many people did. You can feel it, recognise it, believe in it now that the group have attained genuine, irresistible superstar status. Many more people do.

The spark remains constant. Everything else changes. Try listening to U2's 1980 debut album "Boy" back to back with 1988's "Rattle And Hum". Could this be the same group? One determinedly modern, electric combo with big, silvery shards of guitar and stretched, youthful voices, the other a rootsy, rocksy, folksy band with a rough-hewn sound and a growling powerhouse of a vocalist. Over the years the gradual changes can seem almost imperceptible. This is evolution, not revolution. But over seven albums in eight years U2 have redefined and almost completely reinvented themselves.

U2 records are stacked up by my stereo. Twenty-seven of them, including the singles. I've been spinning them all, reminding myself of forgotten pleasures, sometimes opening my eyes to unnoticed weaknesses, trying to see how things look as the dust settles on the rattle and hum. Most of all, catching up on old friends.

I WAS of the feeling it was out of control, I had a crazy notion it was out of control... U2's debut single, "Out Of Control", remains an appropriate anthem with which to have unleashed the group on the world. The song's central image is of an adolescent realising, as Bono has said, "that the two most important decisions in your life have nothing to do with you: being born and dying." And with that vision of personal anarchy, U2 were fired forward into the unknown. The song became, for a time, the mainstay of their live set, opening and closing their gigs, so it is ironic to recall that prior to the release of the record there was a great deal of uncertainty about which of the three songs recorded should feature on the A-side, the matter eventually being settled by a competition on the Dave Fanning Rock Show. At the time "Stories For Boys" was a favoured contender, a poppier and more structured song that, in retrospect, lacks the life-and-death dimension that gives "Out Of Control" its historic perspective.

But how was anyone to know that back then? Our ideas on the band, their own ideas on themselves, were just forming. The "U23" EP, released only on CBS Ireland, introduced a young, new-wave rock group with a distinctive guitar style. Looking

"'Boy' was a stunning album when it came out and it remains an intriguing, original and rewarding one to this day."

back, it all fits quite neatly with the musical preoccupations of the post-punk era (though it should be recalled that, along with bands like The Skids, U2 were establishing the hallmarks of that early 80's sound themselves). This is not a gargantuan, earth-shattering record. It barely touches the feeling U2 were capable of stirring live. The drums are dinky, the playing too fast and, on the third track "Boy/Girl", Bono lapses into singing in a sort of cod-English accent in keeping with the popular style of his Brit-rock contemporaries. Still it has power in the rumbling low bass and The Edge's too sharp but already remarkably inventive and fluid guitar playing, and the songs themselves are more than a little left-field, dealing from four different angles with the character of the Boy, the Bono child, who races in dazed confusion through all three tracks and who was to go on to provide the central theme for all of what can now be seen as the first phase of U2's output.

"U23" now sounds like a public demo, the shaping of things to come — as indeed it was. But the B-side of their second CBS Ireland single is an even rougher beast, an early four-track recording of "Twilight" (later to be improved on their debut album, along with "Out Of Control" and "Stories For Boys"), complete with an unchecked bass mistake, very dubious timing and a contrived, hiccuping vocal. It sounds unformed and naive but, in its exposure of the group's essence, it is somehow far more in character than the A-side, "Another Day". Produced, like the previous single, by Chas de Whalley and U2, this was a relatively new song that brought the Boy bouncing back, protesting about the conditioning of childhood. An uncertain attempt at a bright, modern, new-wave pop-piece, it remains U2's weakest ever single, interesting only in that it reflects an area of sound, structure and approach that ran through a lot of their early live material. It has something in common, for example, with the riffing rock of "Cartoon World", a striking, straight ahead rock song that boasted an unusually concise and exact lyric for Bono at the time (*"Jack and Jill went up the hill/They dropped some acid and they popped some pills!/It's a cartoon world"*) but which they completely abandoned before embarking on their recording career proper.

That began when they signed to Island and released "11 O'Clock Tick Tock", a 45 which has subsequently repeatedly been voted the No 1 Single Of All Time on the Dave Fanning Rock Show. A remarkable record, it showcased an unusual and individual rock group of a character as yet only hinted at on vinyl. It was their first recording in Windmill Studios, which subsequently became virtually their home from home, and they were working with a new and more accomplished producer, Martin Hannett, an eccentric who was briefly British rock's main

Bono and Ali

The Edge

Neil McCormick (badge)

Mount Temple, Dublin, the Class of '78. Bono (then, Paul Hewson) is third from the left in the front row and beside him is his wife-to-be, Alison Stewart. The Edge (then, Dave Evans) is fifteenth from the left and almost in the centre of the fourth row. His lapel badge probably bears the insipient legend, U2. Finally, Neil McCormick, the writer of this and other chapters in the book is sixth from the right in the second row. His lapel badge probably refers to his own first and short-lived band, Frankie Corpse And The Undertakers.

Turn on your radio!

sonic influence due to his early work with the likes of Joy Division and Teardrop Explodes.

In fact, the sound of the record reflects the influence and preoccupations of Hannett far more than it does the still crystallising U2. It's a dark, cavernous aural landscape featuring a white-noise snare and guitars that are not so much metallic as rusty. As the band swiftly moved on to develop a more even-keeled relationship with Steve Lillywhite, "11 O'Clock Tick Tock" has been left as a strange anachronism — a one-off, utterly different to what went before but just as divorced from what was to follow.

It remains an outstanding piece of work, featuring a coruscating riff (which, controversy has it, was pilfered wholesale from Irish contemporaries The Atrix) and giving Bono the long-needed room to say more by saying less. This time the singer isn't all over the song, he's deep in the heart of it. Though his voice is still thin and undeveloped it suits the harsh production and fits the yearning mood. This is a song for and about children of the night, rock audiences and fashion victims desperate to establish individuality in life's identity parade yet sadly channeling their energies in futile directions. *"We thought we had the answers, it was the questions we had wrong,"* he sings. The title does not even appear in the song but stands instead as a guide to how the listener might approach it, defining the mood. The B-side "Touch" (transmuted from an early song called, unconvincingly, "Trevor"), a big, basic, human plot with heavy, heavy guitars, makes an ideal companion piece. It was often remarked (before they became regular fixtures on *Top Of The Pops*) that U2 were not really a singles band yet this record could only exist as a single, the first essential U2 output, made all the more vital

retrospectively by the fact that we would never hear the band sound like this again.

"A D A Y Without Me" is like a white flash compared to the previous record, a speedy, surging, bright, fresh attack, driven by loud clattering drums and, with The Edge's guitar expanded in every way, at long last fleshed out into a more accurate representation of how it sounded live. For U2, Lillywhite was an ideally sympathetic producer, building the sound up from their own raw materials rather than imposing his identity upon them. It is a far more assured and dynamic sound than that of their debut but you can make the connection, trace the development. In fact "A Day Without Me" and "Out Of Control" both deal with similar ideas, a youthful look at death and, in this case, suicide, but production values apart, the earlier song is superior in almost every way. There is no real emotional core to "A Day Without Me", the too-sketchy lyric betrayed by the optimism of the musical feel. Coupled with "Things To Make And Do", a rock instrumental flip of no consequence, it is a less than vital single, though it did serve as an introduction to the redirected sound. And what a sound...

"Boy", U2's first album, breathed with it, was drenched in the shimmering silver rain of The Edge, hammered out with the piledriving reverberations of Larry's kit. It was a stunning album when it came out and it remains an intriguing, original and rewarding one to this day. It was the culmination of years of growth and exploration, but more than that, it was an artefact in itself in which the ideas and talents of the band were distilled in brand new material, as well as established live favourites.

Early U2 songs were built around two characters, The Fool and

Bono on stage at Self-Aid, 1986

The Boy. It seemed the former had been laid to rest without ever having made an appearance on vinyl. Gone were such songs as "Concentration Cramp", "Life On A Distant Planet" and "The Fool". It was probably a very wise decision. Half-remembered lyrics, like *"He's the fool/The street Jester/Hero of society"*, suggest a one-dimensional, even cliched creation. "Boy" could never be accused of those faults.

From the simple, elegant, yet oddly disturbing cover photograph of a young child through to the final, fading after-noises of the album's play-out grooves, "Boy" deals with growth, innocence, adolescence and burgeoning sexuality with an empathy that is rare in the (so often all-too-macho) world of guitar rock. Bono plays at being the catcher in the rye, spreading out his arms to hold on to all the tensions, arrogance, pride, insecurity and irrationality of youth. The lyrics are expressionistic rather than explicit, and sometimes a little too simplistic in language, but they work — perhaps because the group were still young enough to know the feelings they were dealing with. "Boy" evokes, as much as it examines, those feelings.

And it flows. "Boy" is a journey. You get caught up in the opening landslide of "I Will Follow", filled with thundering spiritual promise, and carried without pause to the quiet, closing sadness of "Shadows And Tall Trees", a dripping, acoustic sound picture. "Twilight", "Out Of Control" and "Stories For Boys" had all been re-recorded to dramatic effect, the latter becoming a bellowing anthem. "Another Time, Another Place", a long established set-piece, featuring The Edge impressively on a style of fluid guitar he has not been inclined to since, "A Day Without Me", improving in context, and "The Electric Co", were rushes of pure excitement while other new material — "The Ocean", "An Cat Dubh" and "Into The Heart" (the latter two linking seamlessly together) — was moodier, more delicate and restrained.

Bono has said that he finds it difficult to listen to his early recordings because the singing is so bad. Certainly, in comparison to the grandeur he has since achieved, the singing is weak, but context is everything. The voice here has an identity of its own, radically different to his later dominatingly powerful delivery. It sounds vulnerable but it reflects the song's vulnerabilities. It never seizes the record but it never has to, it is held up in enormous, crashing waves of always riveting guitar. When I listen to "Boy" now I hear the near-perfect creation of a young rock group. But as much as it is the birth of the band who would be kings, it is also the end of a first explosive chapter of growth.

WITH "BOY" U2 exhausted the themes of childhood and

innocence they had been exploring and indeed building themselves upon for many years. They needed not only a new direction but a new core. "I Will Follow" was taken off "Boy" as a single and though it exists very much in the context of that album and the group at that time it also, in retrospect, heralds the changes.

"I Will Follow" is a desperate, driving, optimistic song filled with burning need. Essentially it is a spiritual song and more specifically a Christian one: circumstance may have obscured the point at the time but it seems so obvious now, when Bono sings *"I was blind, I could not see"* and *"I was lost, I am found"*. Spiritual quest — the need to believe and find meaning in something — was present in U2's music from the outset: from their earliest cover version of Peter Frampton's "Show Me The Way", from their first self-penned song "Street Mission" (never released). It is in the fear of death, central to "Out Of Control" in the sense of wonder at the beauty and mystery of the world in "Shadows And Tall Trees", but in "I Will Follow" it is for the first time made direct: it is God, Bono is pledging himself to follow. The song quickly became the centrepiece of U2's live set, replacing "Out Of Control" as a new and more positive anthem.

The single's B-side was a live version of "Boy/Girl", the first of many in-concert performances to appear in an initially futile attempt to capture on vinyl that extra something that U2 always had live. Their touring commitments, as they spread the net worldwide, garnering an ever-growing reputation as an essential live band, meant that, for the first time since they'd begun recording there was a lengthy gap between records. It was nine months before the next single appeared, after added delays due to the band's sensitivity about the song's title in the wake of Dublin's tragic Stardust Ballroom holocaust — a tragedy which occurred in Artane, close to the band's Northside base.

The single was "Fire" and, once again, it sounded like a departure for U2 (though it would turn out to be a misleading one). It lopes and clicks along with a looser, more shambolic, less structured feel than anything U2 had done previously. It is indisputably a rock performance yet it has a slightness of touch about it. The guitar is, for the first time on a U2 single, not a constant, dominating presence, though it effectively steals the limelight as it bursts in and out of the track with spit and fire. Though the lyrics deal with personal struggle, with anger, the music bubbles with optimism and this time the two complement, rather than contradict, each other. It remains one of my favourite U2 records and with the B-side "J. Swallow", a jumbled collage of sounds that might have been recorded under another element, water, it suggested, at the time, a group at ease with themselves, ready to dive off the deep end of possibilities.

> "'October' did not fulfill these high expectations. It reveals a band developing and perfecting their own unique sound, but, somehow, at the expense of content."

"October", their second LP, did not fulfill such high expectations. It reveals a band developing and perfecting their own unique sound — but somehow at the expense of content. The Edge's guitar-work is, once again, the focal point, though the range is wider, more all-encompassing, with an added staccato element making its presence felt. He also introduces a deep, ringing piano, letting it take one solo and fill in where once there was only guitar. Adam's bass playing, often the least noteworthy element of U2, is more assured, with just a hint of contemporary funk influence. The bass sound is fatter and fuller. The drums are like compact thunder with blasts of percussion riding across. The vocals soar with confidence, more assured than before, more varied in texture, though Bono still sounds like a man who's pushing hard against frustrating limits.

The album opens with "Gloria", an all-cylinders-firing patent U2 epic that is one of the most potent hymns ever carved out of rock. And a hymn is exactly what it is. *I try to stand up but I can't find my feet/I try to speak up but only in you am I complete/Gloria in te Domine.*

On "October" U2 embraced their faith and therein lies the rub. With the public revelation that three of them were committed Christians they had been confronted in the press and by their fans with their beliefs, forced to re-examine and reaffirm them, which, as "I Will Follow" had suggested, was something they chose to do with their music. "October" is a spiritual LP, a Christian LP, though it is not preachy, not hellfire and brimstone, not crusading, not evangelical, not even particularly specific. In fact it is not, in retrospect, much of anything. You can tell something is awry with just a glance at the cover. A standard colour photo of four young men in a group, it has no special resonance, lacking the sense of overall vision "Boy" 's cover immediately imparted.

Side one of the album is crammed with excitement, as U2 wail through a sequence of immensely powerful rock performances. "Gloria", "I Fall Down", "I Threw A Brick Through A Window", "Rejoice" and "Fire" all deal in some way with faith and personal struggle, the bottom line emerging on the thrilling "Rejoice": *I can't change the world/But I can change the world in me/I rejoice... *

When I first reviewed this album for *Hot Press*, I was an excitable youth and I was so pleased with the passion, so wrapped up in the explosion of sound on my turntable that I accepted without too much reservation Bono's bare declarations of fealty to his Lord. I no longer can. Lyrically, "October" is a decidedly inarticulate speech of the heart and only on the elegant and quite beautiful title track does it come any way close to conveying the mysteries of faith. In "Tomorrow", a breathy, Uilleann pipe-inspired Irish musical adventure, Bono sings, once again, about death, winding up with a cry to Jesus. It is as if he no longer had questions, he had an answer. But to convince the sceptical,

U2 live, in Dublin, 1979: Edge and Bono

answers have to be supported and defended not simply declared...

On side two only "October" and "Tomorrow" really work for, although the band charge full steam ahead, they are bedevilled by an inadequate sense of direction. "With A Shout (Jerusalem)" is one of my least favourite U2 tracks of all. U2-by-numbers, contrived and lacking in substance, it takes their own sound innovations and abuses them to the point of cliche. "Strangers In A Strange Land" is an impressive evocation of alienation but it is essentially just a picture postcard, a snippet of an idea that drifts off because it has nowhere else to go. "Scarlet"

Bono and wife Ali in 1981

meanders inoffensively but unspectacularly, with Bono litanistically reciting the word *"rejoice"*. And the closer "Is That All?", though it involves a striking band performance, is undermined by Bono's banal repetition of the question *"Is that all you want from me?"*. I suspect he is addressing God but the listener's answer has to be "No!". U2 had already demonstrated that they were capable of so much more.

I have often felt that "October", of all U2's LPs, is the one that has weathered least well. And yet, far from an unequivocal failure, listening to it again reveals numerous pleasures on offer. For one thing, it shows them taking their earlier sound to its full potential: as a hard rock unit, U2 had never before been this cohesive, this tight, this professional... and I suspect that on the whole they never will be again. For, in an odd way, the sound was beginning to let them down: it was taking over, creating a shroud behind which the limitations of the content might be hidden. "October" is an exciting and passionate record even when it completely fails to get to grips with the issues it is addressing. Once the band were plugged in and going, nothing else really mattered: everything they did would sound enormous. For a group so intent on getting right to the heart of the matter, however, this could only be self-defeating. Before we heard from them again there would be more changes afoot...

"Gloria" was released as a single and it remains a classic, possibly the most stirring U2 song of those first years. Once again there was a live B-side, this time a version of "I Will Follow" that adds nothing to the original, though it did provide a sort of double mega-anthem package. U2's next single was to be a one-off, unconnected with an album, the first time they had done this since their Island debut (and, so far, the last). I think I can lay claim to having coined the title (a poor substitute for fame). The phrase 'a celebration' had provided the key point and, as I recall, the headline to my own overwhelmingly positive review of "October". It became a catchword not only associated with but used by the band, getting as close as any word could to the essence of U2's uplifting musical identity. And it became the banner waving heading for their new record — one in which, like "11 O'Clock Tick Tock", the title phrase never appears.

"A Celebration" is a raw, blistering song with a big 60's, Who-like guitar figure, the first hint of a new rock rootsiness. Bono had been making remarks about U2 sounding too much like U2, and though this single had all the hallmarks of their sound, there was something rougher, more aggressive about it. The lyrics too were challenging in tone, still displaying a Christian sensibility but now sounding a warning that Armageddon might be at hand. *"I believe in the bells of Christchurch/Ringing out for this land... I believe in the powers that be/But they won't*

overpower me." Viewed with hindsight it is very much the halfway mark between the old U2 and the band that would emerge on the forthcoming "War".

The B-side, "Trash Trampoline And The Party Girl" is also something of a departure. This bizarre, swinging song has a refreshingly idiosyncratic arrangement and displays an off-beat sense of humour that few would have credited the band with. Not that there are any jokes, you understand, but there is a strange and indefinably poignant cast of characters that might have wandered in off a Tom Waits' track, and when Bono sings *"you know what I mean"* nobody really does. Call it surrealist comedy — but whatever it is, it works. Interestingly "Party Girl" became a live favourite, even appearing on the "Under A Blood Red Sky" live mini-album, while "A Celebration" seems to have disappeared without a trace, rarely having ever been played live and apparently having now been deleted as a single. I suspect the band's dissatisfaction with the song lies in the lyric's inability to quite get to grips with their intent. If it is meant to show an acceptance of the existence of worldly powers while rejecting their personal hold on the singer, lines like *"I believe in the third world/I believe in the atomic bomb"* certainly invite misinterpretation.

"New Year's Day", the follow-up and the first taster of "War" is something else again, a song of which the band can and do remain justifiably proud. It is a pulsing, gently locomotive piece propelled not by the usual U2 guitar figures but by resonating piano chords and a modern, throbbing bass. When the guitar does come in its effect is sensational without being domineering; its figure is linear, travelling with the track, adding bursts of colour with an almost minimalist restraint which only "Fire" had successfully hinted at. And the voice is different. Just as the rest of the band hold back, it moves stage-centre: forced to take charge, Bono is straining at the leash, extending his range, digging for fresh passion and finding it.

This was the band's most contemporary performance to date, fitting in oddly with prevailing rock-dance trends and it provided them with their first hit single. In some ways it is a love song —not this time about the love of God but centering on a more human concept of love and how it can overcome conflict. And not this time interior conflict either but the physical travails of flesh and blood. It is about a moment of quiet on the western front. This is U2 in the real world.

Together with the B-side "Treasure (Whatever Happened To Pete The Chop)" (an obscure title that refers, for no apparent reason, to a character Bono had met in New York and written a never-released song about), it introduced some of the themes which would surface on the forthcoming album. "Treasure" — a

> **"On 'War', The Edge had evidently decided to make things difficult for himself and find new ways to approach playing his instrument."**

A pensive U2 during their first major British tour in 1980

rougher, less well-formed attempt at a track that would evoke a similar feel to the A-side — rails against the endless repetition of the same old songs: *"I think it's time to get it right,"* sings Bono. He's not singing about the charts, he's singing about rebel songs, history endlessly repeating itself. He's singing about...

"War"! After "Boy" Bono had talked to me about making an epic album, their Sergeant Pepper he'd called it in a moment of extravagant enthusiasm, an album about good and evil, an album about struggle. "October", whatever the band's intent, was not it. "War" at least saw them coming close.

It may seem strange to say so now but at the time it was a shocker of an album. Not least because, as I have already suggested, the group were, in effect, abandoning their sound, to build themselves up again along new guidelines. The drums, for example, were surprisingly rough: harder, uglier, more basic than before. A sharp snare replaced the sonic-boom of reverb that had provided such an awesome back-drop to previous recordings. It was as if Larry had sacrificed his special effects to lend the band a tougher feel. Adam's bass playing, though always straightforward and to the point, acknowledged a host of contemporary influences from the dance sphere. And, most noticeably, the guitar had been stripped, not of its power perhaps, but certainly of the automatically giant sound created by The Edge and his way with effects.

The Edge was never a guitar hero in the old mould, never really a virtuoso, a wizard of dexterity. He had relied instead on imagination, and especially an ability to shape and control his guitar sounds. On "War" he had evidently decided to make things difficult for himself and find new ways to approach his instrument. Suddenly here, he's playing rock'n'roll, playing

acoustic, playing rough-cut funk and playing havoc with the atmospherics, all the time underpinning the songs rather than taking them over.

And they *are* songs. Much later in his career Bono was to become publicly enamoured of 'the song' as a special creation, something far removed from old U2 material which he almost disparagingly redefined as existing only as performances within the boundaries of the band's identity. "I've just discovered 'the song'," he was saying with amazement post-"The Unforgettable Fire", as though he had never written one before. But even in the light of his new terms of classic reference he was being unduly harsh on U2's older work. "War" is a collection of distinct songs, melodic and well-formed, with greater *individual* identity and more complex lyrics than anything U2 had done previously. And in writing those lyrics it was as if the singer had decided to take charge.

Bono and The Edge have always been the lynchpins of the group (not to detract from Larry and Adam's engine room contributions) but while Bono's personality was the key to U2's live appeal it was The Edge who starred on the records. With "War" Bono came into his own, stamping his passionate personality on the music, determined to evoke the feelings and express, in his own words, the ideas to which U2 aspired. And the words themselves came pouring out. For the first time in his career as a lyricist, Bono risked being called verbose.

The album opens with "Sunday Bloody Sunday": with its cascading violins, military drumming and roared vocal, it represents an angry, emotional cry for U2's divided country. Not a rebel song, but not a peace anthem, it is, rather, a battle-cry for love. It demands humanity from humans. *"And the battle's just* begun/There's many lost but tell me who has won?/The trenches dug within our hearts/And mother's children, brothers, sisters torn apart... How long, how long must we sing this song?". It is, quite unusually for a U2 song, unequivocal in its stance, not relying on subconscious imagery and not open to individual interpretation.

"Seconds", which mutates in an acoustic fashion from the same drumming and a reversed riff, widens the battleground, railing against the nuclear threat hanging over our heads. Interestingly the lead vocal is taken by The Edge, though, as is often the case within a group, the influence of the lead singer serves to make the two voices almost indistinguishable.

The sense of longing — for peace —conjured by "New Year's Day" is followed by "Like A Song", on which Bono vents his frustration at the impossibility of halting the fighting, whether through violence or love. It is a frenzied, spluttering performance, a long way from the shiny, powerhouse rock of "October". The side ends with "Drowning Man", a sometimes clumsy but moving declaration of love, the singer's voice almost fragile as he finds personal solace in the arms of another, losing himself at the same time in a strange musical landscape.

Side one is a conceptual journey across fields of conflict, supported by the saving grace of love. Side two takes us to America, takes us to the wasteland. It opens with "The Refugee", a sloppy storm of a song, a hard, pummelling African-influenced blow-out in which the victims of war and imperialism keep themselves alive with the hope of the (false) promised land, America — the world's saviour or the Great Satan? Built into the song is a strange, threatening sense of war someday arriving in the US, as if war itself is a refugee. No one can declare themselves immune from this evil.

"Two Hearts Beat As One" is a love song but it too embodies all the tension of violence, though the conflict in this instance is not between two people but between one man and his feelings. It is also a pop song, a pile-driving, slap-happy, rocky U2 version of New York-styled R'n'B funk, which would give the band their second hit single. The New York influence remains through "Red Light" and "Surrender" which utilise the talents of female backing singers from (of all people) Kid Creole And The Coconuts and a superb solo trumpeter, as Bono sings about cities and the people who lose themselves in them.

"Surrender" indeed is a seductively atmospheric track, the music swelling up around the vocalist until it drowns him completely. Appropriately it is about the lack of a will to resist, about surrendering, because there is nothing else you can do. The album's lullaby closer "40" leaves Bono reminding us, wearily, hopefully, of the question posed at the very beginning: "How

"'Under A Blood Red Sky' lacks that sense of adventure which, as anyone who has seen the band live can testify, is crucial to U2's appeal."

long to sing this song?". It is far removed from the unsatisfying query on which "October" ends — "Is that all you want from me?" — for it is a question posed by someone who has just given his all.

"War" is quite an achievement. Like "Boy" it looks at one complex topic from many different angles but it is far more specific in intent. "Whereas the previous two lp's had been inward-looking, 'War' was outward looking," Bono reflected at the time. Clearly it was a band trying hard to relate and to communicate, to apply their inspirational beliefs to something —a band fronted by a singer who no longer just performed with passion but who examined it, confronted it and revealed himself through it. The character of Bono that could be felt on stage, that was so evident in person, could at last be heard on record.

U2's third lp can stake a claim to greatness but it has its share of weaknesses. U2 had stepped from a bright place into the shadows, stepped down off the unique rock pedestal they had built for themselves and moved into the bustling market-place of wider rock influences. They had reworked their patented sound and replaced it with something powerful... but not yet, I think, equally powerful. "War" is far superior in concept and content to "October" but it does not leap off the turntable with the pure sonic strength of that record. The decision, if it was that, to hold back The Edge and unleash Bono was brave, but without Edge and Larry's Wall Of Sound, Bono's voice is sometimes left too open, exposing ragged and uncertain edges. When "War" is sloppy it sounds less like deliberate punkiness than a band overwhelmed by passions they can't quite control. In retrospect it is clearly the work of young guns, coming out with all barrels blazing and shooting up everything they see. Musically it is a precursor to "The Joshua Tree" but, in comparison, that Western Odyssey would display the dangerous mastery of sharp-shooters.

The single "Two Hearts Beat As One" featured, in response to the style of the times, a variety of mixes on the 7" and 12" versions. With a band for whom the spirit, the inner strength, of the performance is everything, the lengthier club mix and the hip Francis Kervorkian remixes of the title track and "New Year's Day" seem almost entirely pointless, marketing gimmicks that amount to little more than meddling. Still it made a change from the extra live tracks that usually cropped up on U2 12" and double-pack singles.

Including the previously mentioned B-sides "Boy/Girl" and "I Will Follow" there had been 10 live takes issued with U2 singles, almost an album's worth in quantity if not quality. "11 O'Clock Tick Tock", "The Ocean", "Cry" (a short inter-linking passage that had gone on to form the basics of "Is That All?") and "The

Electric Co." had appeared as added extras with "Fire".

"Fire" itself, "I Threw A Brick Through A Window" and "A Day Without Me" had featured on "New Year's Day". This material was not dishonourable but neither did it ever really capture U2's overwhelming live appeal. The band's next release would attempt to do just that.

"UNDER A Blood Red Sky", billed as a mini-album, featured eight live tracks from three separate gigs during 1983. This was the "War" tour, with which U2 really caught the imagination of the great gig-going public and the performances are correspondingly gripping.

"Gloria", "I Will Follow", "The Electric Co." (preceded once again by a short blast of "Cry"), "New Year's Day" and "40" are straightforward and efficient, the added warmth from the live setting compensating for any studio losses. Not that there were many...

The Edge has always worked wonders live, defying the limitations of a four-man band with a barrage of effects and quick changes that sustain an impressive and complex variety of interlocking sounds. *Hot Press* writer Bill Graham has dubbed him 'The Edge Orchestra' and here he gets to demonstrate exactly why he deserves such a grandiose title. He also, unintentionally, shows why he is not in Van Halen! On "Party Girl", the old B-side, the guitar is shorn of effects and The Edge offers up a strained, awkward solo that ends in blunder. U2, however, made no blunder in allowing the mistake onto vinyl —it's an intentionally humanising moment of humour from which the song then surges forward, the full weight of the crowd behind it.

It is these sort of touches that really bring a live album to life and "Under A Blood Red Sky" could have done with more of the same. It lacks a sense of adventure which, as anyone who has seen the band can testify, is crucial to U2's appeal. The featured material hardly differs from and rarely improves on earlier versions. Only on one occasion does Bono indulge his habit of playing with other people's lyrics with a nice yet essentially frivolous inclusion of snatches of "I Want To Live In America" and "Send In The Clowns" during "The Electric Co." (his habit was to cost the band considerably in an out-of-court copyright settlement). In this light the album's standout has to be the reworking of "11 O'Clock Tick Tock", stripped of Martin Hannett's gothic touch yet retaining its dark intensity, while the martial and stirring performance of "Sunday Bloody Sunday" might be reckoned a disappointment in comparison to the slower interpretation that featured so powerfully in later tours.

"Under A Blood Red Sky" went a long way towards confirming U2 as a major band yet in retrospect it is little more than an enjoyable souvenir of a particular tour, a moment in time

Larry Mullen in 1982

when the band were about to make a quantum leap live. Subsequent tours were a revelation because U2 were not only powerful and exciting (as they had always been) but also consistently surprising, making the stage a creative musical environment in which their material was deployed as a springboard into other unmapped areas. This is how it had been before they won a record deal, back in the days when their live shows were all they had, and how it was to become again. Marketing considerations aside, "Under A Blood Red Sky" came a little too soon. Nor can it hope to match the later "Rattle And Hum" as a spiritual, truly live creation.

It did mark one departure: producer Jimmy Iovine replaced Steve Lillywhite at the controls. There were far more radical departures on the horizon. "I think you can see that something has come to an end in this group," Bono told *Hot Press* at the end of the "War" tour. "I really feel we're about to start again."

"PRIDE (IN The Name Of Love)" was the clamorous clarion call that brought U2 back to the charts in late '84, after an absence of about a year. An unbridled, defiant and impassioned elegy for the assassinated civil rights leader Martin Luther King, it was U2 at their most anthemic but, though this was familiar territory, they were approaching it from another angle.

Principally there was something different about the texture: it was more seamless, more whole than the often choppy and (intentionally) sloppy playing on "War". The record had a broad, full sound that (as in earlier days) surrounded and supported Bono's voice rather than exposing it (as "War" had done). The singer had by no means been reined in however; continuing to grow in confidence and ability he delivered his most commanding performance to date, a blistering, full-frontal vocal rising all the way to breaking point. "Pride" is stirring stuff, an undeniable display of greatness.

U2 had a new production team in Brian Eno and his associate Daniel Lanois, an unusual choice that on the evidence of their first collaboration was making quite a difference. Eno, a founder member of Roxy Music, had a reputation as a theorist and an intellectual — the ambient music he pioneered was about as far from the full-blooded appeal of U2 as you could get. He did have impressive production credits but unlike Lillywhite, or indeed Hannett or Iovine, he had no track-record as a rock producer. His most contemporary work had been as collaborator on Bowie's electronic projects and Talking Heads' African-derived funk excursions. In fact, "Boomerang 1", a surprisingly sharp funk instrumental and "Boomerang 2", a chanted extension of the idea with African influence, betray a disappointingly derivative Talking Heads' feel. The single closes with "4th Of July", a moody, shivery guitar piece bogged down by a slow and very dull bass. But if only the A-side was remarkable in its realisation, the whole suggests, at the very least, an openness to new ideas on U2's part.

"Pride" can be seen as a bridge between the U2 that "War" had given birth to and the U2 "The Unforgettable Fire" was to deliver. It reveals a more finely-tuned sense of atmosphere and dynamics than had been in U2's capability but it remains within the framework of an identifiable rock song with verse, chorus and hook. In *that* sense of the word song, it is the only one on the album.

The title "The Unforgettable Fire" was lifted from a book of drawings and paintings by survivors of Hiroshima, dealing with their horrific experience at the receiving end of the most appalling weapon the murder machine has ever produced — but that did not make this album the second (World) "War". Images of fear and terrible destruction abound in certain of the record's tracks but to infer that it is some kind of nuclear protest album would be wide of the mark, for U2 also have another fire in mind, a fire that burns in all of us, a fire that's deep inside. In the opening track, "A Sort Of Homecoming" Bono sings, *"Your earth moves beneath your own dream landscape."* This too was where U2 were moving, into the realm of the subconscious...

Bono has always had the greatest respect for the creative powers of the subconscious. As the band's principal lyricist he had never been too inclined to put pen to paper. I recall him struggling to write out the words to all of U2's songs for an early *Hot Press* interview, apparently uncertain what they were exactly. He liked the songs to evolve, taking gradual shape during rehearsal, refining them further on stage, not finally committing himself until the last possible moment, in the studio. His ability to extemporise had stood him in good stead on at least one notable occasion. In August 1984 he went backstage at Bob Dylan's open-air concert at Slane Castle in Co. Meath. (U2 had temporarily forsaken Windmill to record with Eno in a cavernous room at the castle). It was the first meeting between the two and Bono, in the days before he developed a genuine interest in rock music's back catalogue, was more familiar with Dylan's legend than his actual work. So when Dylan asked Bono to join him for a duet he was somewhat non-plussed. He was pleased and flattered at the request but every time Dylan asked him if he knew the lyrics to this or that song from his extensive collection, Bono had to confess that he did not. Finally, afraid the offer would be withdrawn, he seized on a familiar title and agreed to guest on "Blowin' In The Wind". When the moment came he improvised his own version, inventing lines about barbed wire and the Northern troubles to the Irish crowd's roar of approval and Dylan's naked astonishment. Bono rode rough-shod over the chorus but he caught the spirit if not the letter of the song and acquitted himself honourably.

It was this capacity to create on the run — this essence of creativity — that Brian Eno was keen to tap for "The Unforgettable Fire". The key song or piece is actually the record's weakest track, a fatally flawed attempt at spontaneous creation. "Elvis Presley And America" was recorded even as it was being invented, with Bono singing along to a slowed-down tape of music the others had been working on. When, pleased with the result, he suggested they keep working and finish it, Eno

> "To Dylan's naked astonishment, Bono rode rough-shod over the chorus of 'Blowin' In The Wind' but he caught the spirit if not the letter of the song."

Bono, Leixlip 1980 (left) and (right) Cork 1987

informed him it *was* finished.

In truth "Elvis Presley And America" is exactly what the recording method suggests, a sketchy work-in-progress. It is the longest piece on the album (or feels like it at least), a beginning in search of an end. The chord sequence it rides on is simply not sufficiently interesting to sustain endless repetition. And most disappointingly, Bono's vocal is the mumbled, half-formed gropings of a man not yet ready to commit himself.

He says *"You know"* a lot. He repeats *"No one told me"* over and over. Ultimately, the song says little or nothing. Clearly the intention was to evoke the decline of Elvis but for something with such a portentous title and premise, it is sad to discover that the publishing company's copy of the lyrics ends about half way through the song with a hand-written question mark.

Yet its inclusion on the LP indicates much about what U2 were trying to achieve. In marked contrast to "Elvis Presley", the rest of the lyrics are imagistic, colourful and inspiring. They mark a return to the looser logic of pre-"War" U2 but they are considerably more resonant than any that preceded them. And it is not simply through the lyrics that U2 were drawing upon the powers of the subconscious. "The Unforgettable Fire" was and remains U2's most formless, indefinable artefact. From "A Sort Of Homecoming" on, you know you're in entirely different territory. *"I'm coming home,"* Bono sings but he's not taking the listener anywhere they've been with him before. Immediately noticeable is an almost total immersion of the guitar. It's there but The Edge, no longer so much guitar hero as magician, has made it invisible, its presence felt in a tail of sounds rather than riffs. Keyboards loom and swell where once piano chords made more direct statements. And the drums, that other most notable

element of the U2 sound, are rolling not pounding.

"The wind will crack in winter time/A bomb blast lightning waltz/No spoken words, just a scream... " It is an atmospheric piece and you almost, *almost* know what it means. It has an emotional power the equal of U2's rock power, which is not to suggest that they had abandoned the latter. "Pride" states that case to perfection and "Wire", which follows it, is one of the toughest, most adrenalized things U2 have done, complete with scorching guitars, a dirty bassline, alien backing voices and a vocal that starts out pleading and winds up threatening, frightening in its intensity.

It seems — and there can be no certainty with these songs —to be about the living prison of addiction, opening with the line, *"I'm in a cell and innocent am I"* and slamming closed with *"Here's the rope, here's the rope/Now swing on it"*. Addiction certainly provides the key to the album's other most riveting vocal performance. "Bad", a tense, slow-building song of frustration at a loved one's self-destruction, is a *tour de force* of musical collaboration, calling up a vastly wider spectrum of feeling than the lyrics could ever hope to alone. On such tracks the adventure of "The Unforgettable Fire" works unequivocally, giving U2 a depth and substance they had never before attained.

The title track, with a heart-stopping orchestrated middle section, is another of the record's undeniable high-points, lyrics overflowing with drunken poetry, filled with lost love and need. "Promenade" is a lover's stroll, a short musical ramble with a hint of Lou Reed, while "Indian Summer Sky" has the adrenalin rush of "Wire" but this time allied to a purer, lighter feel. The album closes with a short and lovely lullabye "MLK" (another tribute to Martin Luther King) in which Bono exhorts us to sleep, to sink with him into the subconscious: *"May all your dreams be realised."*

"The Unforgettable Fire" is another outstanding work, a strange and rewarding LP that showcased a band prepared to side-step their most obvious commercial appeal to pursue their artistic muse. Yet while it succeeds on these terms it does so occasionally at the listener's expense. It is guilty of being too wilfully obscure and it is hard to draw full satisfaction from lyrics that sometimes fail to offer enough clues for the listener to truly enter into the song. There are performances here driven by demons an outsider is incapable of understanding — which ultimately leaves us outside.

It is, intentionally, an impressionistic record and with it the band re-drew their boundaries but it is also a stepping stone to the realisation of greater potential, one that would wed their painterly sense of feeling and colour to the more defined construction of songs and ideas which they seemed, "Pride" apart, to have temporarily abandoned.

'"The Unforgettable Fire" showcased a band prepared to side-step their most obvious commercial appeal to pursue the artistic muse."

The single "The Unforgettable Fire" meanwhile boasted four extra previously-unreleased tracks, making it an essential fans' purchase. "A Sort Of Homecoming" (which was also the 7" flip) is purportedly a live version of the album's opener which had been shortened and rearranged in performance. The credits claim it was recorded live at Wembley and Good Earth Studios. In fact (I'll let you into a secret) I suspect that the only part recorded live was the crowd noise. The group had preferred the conciseness of the live version to the original and had intended to re-record it as the follow-up single to "Pride", drafting in yet another famous rock producer, Tony Visconti, to do the job. But the results did not meet expectations. I was paying a social visit to the studio and witnessed the dissatisfied shaking of heads while it was being recorded. Imagine my surprise when I spun this disc for the first time only to hear what sounds like the very same performance being greeted by the roaring of a very satisfied crowd!

The other songs were all new. "The Three Sunrises" is melodic and up-beat with an almost Beatlesque flavour to its harmonies. It is delightful, one of U2's finest out-takes, as is "Love Comes Tumbling", a gentle but rhythmic love song on which Bono takes it easy and comes up trumps with an impressively light but muscular vocal, an indication of his ever increasing strengths as a singer. "Bass Trap", finally, is a graceful and civilised guitar and bass instrumental .

"The Three Sunrises", "Love Comes Tumbling" and "A Sort Of Homecoming (Live)" also feature on another interesting U2 artefact from around this period. Titled "Wide Awake In America", this four-track EP was intended only for release in the United States but became a huge import seller in Ireland, Britain and the rest of Europe. The reason was simple — the presence of a previously unavailable live version of "Bad". Extended from its original vinyl incarnation on "The Unforgettable Fire" and replete with taped keyboard intro, this has come to be considered the definitive version of the song, clear-cut recorded evidence of the smouldering power that U2 could conjure up on-stage and which would make "Bad" both a favourite with the fans, and for quite some time, the centrepiece of the band's live set.

O N C E   A G A I N there would be a long wait for new U2 material — this time the longest wait of all. "The Unforgettable Fire" single was released in May 1985. "With Or Without You" did not appear until March 1987. The single's two B-sides clearly indicated some of the changes. Moody pieces that reflect the atmospheric qualities of the preceding album but display little of its rich depth of sound, they provide the bare backing for lyrics that, while as strong on poetic imagery as Bono's last work, were more specific and more direct than anything he had done before. "Walk To The Water" is a largely spoken story of fleeting love, casually if poignantly recounted, while "Luminous Times (Hold On To Love)" builds from a vague beginning to as clear a statement and dedication as the singer could make. *"She is the avalanche/she is the thunder/she is the waves/and she pulls me under/I love you cause I need to/Not because I need you/I love you cause I understand/God has given me your hand/It holds me in a tiny fist/But still I need your kiss/Hold on to love... "* And this is just the b-side!

U2 have not been renowned for love songs, the terrain of the majority of popular music, but they mastered the medium and avoided the cliches on the tender, searching "With Or Without You". Though it has the sense of a ballad it actually — once again — boasts a driving and quite contemporary Clayton/Mullen rhythm section. The mix and arrangement is a long way from the last well-rounded Eno & Lanois production. The band have launched themselves back into the rough-house: drums too sharp, bass too bulky, vocals too loud and too exposed, yet their confident handling of themselves shows just how far they have come since "War". This time the singer can take the exposure, use the room the band have given him to lay his loving confusion on the line. Once again, Bono is dealing with an internal struggle but he is no longer hiding, he allows us access to his thoughts as well as his feelings. Honest, personal, straight from the heart: Bono makes his first confession. But the thing that really makes "With Or Without You" is a little touch, a sideways leap, a phrase that no logic would have found room for, apparently out of place but intuitively right. *"And you give yourself away,"* he sings, giving it all away.

"With Or Without You" was a bold single, tight and

constrained rather than anthemic, returning them to the public eye not with a bang but a whisper. "The Joshua Tree" when it emerged made shock-waves, catapulting U2 to the heights of superstardom, becoming one of the year's best-selling albums world-wide, and alerting the uninitiated that the tired old world of rock'n'roll could still produce a people's champion.

It also marked the integration of the most essential musical strands in their career. It returned to the rootsiness, the rock'n'roll sensibility and the reliance on straight-forward songs that made "War" their most emotionally potent album but it has a depth and maturity which that record lacked. It admitted and made the most of the instinctive, subconscious creative process that initially guided them to "Boy" and which they re-deployed to such potent effect with "The Unforgettable Fire". But there is far more coherence to "The Joshua Tree" than the "Fire" album and far more poetry, in both music and lyrics, than on "Boy". It has the maturity of a band who have proven themselves capable of carving solid rock and also playing mood-games, tampering with the atmosphere. Finally there was a new element, the X factor, in Bono's rather belated discovery of the blues.

"The Joshua Tree" is a tree capable of surviving, even flourishing, in the most sun-scorched desert. U2 had survived and flourished in the often soul-destroying and far too rarely soul-full wilderness of rock'n'roll. Perhaps they had benefitted from a kind of self-imposed isolation, turning a (relative) ignorance of rock history on its head by inventing their own rules, and themselves with them. As The Edge once remarked to me about their early attempts to play other people's material: "We could never play any of those songs. We were the worst cover version band in the world. So the only way we could actually become good..." "... was to write our own stuff!" (the conclusion was Bono's).

They were children of punk rock, knocking everything that went before them without really knowing what it was, and their success came so early on their own terms that they never really *had* to look back. If U2's detractors have accused them of being cliched at least they were their own cliches (usual slights concern their penchant for big-chorused anthems and favouring a quite limited selection of chords). However Bono, after being exposed to Brian Eno's extensive Gospel collection and having met and been impressed with the likes of Bob Dylan and The Rolling Stones was beginning to investigate rock's past and (though "War" had made mainstream musical connections) for the first time identifiable pre-70's influences began to show in U2's work.

Bono was frequently to be seen with an acoustic guitar and wrote and performed a solo, bluesy track called "Silver And Gold" for Little Steven's Sun City anti-apartheid album. He wrote a (never recorded) country ditty called "Lucille" that he would proudly play as a party piece to anyone who cared to listen. A whole new world had just opened up to him and he was awed

Bono: doing the Harley Shuffle

and impressed by it — but not intimidated! It was his self-confessed ambition to write a truly classic song, in the classic mode.

And there is at least one classic song on "The Joshua Tree", one timeless creation with meaning and melody enough for anyone, "I Still Haven't Found What I'm Looking For". Before the album's release, Bono proudly told me that title and I knew he'd cracked it. That one line catches so much, traps the essence of every restless spirit (though it should be noted that The Edge has laid claim to coming up with it!). With a simple three-chord tune and an honest lyric, Bono built it into something entirely special, took it to a place where even his Christianity and his own personal answers became unsatisfactory as they ultimately can never fully satisfy the enquiring mind: *"I believe in the kingdom come/When all the colours will bleed into one/But yes I'm still running."*

It is not only written with painful honesty, it is sung with it. Bono's constant improvement as a vocalist is a cause for hope for every tone deaf would-be singing star. In school, as the band began to become local favourites, he remarked amusedly that his brother told him not to waste his time, he couldn't sing and that was that. He's managed surprisingly well given this handicap. He has dealt with his limitations and either overcome or used them. But could he (or his brother) ever have suspected that one day he would wake up and be the greatest living rock vocalist in the world? For that is what many would consider him after the revelations of "The Joshua Tree".

Listen to him tear down the walls of sound in "Bullet The Blue Sky". He's surrounded by The Edge's unbelievably psyched out guitars howling like Led Zeppelin after the levee broke, but this time Bono needs no cushioning, he can punch his way clean out of there. The track's appalled look at the least romantic, most capitalistic, self-serving side of American imperialism was the darkest thing U2 had produced since "11 O'Clock Tick Tock" and it ripped out of the speakers, demanding to be seen and heard live — though for all intents and purposes it already was live! The gap between U2 on stage and U2 on record had always been the gap between The Edge and Bono. On "Bullet The Blue Sky", the two came together with a vengeance. Not surprisingly, the track would, on "The Joshua Tree" tour, assume the centrepiece role that had previously been the preserve of "Bad", its apocalyptic sound and vision drenched in blood-red lighting.

> **"Bono was embraced as rock's latest mystic healer, a sort of holy cross between the Morrisons, Jim and Van. There was craziness in the air..."**

Not every track was such an achievement. The least satisfying songs are two that seem to have evolved from their post "Unforgettable Fire" live set and are curiously incomplete. "Running To Stand Still" comes out of Lou Reed's "Walk On The Wild Side" via (believe it or not) Elton John's "Candle In The Wind", both of which Bono would often sing snatches of —songs with drifting, shifting melodies that have been borrowed (we won't try and start a law suit with the word 'plagiarised') to form the basis of this sad tale of heroin addiction. Although lilting and lovely, it adds up to less than it might.

"Exit", on the other hand, attempts to capture the bleak, black feel of their punky live cover of Dylan's "Maggie's Farm". On record this murderous tale of the most negative side of love (*"The hands that build/Could also pull down"*) is harsh but too lacking in form. On the subsequent tour it became increasingly crazed until it reached the intended terrifying proportions. The version that features in the "Rattle And Hum" movie (but not the album) takes the song into the twilight zone, where it truly belongs.

But if those might be considered the album's weaknesses they hardly detract from the whole. Both are brave songs. More than any other U2 LP "The Joshua Tree" is a collection of songs with interlinking themes but no overall concept. The main connection is a sonic one. This is U2 bared to the bone and fleshed out again. It makes the U2 of "War" sound almost amateur, certainly confused. Here U2 know what they want from the beast of rock'n'roll. "Where The Streets Have No Name" is the only track where they actually sound like U2 as we might have come to expect them to sound, yet they could be no other band, even

when dipping into the country-rooted upbeat American thrashes of "In God's Country" and the lusty "Trip Through Your Wires". In getting to grips with some kind of roots music, Bono opened himself to a basic emotion that he had never previously embraced in his lyrics: desire. For "The Joshua Tree" U2 got off of their cloud to prove that they were really flesh and blood for the first time (though religious imagery lingers to torment the singer who seems bedevilled by temptation, uncertain whether he is faced by *"angels or devils"*).

There was one bona-fide anthem on board too, in "Red Hill Mining Town", an earth-breaking slice of mega-chorus rock — yet unusually it had a tender and bittersweet core and a bleak message. It was a song about unemployment seen from the inside, where only love can save a man's dignity and even that is sometimes not enough. The rich tones of "The Unforgettable Fire" are evoked on the beautiful, forceful, funereal elegy "One Tree Hill" (inspired by the motorcycle death of their friend and employee Greg Carroll) and there are lullabye echoes of "40" and "MLK" on the hushed tribute to the long-suffering Argentinian "Mothers Of The Disappeared". This was U2's most varied set to date, a work of natural power and assurance that suggested a band at the height of their talents.

It was also their most successful record, the fastest selling LP in Britain ever, and number one on both sides of the Atlantic. Suddenly U2 were being hailed as the torch-bearers for rock'n'roll, on the cover of every kind of magazine, analysed in newspaper editorials, snapped by the papparazi. Bono was embraced as rock's latest mystic leader, a sort of holy cross between the Morrisons, Jim and Van. There was craziness in the air as U2 embarked on an extensive, exhausting world tour further bolstering their reputation and the record's sales. It has become common for groups to promote such a top-selling album like a selfish jockey flogging a racehorse: until it dies, and then some more, for good measure. Many American stadium groups only produce an album about every three years, taking plenty of time after the record has been finally laid to rest to carefully craft another multi-million seller.

No one could have blamed U2 for taking a long sabbatical from the studio: even prevailing marketing opinion holds against flooding the market with too much product. Michael Jackson, the biggest-selling artist in the world, has only managed to release three albums in the last 10 years. Yet "The Joshua Tree" had been something of a creative brainstorm. The band had never been so prolific and all the evidence suggested that they weren't about to let up now.

The next two singles they released in Britain off "The Joshua Tree" contained a plethora of impressive songs on the flip-sides

Adam Clayton, Bono and the late Phil Lynott of Thin Lizzy, together for a *Hot Press* rock awards ceremony in Dublin in 1983

that hadn't, for reasons of space, made it on to the album. The final track listing for the album had actually been the cause of fierce debate within the group, leading Bono to later remark, "The album is almost incomplete." The B-sides would provide the final touches to the picture and a broad hint of what was to come.

"Red Hill Mining Town" had been the first choice as a follow-up to "With Or Without You". Catchy, epic and politically resonant it seemed a natural for a single, another in a line of impressive U2 anthems, but it was dropped from the schedules at the last minute. The reasons for this were never made clear. There was talk of dissatisfaction with the video that had been made by renowned Irish film director Neil Jordan but, given that the band did not even include the song in their live sets the truth may be closer to a flippant remark Bono made to me: "It's too high for me to sing. It wrecks my throat!".

The honours fell instead to the soaring, self-contained classic "I Still Haven't Found What I'm Looking For". On the flip was "Deep In The Heart", a pleasantly loose, shambolic, probably half-improvised ramble and "Spanish Eyes", a blaring, thrashed out, simplistic rock'n'roll song, the first sign of just how basic U2 were prepared to get. "Where The Streets Have No Name" came with three additional tracks including a song so astonishingly good I find it hard to believe it was relegated to a B-side. "Race Against Time" is, frankly, a boring near-instrumental (something U2 have never quite mastered) while "Silver And Gold" is a souped-up and much improved band version of Bono's South African protest song that would receive an even more definitive reading on their next album.

Pride of place, however, goes to "The Sweetest Thing", a love song in which the singer is skewered on the wrong end of the stick yet still making the most of it. It is light, sweet, romantic, delightful and piercingly accurate. It is actually the closest thing to pure pop U2 have produced, hopping on a stop-starting bass, a delicate piano and a spacious drum pattern, as Bono sings in a high, tired and breaking voice of his heart's dilemma: *"My love she throws me like a rubber ball/She won't catch me or break my fall... Baby's got blue skies up ahead/And in this I'm a raincloud/You know we got a stormy kind of love."* When he sings so sadly *"I'm losing you"* only to follow that confession with, *"Ain't love the sweetest thing"*, I feel the zing of my heart strings. How could anyone treat such a sensitive soul so bad?!?

There were two more unusual releases before the major project and both offered clear indications of what was coming down the line, the results of U2's broadening relationship with music of the past. The tracks featured on two charity albums and marked the first time U2 would commit another person's songs to vinyl. The first was a relatively faithful and appealing version of Phil Spector's "Christmas (Baby Please Come Home)" that U2 recorded at a soundcheck for the all-star "A Very Special Christmas", released on A & M. The second was an unbelievably rowdy and uproarious version of Woody Guthrie's "Jesus Christ" that appeared amongst a variety of versions of Guthrie and Leadbelly material on "Folkways...A Vision Shared", released on CBS. The group sounded like they had a good time making the record, with its rip-roaring flavour that brought folk's punk heroes The Pogues to mind. U2 were loosening up again.

Such was the anticipation built up about U2's return to the market place, only a year after their greatest success, on the back of a world tour with the praise still resounding in the media and

Eamon Dunphy's (inflated and inaccurate) biography having only recently topped the best seller lists, that the new single leaped straight to the top of the charts, giving U2 their first British number one. "Desire" was an anachronistic hit (and its fall was as rapid as its rise), a noisy, no-nonsense stomp whose old-fashioned Bo Diddley-derived riff sat uneasily amidst the sequenced Euro-pop of Stock, Aitken And Waterman which then dominated the charts. Even given U2's new enthusiasm for rock's back pages it was surprisingly rootsy, a chaotic whoop of black-leather-jacket rocker's lust, like U2 rumbling with The Clash on dead man's terrain. I couldn't make up my mind about this record when it was first released. It is revivalist, derivative, backward-looking, even unmelodic... it is also thrilling, a pure adrenalin rush, red guitars on fire, weird, phased choral vocals shimmering with *"Desi-i-i-i-ire"*, Bono's voice rising to a raging bellow, *"Hey sister! I can't let you go/I'm like a preacher stealing hearts at a trampoline show/For love or money? Money, money, money, money, money, money... "* In his own words this is *"Where the bright lights and the big city meet."* For U2 the old was new and on its own terms "Desire" is an uncompromising record, bold, brave and burning, burning with the emotion its title evokes. It stands as an exciting and impressive single but there is a nagging voice in my head that whines, carpingly, "I've heard it all before." And not on a U2 record.

There was, embracing more contemporary tastes, an extended version, "The Hollywood Mix". 9 minutes and 23 seconds of riffing decorated with newscasters' voices and a gospelly woman's vocal it does make for a city-in-chaos impression and is certainly a more successful remix than the "War" ones but ultimately the basic blast of the rhythm section is too limited to sustain a groove of this length. The other B-side was "Hallelujah (Here She Comes)", a lilting, gospel-styled song riding on a strummed acoustic guitar and filled in by soul-man and former Beatles collaborator Billy Preston on hammond organ. The lyrics deal yet again with one of Bono's most enduring concerns, oncoming death. Yet, as befits the richly spiritual Gospel medium, the singer seems to be welcoming the great unknown for the first time, without fear or confusion. It is a fine song and one that again confirmed U2's growing enthusiasm for rock's musical heritage.

Like the single that preceded it, U2's new long player leaped straight to the top of the charts on advance orders alone. For perhaps the first time U2 were living up to their early gigging mantle: The Hype. "Rattle And Hum" was a multi-media event: see the film, read the book, play the record. It was difficult to know exactly how it should be judged — there were moments on the record that the film would make sense of and vice versa, yet

> **"'Desire' is revivalist, derivative, backward-looking, even unmelodic...it is also thrilling, a pure adrenalin rush."**

though the two were interlinked they were not entirely interdependent; there were for example, major differences in the track order and selections (the film being considerably more live than the record) and unusually for an album that was billed as a soundtrack it was capable of standing up and being counted on its own right.

"Rattle And Hum" was U2's first double album and it was packed to the limits with music. Still in the midst of an explosion of creativity, U2 had been writing, recordings and performing new songs even as they toured and "Rattle and Hum" tries to wrap this all up in an ambitious and unorthodox manner. Mixing live and studio work, re-interpreted favourites alongside brand new material, it goes where "Under A Blood Red Sky" never could and managed what few live albums ever have: it captures the true flavour and character of the band in a wheels-in-motion portrait of a tour.

As The Edge had previously commented, U2 had once considered themselves the worst covers band in the world. Opening "Rattle And Hum" with a Beatles' song heralds the changes in the band's self-perception and places them firmly in a context of rock history. "Charles Manson stole this song from The Beatles, we're stealing it back," proclaimed Bono as they launched into "Helter Skelter". The wild sexual-fairground song could be viewed as an appropriate introduction to the organised chaos of a touring album but their sloppy version could never hope to match the raw anarchy of the original and Bono's declaration still leaves me with an uneasy feeling. No one has the right to declare themselves heir to popular music's most inspired originators and whatever else U2 were and are, Bono, Edge, Adam and Larry will never be John, Paul, George and Ringo.

Their other choice for a cover also put them in rock legend territory with a rapidly thrown together version of Bob Dylan's "All Along The Watchtower". When Jimi Hendrix recorded that song he made it his very own — U2 just about make it in the end. In interviews they spoke proudly of the achievement of learning a song minutes before playing it live and then wham-bam-thank-you-man sticking it out on a record as if this endorsed some punky notion of the birth of rock music. But the result is the trouncing of a wonderful song already redolent with meaning to rock audiences and it begs the question: are they suggesting there really are 'no more heroes' in the anyone-can-do-it world of rock, or are they getting away with murder because of their heroic status? U2 would probably counter that it was just a bit of fun but the doubts would linger in the light of similar cavalier performances on the B-sides of "Rattle And Hum" singles.

Their flirtation with rock legends continued in the newly recorded material, most notably on one of the album's standout tracks, the most potent *rock* song of the new set, "God Part II". It is their sequel to John Lennon's myth-shattering "God" which climaxed his first post-Beatles album. Lennon is both acknowledged and defended in a pointed couplet that threatens character assassination of the great character assassinator himself, Albert Goldman, whose biography of Lennon had recently stirred up much controversy: *"I don't believe in Goldman, his type like a curse/Instant karma's gonna get him if I don't get him first."* Bono is at his sharpest as he snaps out short verses acknowledging the contradictions in his lifestyle, his image and the world around him: *"I don't believe in excess, success is to give/I don't believe in riches but you should see where I live,"* he sings. And, *"Don't believe in forced entry, I don't believe in rape/But every time she passes by wild thoughts escape/I don't believe in deathrow, skidrow or the gangs/Don't believe in the Uzi it just went off in my hands."*

Each verse concludes with an almost wistful, defiantly out of date declaration: *"I... believe in love."* It is a forceful band workout, a monotone bass and drum track attacked and divided by a savage guitar that is reminiscent of Lennon at his angry best, yet Bono's faith in the power of love seems somehow unconvincing in the harsh and cynical 80's context of his lyrics. I am reminded of John Lennon's weary, poignant put-down on his own failed idealism: *"I really thought love was gonna save us all."* That could be the ironic inscription on his gravestone, the famous last words of a peace advocate slain by one of his own followers. Bono's revival of that idealism has the curious air of a naive 60's hangover, at odds even with the bleak things he has to say.

It too, like much of the music, is backward looking. The most perplexing contradiction of the song is when Bono sings, *"I don't believe in the 60's, the golden age of pop/You glorify the past when the future dries up."* This bold statement is made on a song in honour of a 60's icon, on an album that glorifies the past in its very choice of musical styles and points of reference. The very next track is introduced by an excerpt from the work of another dead 60's star, Jimi Hendrix playing "The Star Spangled Banner".

The tainted, insulting take of America's national anthem erupts into a showstopping version of U2's own assault on the States, "Bullet The Blue Sky". They bring an apocalyptic tension to their delivery of this awesome song, the guitar sliding across it with a noise like missiles in flight, Bono shaking with anger as he extends the spoken outro, railing, to the American crowd's delight, against TV evangelists: *"The God I know ain't short of cash, Mister!"*

A similar dark, challenging mood infests a raging live version of "Silver And Gold". *"Am I buggin' you?"*, Bono asks at the tail of a punchy anti-apartheid speech. *"Don't mean to bug ya!"*, he adds, unpleasantly punching out the words. "Pride (In The Name Of Love)" was a straightforward crowd pleaser but the

Bono at the Slane Castle rock festival in Ireland when U2 supported Thin Lizzy

only other live version of a hit, "I Still Haven't Found What I'm Looking For", saw the song utterly transformed by a black New York church choir who recognise the spiritual, gospel core and raise it right up to the ceiling.

Six of the album's fifteen U2 tracks (apart from Hendrix' contribution there was a short burst of buskers recorded on the street) were recorded live at three American concerts but the nine studio songs maintained the sense of a tour, with backing tracks recorded in a live demo fashion and lyrics that had a sense of travelogue about them, exploring American dreams and nightmares. "Heartland" was almost a love song to the nation, personal and geographic imagery mixing in a tumbling poetic cadence over a breathy, dreamy backing (it is the only Eno and Lanois production credit and shows their influence. The rest of the album was produced piece-meal by the band and various engineers with Jimmy Iovine in overall control). You can almost feel the wheels of the tour bus ceaselessly rolling beneath the song, the words drifting off like reflections glinting on a windscreen...

The title of "Hawkmoon 269" was actually taken from a road sign seen from the bus. This evocative image provided the inspiration for a brooding love song of slow-building stormy power, filled with a sense of deserted ghost towns and rootless drifters. Bono's stunning vocal grows from a deep, romantic request to a booming demand as he delivers a list of metaphors for desire, piling them up until they overwhelm. It is one of his personal favourite songs and shows how far the band had come on their journey: it is by turns restrained and unchained, expressionistic and to the point, poetic and concise. It is not a rock song or a pop song, bears little relation to their own early records and even less to the musical past they were so enthusiastically exploring (and exploiting). It simply exists in its own space.

The same cannot be said of the other tracks, as enthralling as most of them are. There were three songs recorded (in large part) in Sun Studios, where Elvis Presley made his debut, and they reek of reverence to rock's history. "Angel Of Harlem" is a sensational, up-beat tribute to blues and jazz legend Billie Holiday that proved U2 can play sweet soul music. It is entirely predictable but it exults in the pleasures of the genre with a soaring chorus and a steamy horn section breathing down its neck. "Love Rescue Me" is a soulful, country stroll, again built around a familiar chord sequence. The genesis of the song lies in a strangely synchronistic sequence of events. Bono told me that while he was staying in LA he had a strange dream one night about Bob Dylan, woke up and began immediately writing a lyric about a man people keep turning to as a saviour but whose life is increasingly messed-up and who could use salvation of his own.

To his surprise Bono got a call asking him if he wanted to go visit Dylan and later the same day found himself finishing the song off with the man in his dream. Dylan recorded a lead vocal to the track with U2 but later asked for it to be withdrawn. Bono said the vocal was astonishing and taught him more about phrasing than he ever imagined he still had to learn. The excuse for Dylan's withdrawal was his involvement with The Traveling Wilburys but one wonders was the despair and regret of "Love Rescue Me" a little too close to the bone?

U2's other collaboration with a figure from musical history was a triumphant blues duet with BB King, "When Love Comes To Town". The Edge, who from his earliest days in the band had consciously rejected and even despised the blues (or at least its 70's hard rock vulgarisation) found himself playing second guitar to one of the form's most celebrated champions. BB cuts it up with obvious pleasure, chewing on a lyric of such wit and maturity that the old hand expressed astonishment that so young a man could have written it. Again it dealt with the saving power of love, but balanced against the temptations of evil and, in a wicked twist, Bono, so often cast as some kind of saint, saved the nastiest parts for himself: *"I was there when they crucified my Lord/I held the scabbard when the soldier drew his sword/I threw the dice when they pierced his side/But I've seen love conquer the great divide."*

The Edge also contributed a lyric on the solo, folky "Van Diemen's Land", an austere tale of repression from Ireland's history that fades out with a frightening rapidity as if concerned not to overstay its welcome. The double album closes with a track that enters similar terrain to "Hawkmoon 269", another slow-burning song of need, "All I Want Is You". The lyric is bare and to the point, the music sombre and haunting, ending on a long, enchanting orchestral workout arranged by maverick genius Van Dyke Parks...

Before "Rattle And Hum" Bono had warned Bill Graham in *Hot Press*: "You may not like it, U2 fans may not like it, but we need it." They were on a personal journey into the past and the result is a wonderful trip down the back alleys of rock'n'roll: sprawling, strange, forceful, raucous, intense and seductive, it celebrates the music-making process, and has fun doing it. "Rattle And Hum" is almost a live classic. My personal doubts stem less from a dissatisfaction with the record than a sense that, after a decade of uniqueness, at the peak of their popularity they were making the least original music of their career. And one more thing, an uncomfortable feeling that they had lost the thread, fallen for the self-inflating mythology of rock that, in their earliest days, in the Big Bang of punk rock, they had striven to avoid and, by their individual personalities, by their faith, by (who knows?) whatever means, had created something special

"Dylan recorded a lead vocal for 'Love Rescue Me' but later asked for it to be withdrawn. Bono said the vocal was astonishing."

U2 circa "The Joshua Tree"

without. U2's roots had been their own. After "Rattle And Hum" they must share the same ones as everyone else.

Where does that leave them and where is there left to go? The evidence of the last new tracks they released, the B-sides of the "Rattle And Hum" singles, is not overly encouraging. In stark contrast to the wonderful work on the flips of their Joshua singles, their most recent releases have contained some of their weakest out-takes ever, a thin original, unnecessary remixes, sloppy live performances and cover versions that verge on the insulting. "A Room At The Heartbreak Hotel" on the "Angel Of Harlem" single is a sketchy repetitive song that builds in strength with some superbly integrated female backing vocals and a cavalry charge from The Memphis Horns but which is sabotaged by a muddy mix that almost completely buries the vocal.

Bono confronts rock deification with a lyric that is less a tribute to Elvis Presley (whose picture adorns the label) than an expression of disgust at those who would seek R'n'R glory at any cost. The original spoken introduction (left off the final version) was "Everyone wants to live like Elvis, but nobody wants to die like him." Yet the track that follows comes straight from a room

at the Heartbreak hotel, a dreadful live version of "Love Rescue Me" featuring one of rock's least dignified survivors, Keith Richards, on a lazy lead guitar that calls to mind all that was worst about the 70's approach to blues rock, that The Edge once so vehemently rejected. It was recorded at the Smile Jamaica charity concert and Ziggy Marley also makes a guest appearance, clearly on unfamiliar terrain and struggling with the lyrics. Though it has its moments, particularly when the horn section once again arrives to save the day, the fact that the proceeds from the track were going to charity is not enough to justify its release — U2 would have been wiser just to dip into their own pockets and quietly bury it.

"When Love Comes To Town" was a little better with a scorching live version of the single in which BB took it upon himself to preach to the crowd and an interesting "Hard Metal Dance Mix" of "God Part II". There was also a curiously straight version of Patti Smith's "Dancing Barefoot" that, like the "Rattle And Hum" covers, simply had nothing extra to offer over the original. But the worst lapses are with the two old love songs that appear on the flipside of "All I Want Is You". In contrast to that dignified recording, both "Unchained Melody" and "Everlasting Love" sound like they've been learned as quickly as possible and thrashed out in one take. This is neither punky nor funny and certainly not emotional; it is more like garage-band rock that should have been left in the garage. There is nothing glorious about playing below your capabilities and though self-belief is always an essential ingredient of success, there is very real danger to a band's sense of quality control if that characteristic swells to self-regard.

Call it the Midas syndrome, when everything you touch turns to Gold records.

"YOU'VE SEEN the pits, you've seen where we've come from, you've seen the child eating the coal," said Bono to me after the release of "Boy". "To get from there to here you'll admit is rather interesting. To get from here to a Gold album is nothing, a small step." Now they've had their gold album and much, much more besides, perhaps the unprofessionalism of recent tracks is an attempt to get back to the coal pit and find out, after over 10 years together, just what it was that gelled them in the first place. Certainly, they have done enough to earn the benefit of anyone's doubt with a restless and rewarding creativity that has led to the creation of some of the finest rock music of the 80's.

I recall another conversation in twilight hours back in the days when a seven album retrospective would have been an idle fantasy. A few musicians were gathered round, talking about music, plotting, bullshitting. I was discussing my plans for fame and fortune with my own group, Frankie Corpse And The Undertakers. Ever the svengali I was suggesting the way forward was to start out with simple, poppy material and win over a large commercial audience before introducing more complex and personal work. "Step by careful step," I was saying.

"Oh no," said Bono, abhorred. "You've always got to do the very best... the best stuff you can."

The world never did get to hear of Frankie Corpse.

THE MAKING OF A LEGEND

August 1989

Bono studying lyrics at The Point Depot in Dublin during filming of "Rattle And Hum"

THE U2 FILE

1985 - 1990

U2

Saturday, July 13th, 1985 will

go down in history as Live

Aid Day, the extraordinary

culmination of Bob Geldof's

attempts to mobilise the

THE GREAT LEAP OF FAITH

international music industry

behind urgently-needed

famine relief in Africa. Among

the stellar cast performing for

72,000 people at Wembley

Stadium, London are U2, a

band determined to rise to

the occasion.

Report: Neil McCormick

FROM A distance Wembley Stadium looks like a leftover from a Hollywood film set, dream architecture somewhere between "The Thief Of Baghdad" and Metropolis, its rolling, smooth, carved stone oddly out of place at the end of a long, bare, modern road.

Huge crowds of people were filing towards it — happy and colourful in t-shirts, shorts, jeans, summerwear. What a day! What a glorious day! Not only was the sky a rich, cloudless blue with a bright, hot sun beating down, but these people were going somewhere special, clutching tickets to (at long last, after centuries of extravagant, boastful circus posters) THE GREATEST SHOW ON EARTH!

Touts moved wearily through the masses, enquiring cautiously: "Anyone need a ticket?" Rumour had it that the police, visible at every juncture, were taking the unprecedented step of arresting these mercenaries. "We're not doing anything illegal," said one tout, quickly returning his wares to his pockets as three members of Her Majesty's Constabulary strolled by. "We're just discussing tickets between ourselves, aren't we? You can go anywhere with this ticket, it's not seated... it says Gate B but once you're inside you can sit or stand where you like. Look — there's no seat number, see?".

The ticket was an attractive and complex affair, worthy of any mint. "Of course it's not a forgery," insisted the tout. "It'd just be stupid to sell forgeries. Then you could really get nicked!"

The touts' asking prices varied astonishingly, depending presumably on the gullibility of the purchaser. "I managed to pick up a couple of tickets last week for 80 quid a shot," someone from a record company told me proudly. His companion turned to him and said nonchalantly, "they're selling them over by the gate for 35."

To the respectable purchaser a ticket was £5... plus a £20 donation to the BAND AID charity. 72,000 of these had sold out in a matter of hours. Nobody had thought the asking price steep. Outside the stadium official stands sold BAND AID videos, LIVE AID posters, t-shirts and programmes, David Bailey's book of Ethiopian photographs "Imagine" — everything bearing the legend "This Saves Lives". People thronged around the stands,

world calling   Pic: Mick Quinn

While my guitar gently weeps

keeping the volunteer helpers on their toes, most people buying a number of items, some buying as many as ten programmes at £5 each. THIS PROGRAMME SAVES LIVES...

And you were there. That was the main thing, as your ticket stub was torn at the turnstile, you were there, in person.

THE SIZE of the crowd really hit me as I stepped into it. Not just enormous but... bustling with life — it was momentarily frightening, the mood so raucous and jubilant that it seemed any small movement onstage could trigger a crazy stampede. But I soon realised the atmosphere was probably a little bit more picnic than carnival in most of the stadium. I had walked straight into the most manic area — directly beneath the celebrity seating.

"It's fuckin' Bowie, man, fuckin' Bowie," exclaimed a half tanked, beer bellied, sunburned man with (believe it!) a handkerchief tied to his head and a north of England accent. He was pointing at the stand and nudging his slimmer but similarly naked and burnt companion. "See — the first row —grey suit... fuckin' Bowie, man, fuckin' Bowie!" Another young man drew his friend's attention to Bowie with the more sedate "There's David — can you see him?", sounding for all the world like an old friend of the rock star.

A bearded George Michael appeared amidst the screams of those girls close enough to recognise him. People climbed up the stand as close as they could get to the celebrity area, passing programmes over to be autographed.

Someone was announcing the start of the concert as Prince Charles and Lady Di took their seats to a roar that drowned out the PA. Photographers, amateur and professional, jostled for the closest position. "Did you get the picture of Diana?" yelled a girl at her boyfriend as he and his instamatic were elbowed away by very serious looking papparazi. Bob Geldof, in denim and bristle, followed the immaculate heirs to the throne, and was as much a recipient of the standing ovation, from celebrities and crowd alike, as were the Royals.

On stage, a small military band played what seemed about 2 bars of the national anthem, for which nobody remained still. People who had started to sing were caught out when the music stopped short, and they began to shout instead...

NOISE AND excitement filled the air in the stadium. It was shaking. It took a moment to realise that Status Quo were onstage, barely visible through the ranks of arms held high, barely audible through the bellyroar of the thousands present. You could hear a snatch of that familiar, loping sound... "Rockin' All Over The World".

It was the first of many songs that bands pulled out of their

personal hit parades as appropriate to the occasion, the huge video screens on either side of the stage showing the pictures that were being beamed out to the invisible satellites. The crowd sang along full throat, delighted by the familiarity and friendliness of Quo's short set, the masters of 12 bar repetition packing a punch in 3 songs that they had probably never achieved before in their long (long, long) gigging career.

A couple of Status Quo banners were held high as the band left the stage. While most people were indistinguishable in their shorts and Live Aid t-shirts as fans of one band or another, there were some visibly partisan elements in the audience. Denim jackets with QUO sown in, several U2 banners, old leather jackets studded with The Who and, most strangely, one character with long hair and a headband who sported the name of Randy California on everything he wore and carried (including several copies of the same Randy California album). Did he know something we didn't? (Fortunately, the answer turned out to be NO).

A five minute gap between the openers and The Style Council allowed the atmosphere to calm down considerably, and Weller & Co, through warmly received, did not deliver the kind of stadium set that would have kept people on their toes. Some stretched out amidst legs that earlier looked ready to stampede and crush.

"Shall we stay here?", a girl asked her boyfriend, mid-crowd, "At least we can see the video!". "I didn't come to Wembley to watch TV," he replied, pushing forward.

At the very back there wasn't much else you could do, the dots on the stage being so unrecognisable that your eye was naturally drawn to the large screen close-ups. By the time the sound reached the back, however, it was out of sync with the picture. Some found those stands ideal however. "There's just about room to sit down," said a 30-ish denim-clad man, "hear some music, watch all the people enjoying themselves and" — he patted a wooden box with six plastic pint cups of beer — "drink up some atmosphere."

The three stages-in-one system had revolved once again, and, although Ultravox were next on the programme The Boomtown Rats were announced. There was a hefty cheer that grew and grew in volume as Geldof ran onto the stage. Even in the seats where no-one had stood thus far, people stood for a moment to applaud the man who made the day possible...

Despite being, in terms of international success, the most dubious band on the bill, there only because of 15 minutes of fame which had long-since ticked out, The Rats acquitted themselves superbly. Their sound was full (the best so far) and their hits memorable enough to have a crowd

> **"A strange guitar sound filtered in from the stadium. 'U2?', said one guy, torn between losing his place in the beer queue and seeing the band whose name he bore on his back."**

Of youth... Pic: Bono

that (in an odd role-reversal) wished to please — more than be pleased by — its hero. They sang along noisily, waving arms and applauding when Geldof paused meaningfully on a line from "I Don't Like Mondays" — "and the lesson today is how to die!"

During "Rat Trap" the first sound problem of the day manifested itself when the lead vocal vanished completely, causing some confusion as Simon Crowe's harmony lines interrupted what many took to be an extended instrumental introduction, while Geldof cavorted about the stage, hearing himself on his monitor and looking rather ridiculous on the video screens, as he silently mouthed the words of the song.

His voice, it must be conceded, was not sorely missed, the crowd doing a sterling replacement job, the vast majority of the 72,000 proving themselves to be better singers than Geldof (I sometimes wonder how someone could be dumb enough to think he could become a pop star with a voice like that and yet smart enough to do it!). And anyway... "I've just realised today is the best day of my life," he said before we lost his voice, and no accident of the PA could take that away.

THE VIDEO - screens went dead as the Rats left the stage and failed to come back on when Adam Ant and his band ran on to play "Vive Le Rock", his current single which no one seemed to recognise (despite the presence of lead vocals). He immediately ran back off after his one song set, leaving the stadium a little baffled.

Most of the press corps, however, could not have been the slightest bit confused, their seats (which probably for the first time in reviewing history had been paid for, at a cost of £100 each) remaining conspicuously empty throughout his set. In a

stadium overflowing with life, packed out with partying people, the press and VIP (£250) areas were starkly deserted for much of the gig. The same could not be said of the private bar.

"We got ten tickets into the office," moaned a record company representative sitting at the very back of the stadium, "and the bastards that grabbed them didn't give a damn about the gig. They just wanted to hang out at the bar. I wanted to hear the music!"

"So? You can hear the music all over the stadium," I observed.

"Yeah, but it would be nice to be able to get into the bar as well," he grinned.

Between sets the wide corridor that ran around the stadium filled up with people buying beer, coke and burgers (and more programmes and posters). One bar was so swamped it ran out of beer by 1 o'clock and someone had to stand shouting "Only Coca-Cola here!" to disperse the rapidly forming and potentially belligerent queues. "We should do the business like this everyday," said a sales woman. "No bleedin' thanks," said another, pouring coke out as quickly as she could get the cap off another litre.

A strange guitar sound filtered in from the stadium. "U2?" said one guy, torn between losing his place in a beer queue and rushing out to see the band whose name he bore on his back. Eventually he ran off to find Ultravox playing "One Small Day". I wonder if Midge Ure would take that as a compliment?

The heat in the crowd was intense — the sun beating down with a directness we hadn't experienced all this English summer. Somebody stripped down to his loose Y-fronts. "We could throw you out now," joked a steward.

Ultravox's playing was at first ham-fisted for a major

rock group, though it finally came together in a rousing "Vienna". "It's just like *Top Of The Pops*, isn't it?", said a young girl who had hitched her top as high as it would go and removed her trousers. "*Top Of The Pops* in the sun. It's lovely!" She had never been to a big live gig before. Perhaps, accustomed to seeing rock stars on fast moving TV shows, this was what she expected all live concerts to be like...

T H E   S T A G E revolved once again, bringing with it a new set-up and more roadies testing microphones. A heavy metal band played on the video, Kerranging its greetings from another part of the world to the apparently total disinterest of Wembley. The sound did not have the full weight of the PA and was (mercifully) constantly interrupted by the road crew thumping drums and counting up to two. It cut out completely mid-solo, to be replaced by a voice welcoming Spandau Ballet.

An extremely obese girl, stripped down to her bra and underpants with a t-shirt tied round her waist to act as a crude loin cloth, pointed excitedly at wide boy Martin Kemp. "My sister's boyfriend looks just like him!", she informed her companions. Kemp, in his regency finery, smiled benignly out at the crowd. "He's horrible," said one of the girl's friends.

Spandau, the first real heart-throb showbiz glitter act of the day caused a female surge to the front. Their first song ended amidst a few screams and wide, appreciative applause. Gary took the mike. "This is a brand new song, written especially for you. It's about any boy or girl that's born today — wishing them luck, cos they're gonna need it. It's called — 'We Are Virgin'," he announced.

"Speak for yourself sweetheart!", the girl in the bra shouted out.

The repartee of the bands we had seen thus far had not been particularly memorable, amounting mostly to a few 'y'alrights?' and a couple of 'Have a nice days'. Spandau, perpetrators of revolutionary chic turned smooth boyos, even let loose the hoary old chestnut: "You're looking beautiful, every one of you!" They obviously couldn't see the section of the crowd I was standing amidst: overweight, underdressed and sweating profusely. The rest of the stadium and the viewers at home could not plead the same ignorance. A television camera swung round in our direction. Arms went up excitedly as people appeared on the video. "Wave to your mum!", shrieked the fat girl as she saw herself and her companions in the middle of the picture. Astonishingly, they all waved frantically at the screen nearest them, not at the camera.

Close by someone was demonstrating greater media experience by holding aloft a hand-painted sign that read "Nicky & Sarah &

Jason & Steve. Hello Mum & Dad (x4). Jill Mary Lesley Bob Class of '77 and TORBAY."

Despite the stadium seething wall to wall with bodies, movement through the crowd was quite easy. The mood by now was relaxed with a total absence of belligerence on anyone's part. At the front, although there were various appeals from the stage for people to move back and make room, it was not dangerously jammed. Stewards sprayed water over the first few rows but nobody seemed in danger of collapsing and, between sets, there was a constant and unimpeded stream of people filing back and forward to the corridors.

> "Phil Collins and Sting... this is what people really wanted to see and hear – the rare, historical magic moment when two superstars meet."

Elvis Costello took the stage to a clamorous, welcoming cheer. A tiny figure on the huge stage, he strummed his guitar and said, "I want you to help me sing this old northern English folk song", before pre-empting the rumoured Beatle reunion by delivering a lovely, personalised, singalong version of "All You Need Is Love". The crowd sang lead, harmonies and even the horn parts without any bidding.

A L T H O U G H   T H E video had now arrived in Austria, it was, once again, largely ignored by the Wembley crowd. Many filed out to the toilets between sets, causing huge queues outside every Ladies sign. A toilet set aside for Physically Handicapped was filled with girls whose only handicap was an uncomfortable bladder. Some avoided queues by stepping furtively into a toilet whose entrance was partially blocked by a sign reading "Out Of Order. No Entry". Such was their desperation that a large queue of embarrassed girls formed inside one Gents, where they waited for cubicles to come free while lining single-file alongside the urinals. This was the cause of a very strange phenomenon — next door was a Gentleman's convenience that boasted only a large number of urinals (no cubicles) but which was curiously devoid of urinating gentlemen, while in the Gents filled with ladies, men *queued* to use the latrines, presumably for the privilege of exposing themselves legitimately to blushing female strangers.

Nik Kershaw took the stage on schedule to play a neat trio of hits. The efficiency of the stage management was stunning given the complexity of the task (and the usual propensity of shows —especially festivals — to run late). Backstage, shabby mobile cabins served as dressing rooms, with each performer allowed only a half hour of privacy before and after the gig, the cabin then being handed over to the next star. For once there were no ridiculous riders or extravagant extras and no complaints about the dull decor, peeling lino or missing luxuries.

Sade, onstage only five minutes late, wondered "Why Can't We Live Together?", her low key operation sounding remarkably convincing in this huge stadium. Oddly, she was the only black

...and age

star — a fact that doubtless accounted for, in an unusually mixed rag-bag of an audience, the very small presence of black people. She was also the first female star to make an appearance — causing the mass male ranks to cheer loudly when she removed her jacket and even more loudly and boorishly when she turned to reveal a backless top. "The best thing about these festivals," confided a young man with a predictably thin moustache, "is the girls." He and his friend went on to discuss someone they had seen in fishnet stockings and not much else. "You paid £25 for that?", I asked incredulously. "You could go to picture shows in Soho for 50p!". "It's for Ethiopia!", he replied honourably. I pointed him in the direction of some near-naked flesh.

Noel Edmunds delivered a lengthy build-up to Phil Collins and then had to run back on stage to shout rather sheepishly over the anticipatory yells of the crowd, "But first... Sting!" Sting and Collins alternated solo guitar and piano songs, winding up with duets on two of their finest moments — "Long Long Way To Go" and "Every Breath You Take". Without the slightest touch of bombast these two completely capitavated the stadium. This is what people really wanted to see and hear — the rare, historical, magic moment when two superstars meet.

This was the main element of the whole gig, of the whole Band Aid phenomenon. It wasn't just the chance to see all your heroes in one day, it was a chance to see all your heroes together, hobnobbing. An excuse to believe the rich and famous really were

different, living in another world, a world of MILLION DOLLAR QUARTETS...

Howard Jones was delighted to be part of this world, grinning from ear to ear as he sat down at the piano to play "Hide And Seek". For the newer and younger stars this must really have been the time of their lives, meeting people who were as much heroes for them as for the audience. The hippy in Howard, never too far from the surface, was brought right to the fore by the occasion —the Woodstock he never knew! "It's a great pleasure to be here with you sharing this experience," he informed everyone smiling.

At least one person was totally prepared to share his experience with the preposterous Mr Jones. A young man who somehow combined an outlandishly jet black mohican hairdo with a furry blond disco bopper moustache, leaped up and down screaming "Howaaaard!" and waving frantically at the stage. Howard, caught up in his own rapture, failed to notice.

The Russians invaded his set with a satellite broadcast of Autograph which sent people scurrying back in search of beer and toilets. A four-foot girl standing close to the stage complained vociferously that she hadn't seen a thing so far. "I've forced my way right up here and I can't even see the video!", she said. "There's always someone in the way." "Try growing," somebody suggested unhelpfully. "They should let the short people stand at the front and make all the tall people stand at the back, staggered by height," another diminutive girl was heard to suggest. "I don't think even Bob Geldof could organise that,'' her 6 ft boyfriend replied.

''BRYAN'S MAIN Vocal, Bryan's Main Vocal,'' repeated a roadie with a civilised voice and a vocabulary that took in more than the first two digits and the word hello. Trust Bryan Ferry to have an educated road crew. The man himself looked as smooth and sensational as always, leading a smooth and sensational band on stage. With exaggerated trade mark dips and shoulder shuffles he sucked the crowd into a set drawn largely from his new album, but delivered with such elan they sounded like family favourites. The PA faltered occasionally, cutting out drums and bass at certain points and almost fatally wiping out the vocal during the high point of the set, ''Imagine''. The loss of Ferry's vocal was a far more severe crisis than the loss of Geldof's had been, but once again voices rose from the crowd to fill in the gaps: ''Imagine all the people living life in peace... '' He closed the song by leading the entire stadium in a mass chorus of the worst whistling ever heard by man or beast, and received, upon his parting wave, one of the loudest responses of the day.

A Scotsman with a stutter listed ''F-F-F-F-Ferry, Paul Young, U2 and The Who'' as his reasons for travelling all the way to Wembley. ''I just want to see everybody,'' said another, ''so I'll be able to namedrop in conversations, you know. Bowie? Oh I've seen him live. The Who? I've seen them live! Status Quo? Queen? Elton John? I hate to bore you but I've seen them live too! Nobody will be able to hit with that 'I was at Woodstock' line again. I was at Live Aid, man.''

Paul Young's band did more stirring sing-a-song work and thankfully there were no vocal problems as another MILLION DOLLAR DUO brought the house down, Young duetting with Alison Moyet, a marriage made somewhere close to pop heaven and sealed with a kiss on the cheek. Matchmaker Geldof made an appearance at the end of their set to welcome America to the proceedings. ''Please, please give us as much money as we know you have,'' he said before the obligatory ''Have a good day.''

Bryan Adams came live but not very loud on the video from Philadelphia as in the thick of the crowd U2 flags were appearing. There were banners for everyone that day from ''Nik Kershaw'' to ''Hello Grimsby'' but there were more for U2 than anyone else. Perhaps U2 just have a flag waving audience for they inspired the loudest welcome since Quo as they launched into ''Sunday Bloody Sunday''.

Bono, as ever, connected with the audience, leaping down an embankment to pull a girl from the crowd during an extended version of ''Bad'' that swept into ''Ruby Tuesday'', ''Sympathy For The Devil'', ''Walk On The Wild Side'' and all of

"Bono, as ever, connected with the audience, leaping down to pull a girl from the crowd during an extended version of 'Bad'."

rock'n'roll. There was something strangely manic and disturbing about the performance but, more than any other of the day, it transcended crowd pleasing while succeeding in utterly pleasing the crowd. ''I w-wish they'd played m-m-m-more songs,'' said the stuttering Scotsman. Well, you can't keep everyone happy.

The Beach Boys, on video from America, were the first band to break down the boundary of distance, inspiring the Wembley audience to sing and dance and applaud as if they were on the stage in front of them. In two parts of the world crowds sang ''Good Vibrations'' — a hippy dream come true through the wonders of technology.

Dire Straits, with Sting on backing vocals, kept the stadium rolling. The crowd, since Ferry, had been getting louder and more agitated as star was heaped upon star and the compound excitement of the day mounted, and the appearance of vast arrays of invisible guitars, their players whining along to ''Sultans Of Swing'' added considerably to the pandemonium. But all hell broke loose for Queen who contributed the most brilliantly constructed greatest hits set of the day, 20 minutes into which they packed ''Bohemian Rhapsody'', (cleverly cutting away before the complex vocal harmonies), ''Radio Ga Ga'' (inspiring the ranks at the front to behave like extras in the video), ''Hammer To Fall'', ''Crazy Little Thing Called Love'', ''We Will Rock You'' and ''We Are The Champions'' — jerry-built crowd-pleasing anthems for every occasion. The band's sound was crystal clear and Mercury led the crowd like a true showman... I may sound like the converted here, but I saw punks dancing and applauding those hoary old pomp-rockers.

Queen even outdid everyone in the programme, tastefully printing the words ''Is This The World We Created'' where other bands had badly written biogs filled with the kind of extravagant claims that seemed out of place in the name of charity. The ads in the programme were another testing ground of sensitivity and cleverness. While some simply sold their products — cigarettes, make-up, stereos, clothes — presented colourfully and a little appallingly after horrifying photos from Ethiopia, many wisely and tastefully pushed the theme rather than themselves. ''Please think of the people for whom one hour seems an eternity,'' said Seiko. Ford Trucks had a cartoon of a packed family transit van on one page under the line ''Suffer Little Children'', while the page opposite stated ''But Don't Let The Children Suffer'' and elsewhere an otherwise blank page simply bore the line, ''this space has been donated by Imperial Tobacco Limited''.

Two other old Queens of Rock, Jagger and Bowie made an appearance on the video screen, singing ''Dancing In The Streets''. They were cheered but not as loudly as the arrival on-stage of the real thing — David Bowie, immaculate in a suit, surrounded by backing singer beauties and a stunning band, playing "Rebel Rebel".

"It's him! It's him!" yelled a girl close to tears. Presumably, elsewhere in the crowd a young man was informing his friends: "There's Dave on stage." "Modern Love" would have raised the roof if there'd been a roof, but Bowie's show-stopper was "Heroes" where he clearly celebrated the crowd and the watching world: *"We can be heroes just for one day... "*

The song, written so long ago, finally found its place on this stage just as Quo's "Rockin' All Over The World", Nik Kershaw's "Wouldn't It Be Good", Sade's "Why Can't We Live Together?", Sting's "Driven To Tears", Phil Collins' "A Long Long Way To Go" and Queen's "We Are The Champions", all had.

Bowie departed to long cries of 'more', returning a moment later, not to play an encore but to soberly introduce a video made by CBC. "The subject speaks for itself," he said. "Please send your money in."

The video — appalling, heart-rending pictures of the Ethiopian tragedy backed by The Cars' aching "Drive" *("You can't go on, thinking nothing's wrong")* — went a long way towards sobering the crowd. Tears filled many eyes as in the midst of the euphoria you were reminded of the cause that drove it, the tragedy that started the party. "I've got £20 here," said a girl. "Who am I supposed to give it to?" "Go and buy some programmes," suggested her friend. "I've already got five," said the girl.

T H E R E   W A S   a large shift of people at the front of the stadium, as the Bowie fans went in search of nourishment, and Who fans took their places. The sky was growing dark and cloudy above. In the corridor, a guy who had queued for five minutes for a burger, spat out his first mouthful. "That's not cooked," he complained loudly. "I'm not getting food poisoning for anyone, not even starving Ethiopians." Those close by laughed guiltily.

Harvey Goldsmith was onstage trying to make an announcement, but he was totally drowned out by Jack Nicholson on the screens from Philadelphia, attempting to introduce the next band in London. "I want you to think about who you'd like to see. Who?" he teased the crowd, his famous grin causing whoops of delight in Wembley. "I wonder if he can hear us screaming over there," asked a girl, "before emitting an ear-piercing "Ja-a-a-a-a-a-ck."

The star continued unabashed. "A working class image... legendary... " The crowd had their answer in seconds — "back from the dead — The Who!". Entwistle, Townshend, Daltrey, Jones and keyboard player Rabbit ran out onstage to have their intro totally blown by sound problems. When they eventually launched into "My Generation" (3 generations on) Daltrey's vocals were inaudible and Townshend's guitar poses looked

half-hearted at best. And yet still, despite their obvious unhappiness at playing together again, as the sound came together, the old magic came alive. This was The Who! For the last time anywhere. Daltrey mike-spinning, Townshend arm-windmilling, the band going through motions that had greatness honed right into them, singing "We won't get fooled again", and pulling the wool over everyone's eyes.

Santana followed The Who onto the huge screen. (What festival would be a festival without them? Don't answer that). The clouds were growing black and ominous above. "I think it's going to rain," said a fat Liverpool man, naked from the waist up. "I *hope* it rains!", he added, holding his arm aloft. "I could do with a bath." Norway's Band Aid song appeared on the video, as dismal as their usual Eurovision entry, and only made bearable by a ham-fisted roadie checking a piano through the PA. The organisers were testing fate showing this — and sure enough fate gave. The clouds burst and the rain came pouring down.

Since no-one had come dressed for this weather, few even bothered to shelter themselves. Many, including the fat Liverpudlian, whooped with delight. "Don't bother covering

The eyes have it Pic: Bono

yourself," he told his companion, "we've got to kip in a train station tonight. We're gonna get wet anyway — so we might as well get wet now!"

Elton John came out amid the downpour and the uproar, and,

huge lights flashing, launched into "I'm Still Standing". The stadium was singing — you should have heard it, you should have felt it. The rain, the dark blue sky, the lit up stage, a Goodyear airship overhead, everyone standing, singing, smiling; that picture is etched on my mind as the occasion for once and for all became truly united and euphoric.

Elton's set was a storm blowing out over the stadium. The exceedingly boring Kiki Dee caused a true sensation, probably for the first time in her dull career, as she duetted on the bubblegum hit, "Don't Go Breaking My Heart". A bearded George Michael gained some kind of grace by singing Elton's "Don't Let The Sun Go Down", with a confidence and style matched only by the day's finest vocalists. Elton pumped it out 'till the rain stopped during "Can I Get a Witness?", and the heat and dancing began to dry everybody out.

Oh, there was a party going on now, alright. The air was filled with plastic bottles being tossed back and forth while most of one stand kept bellowing "Woah!" The noise grew and exploded into a welcome for the return of Queen's Brian May and Freddie Mercury. They sat on stools and waited for quiet to descend, before performing a slow, acoustic rendition of "Is This The World We Created". The crowd swayed from side to side, treating the simple, well-meant ballad almost like a hymn.

Mercury and May left the stage to a buzz of excitement. What was in store for the ending? The rumoured Beatles reunion with Julian Lennon on guitar? "Don't be stupid!", said the fat Liverpudlian man. A lone figure walked out into the light and sat at the piano. "Keep your fingers crossed," said a girl. "That's Paul..."

The crowd cheered but as the noise subsided, no sound could be heard from the stage. Evidently McCartney was playing and singing... something, but the sound gremlins were at work again. The piano suddenly came through the PA. It was "Let It Be", Paul's head bobbed as he sang, blissfully ignorant of his vocal absence. The crowd joined in anyway, and when his vocal finally came through they bellowed their approval.

Geldof, Townshend, Bowie and Alison Moyet came out to join in the chorus. Everybody sang... never mind that the singing was awful (particularly Geldof's), it was together at the end. "There will be an answer, let it be!"

McCartney and Townshend raised Geldof on their shoulders, the stars of the day began to file onstage — each new face greeted with cheers. See Bono standing with Paul McCartney, generations and cultures meeting before your very eyes.

"I think you know the next song. It might be a bit of a cock-up, but if you're going to cock it up, you might as well do it with 2 billion people watching you. So let's cock it up together,"

announced Geldof, as Bowie led the crowd through "Do They Know It's Christmas?" You haven't heard noise until you've heard 72,000 people singing for a cause, you haven't heard the moving power of song. They'll be talking about this for a very long time to come...

The chorus "Feed the World, Let them know it's Christmas time", filled the summer night long after the stage had been deserted. It could be heard throughout the stadium, in the corridors, and in bursts from the crowds as they headed homeward.

"You haven't heard noise until you've heard 72,000 people singing for a cause, you haven't heard the moving power of song."

A LONG time ago, Gerry Moore of Street Talk, a nothing band with big hopes and dreams told me that rock stars could make anything hip. "They can make it cool to be a punk, hip to be a hippy. If the right people *give*, the people that believe in them will give. Rock'n'roll is one of the biggest money-spinning rackets in the world, and it could make giving hip."

Geldof had done it, you realised, heading for home. Rock had done it. Given everyone a night to remember, and finally made it cool to be kind.

I know where the fee for this article is going.

THE GREAT LEAP OF FAITH
July 1985

The British Press wanted a statement from U2. Bono gave some quotes to Island press executive, Rob Partridge, who took it to the Wembley press room but when the hacks saw it, they judged it unsuitable. For the record, this is what worried the tabloids: "U2 are involved in Live Aid because it's more than money, it's music... but it is also a demonstration to the politicians and policy-makers that men, women and children will not walk by other men, women and children as they lie bellies swollen, starving to death for the sake of a cup of grain and water.

"For the price of Star Wars, the Mx missile offensive-defence budgets, the deserts of Africa could be turned into fertile lands. The technology is with us. The technocrats are not. Are we part of a civilisation that protects itself by investing in life... or investing in death?" Later, an Island spokesman commented dryly: "It wasn't what they wanted. They preferred something glib."

In the magical, wind-swept

OUTSIDE IT'S DONEGAL

landscape of Ireland's remote north-west the cameras roll as U2's Bono and Maire of Clannad make the video for their collaborative single "In A Lifetime". Bill Graham joins the entourage at work and at play and talks to the main protagonists.

I HAVE had my share of strange experiences but few as incongruous as driving in convoy with an empty hearse through Northern Ireland on the same day as Peter Barry and Tom King are meeting at Stormont for the first session of the Anglo-Irish Conference. I have seen some strange musical alliances but few as odd as an acoustic guitar, an accordion and, for God's sake, bagpipes being filmed by a video crew in a bar in Gweedore.

Even if Bono is on board for this most bizarre of occasions, the location should immediately identify those really responsible. Gweedore, of course, is Clannad's home. With them, surreal combinations are commonplace. After all, this is a group whose apprenticeship was spent singing versions of The Beach Boys and Joni Mitchell, translated by their grandfather for local Gaelic pantomimes!

In the nicest possible way, I've learnt my lesson: Clannad are impossible to interview. There's always one more anecdote left, one further twist to their tale. You talk to Maire Ní Bhraonáin for two hours, share other informal sessions with her and the rest of the band and think you've tracked down their true trivia secrets when she admits to having had the same juvenile music teacher as Dana and Feargal Sharkey and sharing ballet lessons with the aforementioned Eurovision winner!

Then the tape tucked away, in the sweetest, most endearingly frustrating way possible, she throws you another morsel from her memories. "Ah yes," she'll say, "then there was the time when I was 11 and in my green Irish dancer's dress, playing with my father's band in Glasgow on St Patrick's Day singing 'The Hucklebuck' and 'My Boy Lollipop'."

Quite, quite impossible to interview! The Clannad musical family tree extends backwards and sideways through parents, grandfathers, aunts and uncles in a maze that would probably befuddle even that most resourceful of researchers, Pete Frame. With their background, I think it's highly probable that the family mutt's got his own equally lengthy story of how he's related to Nipper, the original HMV gramophone dog.

In other words, any journalist who travels to Gweedore seeking facts about Clannad's music is likely to end up more confused than ever. But if he or she goes there seeking the feel,

(above) Máire Ní Bhraonáin of Clannad and (below) Bono

enlightenment is certain.

THE GROUP, the video crew and most of their camp-followers were spending these December days in Gweedore for another reason, shooting the screentrack for "In A Lifetime", their collaboration with Bono.

For Clannad, it's a whole other sort of homecoming, their first opportunity to feature the scenery and community of their native parish in a video, an expedition that sends almost 50 of us, cast, crew and camp-followers from the media and their record company scrambling up and down the dreamscaped, windswept mountains of Donegal in dank, raw weather. So many have been called to the colours that Ostan Na Gweedore, the local luxury hotel, normally closed through the off-season, had been specially opened for the video invaders.

This is an expensive video, costing at least £80,000, its budget increased by the group's determination to film in Gweedore, remote from both the media centres of Dublin and London. As Maire accepts, the full budget is more than it cost to record their six pre-RCA albums but that's how the cookie must be crumbled in the video age. Ideally Bono's participation should give Clannad the passport to markets and video outlets that have previously ignored them. Nobody wants that crucial opportunity to be missed through underinvestment.

It arrives at a pivotal point in their career. Clannad view the "Macalla" LP as the true follow-up to "Magical Ring" with this new album intended as proof of their skill as Celtic pop innovators, blending their heritage of harmony and melody with the design science of the hi-tech studio.

But all has not run smoothly since the album's release. Because of the delicate state of Maire's vocal chords, a tie-in tour has been cancelled and in the UK, the album's second single "Almost Seems (Too Late To Turn)" — for me, the album's highlight by virtue of Maire's measuredly heartfelt reading and the poignant balance of the arrangement — was the victim of unsympathetic airplay policies.

The 45 had been released as a fund-raiser for the BBC's "Children In Need" charity but Beeb's left hand must not have known what its right was doing for their own Radio 1 denied it airplay, deeming it inappropriate for its format and thus dooming "Almost Seems... " to chart failure — a definite setback.

More positively, RCA America are finally showing real enthusiasm about breaking Clannad, a group whom the company had previously considered out of sync with the US tastes, though as the experienced Maire will comment guardedly, "Seeing is believing." Whatever, breaking Clannad to the wider world audience they deserve may now turn on the "In A Lifetime" single, its video and Bono's attendant and influential endorsement.

"Remember that Bono and myself never look at each other," says Maire. "This is not a 'love' song, it's a 'life' song."

Which is why this convoy of two mini-buses and the hearse — actually intended as a prop for a funeral scene — leaves Windmill Lane Studios one December Wednesday noon on a definite mission. Seven hours later after blithely driving through the North and bouncing over the mountain roads of Donegal, we finally enter the parish of Gweedore...

PASSING A crossroads, Clannad's bassist, Ciaran O'Braonáin, forever in shades, explains the finer points of the local geography: "On the map this is the centre of Gweedore but the truth is, there's no real centre to it. It's only on the map because this is where the old railway station was."

He's right. Gweedore is nowhere and everywhere, a sprawling collection of cottages, houses and shops patterned for over six miles along the main road without any definable village centre. Ciaran continues, laughing about confused German tourists who arrive at the station crossroads to find no conventional town square.

But then Gweedore has its own law, lore and very special logic. As Donegal's Gaeltacht, it's proudly retained its own identity, a community that's held onto its long-defined tradition without ever denying the late 20th century. Never under-estimate these people. Ireland's most forgotten Western county may be remote but it is the reverse of primitive. At best, as in Gweedore, its people have self-reliance, an individuality, both a sense of community and an outgoing curiosity, and a lack of cant that makes them among the most fascinating on this island.

Okay, holidaying as a child on Aranmore Island means that I've long had reasons to be in love with the county but watching Bono and Adam Clayton, a self-confessed ligger for the week, blending into the landscape, I could see they've both become equally smitten.

But Gweedore is even more unique in many ways. Besides having its own magical folklore, Donegal Gaelic is distinct from the rest of Ireland, a dialect with its own idiosyncratic accents and words which some claim is closer to Scots Gaelic. Yet the Gaeltacht tourist trade means this society can be equally at home with Beef Wellington as Wellington Boots and down the road, in the industrial estate, the girls whose grandmothers were weavers now work in a computer firm. The simple secret is that this is one community that has never lost its belief in the power of education. The same combination of dedication and open-mindedness impels Clannad.

In the exposed outdoors, the video shoot is an endurance test. Partially sheltered in woodland, we're spared the worst of the biting weather but the wind is forever upsetting the accuracy of the smoke-machines and blowing fumes into our eyes. For a whole afternoon director Meiert Avis and cameraman Tommy Forsberg — an Ingmar Bergman graduate who also shot U2's "New Year's Day" video — forever fastidiously figure out their angles as the main actors Maire and Bono continuously pace back and forth through their scene, aloft the wild and wondrous Poison Glen.

Everyone implicitly admits, however, that the real star is the scenery and spirit of Donegal. Later in the hotel, Pól O'Braonáin — who's been dubbed "Fellini" for his efforts — oversees the casting of locals as extras for Friday's shooting, which will take place at a crossroads on a bare mountainside.

That's where the hearse features. Driven by Charlie Whisker, an artist friend of Bono who's stimulated the singer's growing interest in the blues, it's part of a funeral procession that's intended to symbolise the evolution from life to death. As Maire later comments: "Remember that myself and Bono never look at each other. This is not a 'love' song — it's a 'life' song."

Fortunately there are other more convivial settings. Friday evening, Leo O'Braonáin's pub is featured. Beneath the arc lights, the bar's regulars must never have seen the like. Fiddlers saw away, a group of local children give a Christmas mumming routine and that's when Leo on Cordovox accordion, the bagpiper and Noel O'Dugáin on guitar play their magnificently bizarre set.

Leo is a most alert and hospitable presiding spirit, always ready to pull out his accordion for a song. In his presence, you understand both the closeness of the Clannad extended family and how music is among the necessities of life for them.

Close to the bar, Bono soaks it all in. In the last year, he's allowed his conviviality overcome any remaining puritanical streak, albeit he still paces himself, preferring to slowly sip glasses rather than pints of Guinness. But he can't completely escape the duties of stardom, for by night's end he must have signed almost a dozen autographs for everyone present.

When the camera and lights are packed away, it all gets quietly mad. The autograph seekers are even propositioning the video crew, Clannad manager Dave Kavanagh and, of all people, myself, the *NME's* Adrian Thrills and *Smash Hits'* Peter Martin. Behind the bar, Bono and Maire are pulling the pints.

Truly a family affair. Later Pól gives the best summary for the expedition: "It's something I'll remember for a long time. To me, there's a whole circular thing about going back and using people who, when I was 12, were directing me in my forays on the stage."

B O N O   W I L L   admit that recording "In A Lifetime" with Clannad was part of his musical higher education. Like many of his generation, he'll confess to having wrongly believed there was no life before '76, other than the obvious landmarks from Marc Bolan back beyond to Elvis Presley.

The same exploration through the past links both "In A Lifetime" and his impromptu blues recording with Keith Richards and Ron Wood, "Silver And Gold", on the "Sun City" album. Recently Bono's been taking his musical history lessons and as we talk, the theme's just as likely to slide off towards English folk music, gospel or Richard Thompson.

He believes the process began when he saw Ridley Scott's futuristic flick, "Blade Runner". "It seemed to be set some place where Los Angeles meets Tokyo in the '90s or towards the turn of the century," he reflects. "Well, somehow I felt that the

Bono: "We don't believe in videos with storylines."

Vangelis soundtrack didn't click, somehow I could imagine an ethnic soundtrack as being more suitable. And then I was talking with Chris Blackwell and he thought people wouldn't want pure electronic music in the '90s because it would remind them of whatever loss of humanity they might be suffering. He thought they'd be looking for musics that would encompass ethnic sound, cajun, reggae, Irish, blues or hybrids that would be a merger between the available technology and ethnic sounds."

That theme led him to German producer, Conny Plank, who'd briefly worked with Clannad in their pre-RCA career and who's long been intrigued by the possibility of a marriage between Irish and electronic music. But that was theory; for Bono, Clannad's magnificent "Harry's Game" was proof.

The first time he heard the group's ground-breaking single, the effect was devastating. "I almost crashed my car," he recalls. "There were bass synths and vocal banks, people keying vocals. Through keyboards. There it was under my feet, more developed than anything else."

Simultaneously Bono had been talking with violinist Steve Wickham about ways of modernizing Irish music. "Now with Clannad," he continues, "I was beginning to see the future of something, whatever it might be, something that could avoid the trappings of rock'n'roll, places like the Marquee or the Ritz in New York, and go straight to Carnegie Hall. They're not the same as modern classical composers like Philip Glass or Steve Reich but Clannad deserve to be categorised in some place near them."

If he has one worry, it's that Clannad can "be more interested in pop music. It's their experimental side I prefer."

One thing was destined to lead to another. "Harry's Game" became the atmospheric theme that closed U2 concerts. Previously strangers, U2 and Clannad gradually began to huddle together. Maire takes up the story.

"There's total musical respect between the two bands which is lovely to have, especially because when two bands meet, there's often so much bickering. RCA had been edging in for some time, suggesting I should do a duet. And there were a couple of big names there but it didn't turn me on. If it didn't mean anything to Clannad, it didn't mean anything to me."

Bono and Maire first met in the wake of "Harry's Game". "They started to play it and we were introduced in Windmill one day and he said they were on an American tour and in some of the university interviews they were being asked about this song, so please tell me more so I can talk about it... but some of the band didn't know him or the rest of U2 before the recording. We were gradually meeting up because of using the same studios, because both managers are close friends... I think the first band-to-band

meeting came because of going to Croke Park. But it was a gradual thing. We didn't meet like our five members and their four members — like, I've only just recently met The Edge."

Maire first suggested the alliance but all agreed "if it wasn't great, it wasn't going on the record, no matter how much time was spent on it."

Bono truly disrupted the proceedings: "This was our ninth album and you could lose a little bit in terms of different ways of performing. It broke our routine... So myself, Ciaran, Pól and the producer, Steve Nye, went into the studios and played him the instrumental track without a guide vocal once and he immediately learnt it and turned around to the engineer and said 'Kevin you know the way I like it, give me a mike.' He'd never heard it before and he immediately started singing with it.

"We all just sat there with our mouths open. We didn't expect someone to spring this on us. Because some of the actual lines he did put down were, in the long run, it. The way he works, it's sometimes a spontaneous thing where what you do right away can work."

Bono has similar memories of the session though he thinks the second take was the good one. "I was copping out from being a 'musician'. Pól was giving me timings but I just said 'play the track and give me the microphone."

WITH, AS Bono says, "Radio 1 DJ's playing it twice in a row", a video was inevitable. Bono co-directed it though he left most of the location direction to Meiert Avis while he and The Edge came up with the basic scenario. "We don't believe in videos with storylines," he explains, "we're imagistic. We don't think you should explain a song. You should add other images that you didn't know were there in the song."

But relationships now extend beyond the studio. Donegal is close to his heart. After the pressure of American tours, Bono says he and his wife Ali often retire there or to Scotland because, he jokes, "we're sure it will rain there."

Gweedore and the extended Clannad family also loom large in his affections. "You can see the love they have for each other. They're very physical in their affections. And then there's their father, a tee-totaller, running the noisiest pub in Ulster."

Bono's explorations were also prompted by Bob Quinn's Atlantean trilogy, the television series that heretically argues that the roots of Irish culture might be in the Middle East among the Copts. "Both myself and Brian Eno were very interested in that," he says, "and I met with Bob Quinn a few months ago. He's a very unpretentious man, humble yet at the same time the sort of Dublin hard man I could relate to — not a flowers in the hair hippy you might expect to drop out in Connemara." Quinn gave

> "Meeting Keith Richards was a highlight for me. I hope I'm still in love with music at 45, though I'd prefer to get there by a different route."

him a list of contacts which Bono used on a recent African sojourn, *en route* to which he stopped off in Cairo.

The Irish/Atlantean connection could be seen coming perhaps, but hardly the ravaged, viscerally emotional blues of "Silver And Gold". Bono was hardly a day out of Africa when he jetted into New York for the "Sun City" video, meeting up with Peter Wolf, the J. Geils Band's former mouthartist, and they both went off to The Stones' session which was under the thumb of ex-U2 producer, Steve Lillywhite.

"I didn't go to bed much. It was like a dream sequence for me," he recalls, "meeting Keith Richards was like a highlight for me. I hope I'm still in love with music when I'm 45 — though I'd prefer to get there by a different route. When he put on his guitar, you could see the lines disappear from his face."

These memories can seem an absurd over-romanticization, particularly when I remember Bono's unhappiness at the Dylan/Richards/Wood "Live Aid" performance. Yet the musical evidence is on his side. "Silver And Gold", written overnight in something close to a frenzy, is very special.

Now the "Sun City" cabal want to release "Silver And Gold" to give extra momentum to the album and liberation cause and that may mean another video.

Bono's rather torn. He sees the necessity for supporting the "Sun City" project and will probably go ahead but he's worried these solo projects might detract from U2. "After all I'm only one of four," he reminds me, "my favourite group is still U2."

All this activity leaves the future in fascinating flux. At the start of '86, Bono seems to have more ideas and stimuli than he can easily condense and refine and refuses to give an exact prediction of when the next U2 album will appear.

But hints regarding how it might evolve can't be avoided. "I'm torn between two continents," he says, "whereas The Edge has a more European sensibility. I think the justification for that combination is that U2's music has both. It can reach into Europe and reach into America."

And perhaps beyond. If Bono seems to be teetering between continents, he also has a new confidence in his singing. "Somewhere in the last six months, I've learnt how to sing," he says. "It began on 'Unforgettable Fire' but now I think I've come onto something. I've been uptight for the last few years; now I think the voice may be coming into its own. I may be learning how to find something else, how not to howl."

I suspect that the wait may be worth it, that the next album may be as different from "Unforgettable Fire" as it was from its predecessor. But his last words are about Clannad and Irish music.

"I prefer the experimental side of Clannad to their pop side. I think there's a huge hole in Irish music ready to be filled, to which they can contribute."

For Clannad, U2 and whoever else may enter, the race is on.

Máire exults on stage

WIDE AWAKE IN AMERICA

In what may well be the most effective marriage yet of rock and pragmatic politics, U2, Sting, Peter Gabriel, Lou Reed and others are pushing the Amnesty International message on the 'Conspiracy Of Hope' tour. Pat Singer joins them on the road.

ALREADY AT 10.30 am "I Will Follow" was blasting from a van swathed in a white U2 banner in the parking lot of Giants Stadium in the swamps of Jersey, not far from New York city. It was Sunday, Bloody Hot Sunday, June 15, and it was 11 hours and twenty-two acts later that U2, in the flesh, took the stage for the benefit of Amnesty International USA. Bono, head bowed at the mike, lulled the clamorous crowd momentarily with the opening lines of "MLK" before launching into "Pride" — could he see the large photo of Dr. King held aloft by some attentive fans in the field? Next came "Bad", and "Sunday, Bloody Sunday" —"Are you tired of reading the papers, and watching the news? Have you had enough of Beirut? Have you had enough of Nicaragua? Have you had enough of Belfast?". Then "Maggie's Farm/Cold Turkey" — more focussed and thus more mesmerizing than at Self-Aid (and with a smaller spotlight). And to dispel that dark mood, a soothing end to the set: a balladic version of "Help", the audience singing its help out to the mike turned towards them.

The show wasn't over yet, though; the Police had yet to play.

THE MARATHON concert was the last gig of a six-city tour by U2, Sting, Peter Gabriel, Lou Reed, Bryan Adams, Joan Baez, and the Neville Brothers, marking Amnesty International's 25th anniversary.

Dubbed a "Conspiracy of Hope", the pop caravanserai travelled across America, playing 15,000-seaters in San Francisco, Los Angeles, Denver, Atlanta (where the Police reunited), and Chicago before winding it up for the sweltering sell-out crowd of 55,000. Just in case the headliners weren't your cup of tea, Sunday's roster included Jackson Browne who played San Francisco and Los Angeles too, Miles Davis, Peter, Paul and Mary, Little Steven and Bob Geldof, Joan Armatrading, Howard Jones, The Hooters, Ruben Blades with Carlos Santana and Fela Kuti (released with help from Amnesty), Yoko Ono, Joni Mitchell, Third World, Stanley Jordan and John Eddie. Just in case you couldn't get a ticket, the entire concert, noon to 11 pm was televised on MTV, the national pay-TV music television channel, and the evening portion was on free TV channels as well. It was also simulcast on radio all day long.

To some, U2 playing for free, again, may be losing its

noteworthiness, but their role in boosting a benefit *tour*, and Amnesty's aims for the show made the occasion not just another euphoria-in-the-service-of-conscience-salving one-night-stand.

In December of '84, the band had donated proceeds from a New York concert of Amnesty, and Jack Healey, ex-monk and Executive Director of the USA branch, had seen the show and been impressed. Healey wanted 1986 to be the year that Americans learned about Amnesty. Here, in the land of the free, a country with a voting population of over 170 *million* people, the group had just 150,000 members and its work was largely unfamiliar to most. Healey had a notion that music would do the trick.

His metamorphosis from obscure human rights activist to big-time rock 'n'roll impressario took all of ten minutes, and it happened — not surprisingly — in Dublin. One day last August, in the time it took to outline his idea to Paul McGuinness and Bono, Healey found himself holding a letter of intent from U2, promising Amnesty at least a week's time in the summer of 1986.

"Healey found himself holding a letter from U2 promising Amnesty at least a week of their time."

This bona-fide commitment made it much easier for Healey to convince artists, managers, and record companies that the shows would indeed take place. Even so, he didn't get everybody he wanted, some were locked into summer tours already, some, who will remain nameless, were unresponsive. (Eventually promoter Bill Graham — you read about him in Geldof's book — came in to help run things). Other artists, though, were happy to juggle their schedules — Sting, who had recently come off the road was willing to go back on. "The only thing," he said, "that could possibly get me out of bed is Amnesty." Lou Reed said that he couldn't think of a better way of using his time, and Peter Gabriel wrangled his way out of a "So" promo tour in Japan.

Such commitment was essential to the success of the tour, not only in terms of drawing large audiences (demand for the $36 tickets far exceeded availability) but also because the artists were to become the primary spokespersons for the cause. For, the whole point of the tour was not simply to swell Amnesty's coffers but to enlist young Americans as 'freedom writers', to motivate people to actively work for the release of prisoners of conscience. This time, a cheque alone would not suffice. They needed to join the "Conspiracy Of Hope", a conspiracy that by its unabashed overtness was a perfect counterpoint to the secretive practices of torture and imprisonment Amnesty works to eliminate.

To wit, you couldn't go to the concerts without learning about Amnesty. At every venue, there were tables set up with literature, and postcards to six governments, urging the release of the six prisoners who had been 'adopted' for special attention during the tour. Once they've sorted the tens of thousands of cards,

Amnesty will hand-deliver them to the embassies of the countries in question. (Scroll-like petitions to P.W. Botha protesting the state of emergency in South Africa were timely additions to the scene at the last concert).

Shown at the concerts was a clip comprising actual footage, interspersed with some of the compelling public service announcements quoting first-hand accounts of torture, and describing Amnesty's work and how anyone could participate.

Even juxtaposed with deodorants and shampoo commercials on the telecast, these momorable announcements, by Elvis Costello, Keith Richards, John Huston, Meryl Streep, John Taylor, and many others lost absolutely none of their impact. Pat Benatar made it clear that buying a t-shirt wasn't enough, prodding viewers in a very non-didactic, down-to-earth way, acknowledging the extra effort requested: "It'll involve some work on your part, that's right, work…you still payin' attention?…in over fifty countries, you could be arrested for listening to this message."

Comic Robin Williams did a brilliant, scathing vignette in the persona of a Central American tyrant — "I keep getting these damn letters … OK, one letter, big deal…I get another bag of letters … another bag of letters. They make me feel baaad about myself! Oh, Deectatorsheep is a Beeetch!" (By contrast, the on-air hosts, actor Elliot Gould, and comic Richard Belzer, were appallingly insensitive and phony during scripted interviews with the artists, visiting politicians, etc).

Aside from the in-house publicity, once the tour was underway, the press pounced, especially TV. America started having breakfast with Bono, and Sting, and Peter — interviewed on network morning shows, each of which is seen by, oh, 7 or 8 million people every morning.

Throughout, all the artists showed unprecedented patience with the press, graciously reiterating their reasons for taking part in the tour, Sting and Bono stressing that they'd become supporters and letter writers themselves through entertainment — specifically the "Secret Policeman's Ball". Even the morning after the big bash, Sting, Peter Gabriel, Jack Healey, and Bill Graham appeared on the *Today* show, at 7.30am, hoarse but articulate proponents of what Gabriel termed "the politics of embarrassment."

THOUGH THE tour in itself was an innovation in the prophets to profits category, the national telethon a lá Live-Aid/Self Aid of the expanded Meadowlands show was as essential to the whole undertaking as a great hook is to a hit song. Transforming the final concert into an "EVENT" made the

Guitar man: Bono

This is The Edge

music and the message more newsworthy *and* fuelled the anticipation for the Sunday show — thereby increasing the potential home audience, who would then learn about Amnesty International. (The tour played live to about 150,000; 32 million households have their MTV, and the syndication of the 8-11 pm part could be seen on half the televisions in America, some 43 million. Fortunately for Amnesty and the advertisers, the US Open Golf Tournament ended before the syndication began).

The telecast wasn't only a news peg, it was a carrot to dangle in front of major advertisers. Not that it was easy to sell something called a *conspiracy* to squeamish corporate types, especially if the firm did business in, say, South Africa. Not only that, television station managers outside the larger cities complained that the headliners weren't "real" stars, like Madonna and Lionel Richie, meaning the kind who make the cover of *People* and *Time*. What's more, plans were finalised at the beginning of May, meaning that many advertising budgets were already set for the year.

Still, despite the 'off-putting' title and the uncompromising nature of the talent on board, corporate sponsorship and TV advertising from the likes of Seagrams, Coke and Honda Scooters added up to big bucks — over $1 million. (Not bad at all, if you consider that Live-Aid media sales were in the area of $3 million). These monies will go towards paying tour costs, which will certainly top the $1 million mark. The artists took no fees, but running the tour, promoting it, and filming the public service announcements were all Amnesty's responsibility. Ticket revenues — in the $5 million range — will also help to defray costs.

Along the way, the "Conspiracy Of Hope" elicited lots of

rate-cutting, saving hundreds of thousands of dollars. Hotel rooms for the 180 on the tour were had for free or cheap. The Boeing 707, scene of jam sessions, general bonhomie, and at least one pillow fight (instigated by P.G.), was also had for a song, maybe a bit more. Amnesty kept a higher percentage on t-shirts etc than even Springsteen gets — they stand to net something like $300,000 from merchandise sales. (T-shirts sales at Giants Stadium were frenzied, one booth sold one thousand $15 shirts by 12.30 pm).

The final tallies aren't in for Giants Stadium, but it would be interesting to know if more t-shirts were sold than postcards signed. Events tend to attract generic event-goers, automatic souvenir buyers. To paraphrase P.T. Barnum, something of an event expert himself: You can reach some of the people some of the time, but you can't reach all of the people all of the time.

THE CONSPIRACY Of Hope finale, with its staggering musical diversity and quality, posed the thought that America is not a big market, it is many markets, sharply segmented and defined — largely due to the way radio programming is formatted here. So while one market was into the music and dancing, the other markets were making paper airplanes out of Amnesty literature, playing beachball, throwing toilet paper rolls off the upper tiers or having noisy water pistol fights.

Many of those who fled the scorching heat into the perimeters of the stadium passed the time drawing hearts and testaments of love (Michelle 'n' David) on the Botha petitions taped to the walls. (The petitions on tables manned by A1 volunteers received more dignified treatment).

Perhaps part of the preponderance of 17 year-old Red Hot

Chilli Pepper clones in the audience was due to ticket giveaways by several local radio stations. But the lacklustre response to unfamiliar artists, especially quiet ones like jazz guitarist Stanley Jordan (who came over very well on TV though) was disquieting.

Jamaica's Third World did a great job of getting the mostly white, middle-class kids on their feet, as did Little Steven, and the Neville Brothers with Joan Baez. In short, if you weren't mainstream but you *were* loud, you did okay. This isn't to say that they didn't play very well too, but why wasn't Geldof's raucous, on the mark version of Marley's "Redemption Song" better appreciated?

The reception for top forty acts were audibly different. When Howard Jones came out for one song, the roar was deafening. The same went for The Hooters, who got their big break last year opening Live-Aid in Philadelphia. Their set of songs especially chosen for appropriateness to the spirit of the day included "Lucy In The Sky With Diamonds". So there. This year's career-boosting slot was given to John Eddie — an unknown whose video went into heavy rotation on MTV the week preceding the concert. (He's a sort of Elvis Cougar Springsteen and he's all over the radio now).

The quality of the sound was not at all what it should have been at an event of this calibre. It was muddy, miking was bad and there was inexcusable feedback. Anyone who was at Self-Aid should consider themselves spoiled rotten, and forget what minor glitches occurred there. The sound did seem to improve somewhat, however, when the headliners, starting with Lou Reed, came on in the early evening. The tenor of the crowd was much more unified too. Peter Gabriel, in great voice, had them in the palm of his hand, opening with "Shock The Monkey", "Rain", "Shoot Into The Light"; gyrate dancing through "Sledgehammer"; then bringing things down with a riveting, mimed "San Jacinto" and closing with "Biko", dedicated that day to all those detained in the state of emergency.

Bryan Adams' rock'n'roll was not a jarring successor to Gabriel at all. Even "I Need Somebody", like several songs by other artists on the tour, took on additional meaning in the context of the show. His energy cranked the fans up a few notches, but anticipation turned to exasperation when Joni Mitchell took the stage in the slot before U2. A victim of wildly bad pacing, somebody (Bill Graham?) had shoved her into Pete Townshend's time. (Townshend had returned to England the day before when his father fell seriously ill). Despite a bag of water exploding near her on the front of the stage, she finished her brief set of new material, subtly jamming with her husband (on bass): another performance which shone on the tube but was lost on the arena, where the tired fans couldn't stand to wait any longer for U2 and their superb set of cover versions and originals.

BEFORE LEAVING the stage, U2 reprised "Sun City" with Little Steven, Nona Hendryx, Ruben Blades, and Lou Reed sharing vocals with Bono, and the fans, of course.

And so The Police, who, having turned down huge sums to play stadia this summer, decided they could bear each other's company for the sake of Amnesty. They sure didn't sound as if they'd been apart for two years, offering much more than rota versions of "Message In A Bottle" and "King Of Pain", Stewart on the xylophone, Sting a little raspy but completely wound up. With Kenny Kirkland backing up on keyboards, "Driven To Tears" was an interesting hybrid of the Blue Turtles' rendition punctuated by Andy's guitar. Then on to the real sentimental favourites, "Every Breath" and "Roxanne".

> "If one per cent of the millions of people exposed to Amnesty's message maintain an interest, the tour will have been a success."

The denouement was "Invisible Sun", soulfully slowed so the words weren't thrown to the breeze. A reserved Bono came out with a bashful smile and duetted with Sting on the last verse, Sting's head bumping Bono's hat as they shared the mike, counting to six, a reminder of the six prisoners adopted by the tour.

For the finale Bono took the lead, and U2 became the back-up band, borrowing some instruments — Sting handing over the bass to Adam, and giving him a hug and an avuncular buss on the forehead. Eighteen special guests were introduced as everyone assembled on the stage sang Dylan's "I Shall Be Released" —eighteen former prisoners of conscience, freed thanks to the work of Amnesty International.

As they stood looking out into the multitude (having been shooed to the sides of the stage by Bill Graham), Bono kept singing the refrain as "They shall be released", ever mindful of those prisoners who have no inkling of the effort being made on their behalf on the day — yet.

For it is the conspiracy's hope that the cards and petitions gathered on the tour will indeed mean "they shall be released."

THE "CONSPIRACY Of Hope" tour will be remembered for the artists as well as the cause, although Amnesty's message was never subsumed by the entertainment. Certainly, many will have discovered U2. The energy and the intensity of their performance and Bono's charisma were not diminished on the small screen, especially with the radio simulcast.

The tour did prompt at least one New York area record store chain to promote the entire U2 catalogue, putting all their albums on sale soon after the tour started. The week after the telecast, it had sold four or five times the usual volume of U2 records, and other branches were re-ordering. (Managers in three different chains stressed that U2 represent one of their most consistent sellers).

U2 sales were also up somewhat at Tower Records downtown, an indication of the kind of beneficial effects which can accrue to bands as a result of this kind of event. But while sales of Peter Gabriel's "So" were also given a boost — not that the album necessarily needed one, arriving as it did, on the back of "Sledgehammer" 's success — there was no real evidence of any of the lesser-known artists featured on the broadcast, achieving a breakthrough.

At the end of the day, exposure is simply not enough. The music must first capture the imagination of the public and it's precisely because of the passionate response their music and performance inspires, that U2 now rate as one of the most popular bands in the US — and the world.

Adam Clayton

While the exact figures aren't in yet, Amnesty will probably reach its goals, which are realistic rather than greedy. They hope that through the broadcast call-in and targetted mailings tied in with the anniversary year and tour, membership will increase by 40,000. That's active members, writing 12 letters a year. This seems reasonable, since reports from the cities the tour went to were that inquiries and donations had already increased. It's important to recall that network shows with tremendous viewership featured the story more than once.

People will have heard their children, their brothers, and sisters talking about the concerts and the cause, and so the name will be perhaps more readily recognised when mentioned in the press. It's possible the press will be more conscious of the issues Amnesty addresses and find stories in them.

Amnesty can also continue to keep their work in the public eye, using some of the $3 million it should be able to raise from this year's activities. If one percent of the millions of people exposed to Amnesty's message maintain an interest in the organisation the tour will have been a success.

On a turnpike tollbooth near the arena, a scrawled sign directed concert-goers to keep left for the "Amnesia International" concert. Amnesia International? Hardly likely.

WIDE AWAKE IN AMERICA

July 1986

U2

THE DRUMMER'S DISABILITY

**Amid rumours and press
reports that his career could
be at an end, Larry Mullen
reveals the truth about the
extent of an injury to his hand
that is becoming a common
problem for rock drummers.
Interview: Niall Stokes**

WHEN THE news first broke, it had a desperate ring of finality. Larry Mullen of U2 was in hospital in New York. There he would be operated on, for a mystery injury to his hand. If the operation wasn't successful, Larry would never drum again.

"We're all behind you," DJ Marty Whelan of Radio 2, in Dublin, assured the U2 drummer in faraway Manhattan, "hope you get well soon." And thus a snippet in the *Daily Mirror* had been elevated to the status of hard fact. The *Evening Herald* and the *Irish Independent* followed with stories confirming that Larry was indeed in hospital in New York and that his career was on the line.

The information was announced again on Radio 2 and U2 fans all over the country were thrown into a state of shock.

The idea of U2 without Larry just doesn't seem feasible. For one thing, U2 as a band are more than the sum of all individual parts. Besides, Larry ranks alongside Bono as the fans' favourite. A sex symbol of unusual potency, he's always been the target for a significant proportion of the band's female fan mail. And yet here were the national media, announcing that his ability to carry on

drumming was dependent on an operation to cure a mystery ailment. The first U2 fan to alert *Hot Press* to the story was in tears. It was unbelievable — but it had to be true. They'd said it on the radio.

Like *Hot Press*, the U2 office had been inundated with calls throughout the morning after Marty Whelan's first announcement. They were baffled about the momentum the story had built. "No, it's not true," a spokesperson told *Hot Press*. "Yes, he does have a problem with his hand. It's *not* piano hand. And it's not going to impinge on his career."

So Larry was not, even as we spoke, undergoing emergency surgery in New York? Far from it, Larry was in rain-soaked Dublin, carrying on with the essential business of working on U2's follow-up to "The Unforgettable Fire".

"The band are currently rehearsing and Larry is playing drums. He *can* play drums. He is playing drums and he will be playing drums," the spokesperson added definitively.

With the level of disinformation which had already been spread, they were anxious to clarify matters firmly and definitely.

BY THE second day when Ireland's largest-selling daily, the *Irish Independent*, followed the *Herald* into print confirming the story, Larry Mullen had decided to talk to *Hot Press*, to get the story straight once and for all.

"I'm surprised at the people in the *Independent* and *Herald* 'cos I know those guys," he commented. "I expected more from them. But just running that story without checking it is descending to the level of the tabloid rags in Britain. The *Daily Mirror* piece is full of shit."

As ever the truth is a good deal more complex than the tabloids would allow. To begin with, however, Larry does have a problem with his left hand.

"The hand had been a bit sore for a while but the first time I became aware that there was a problem was in San Francisco during our American tour. That was less than a year ago. I suddenly realised that I wasn't going to be able to play the gig that night — I was in too much pain. So I was whisked off to hospital immediately and the doctor there told me to take the next two weeks off."

"I was so freaked out. My hands are my livelihood. A serious problem with them could affect me very badly."

With a highly pressurised touring schedule to be completed, that kind of complete rest wasn't on the cards. A compromise was reached, with the hand being put into a sophisticated plaster which could be removed for the duration of gigs. A course of serious pain-killers was prescribed to take Larry to the end of the tour.

"I was so freaked out," Larry admits. "My hands are my livelihood — a serious problem with them could affect me very badly."

A number of cortozone injections having failed to cure the ailment, Larry talked to Max Weinberg of Bruce Springsteen's E-Street Band about it. As someone who's suffered badly with a similar problem, Weinberg was categorical in his advice.

"He's had eight operations on each finger in his hand. He's had a problem for years and he hadn't taken care of his hands — he was in serious pain. So he said to me, 'Don't be a martyr.' Having seen the damage that had been done in his case, I was aware of the need to take care of my hands."

RETURNING FROM the American tour, the lengthy process of looking for a solution was undertaken in earnest. "The problem is that nobody can identify what's the cause. Something causes the tendons in the hand to swell — if you're using part of your body wrongly or if you push it too hard, this kind of thing can develop. But there are a lot of different opinions as to what exactly is the root cause."

Larry has seen top hand surgeons in the States, Europe and Britain. The ailment has puzzled even John Varian, whom Larry describes as "the head of British hand surgeons." Along with other specialists Varian has recommended surgery to explore the hand, to identify what might be causing the swelling.

The idea doesn't appeal to Larry Mullen, who admits that he's trying to avoid an operation. "I've been seeing doctors in Ireland and one of them found this anti-inflammatory tablet which has helped enormously. It's not a steroid and it's not a drug. I don't know how it works but it reduces the swelling and there's less of a problem now. It's a question of knowing how far I can push my hand and then taking care of it, bathing it in cold water and resting it as much as possible."

In the long run it's possible that Larry might have to submit to the logic of surgery but for the moment he's happy that the injury is under control. In achieving that, he's set a headline which other musicians can follow. A lot of drummers in particular have problems with their hands and play on regardless, crucifying themselves as they pound the skins. By the time they wake up to the fact that the problem is serious, it's often too late.

"That's why Max Weinberg asked me to talk about my injury. A new hospital has opened in New York to deal with injuries to hands and he's lecturing there. He rang me to ask me to do an interview with *Musician* magazine, to launch the campaign to make drummers aware of the need to take care of their hands.

'Take a look at these hands.'

That must be where the *Daily Mirror* got their initial information.''

O N L Y   T O   distort it, as they have done with a number of spurious stories about U2 in recent months. ''They had one about me with a copy of the bible in my hand, preaching on the 19A,'' Bono told *Hot Press*. And they also carried a full page piece, including a large picture, about Bono's 'gasometer-like' home.

''We're a most unlikely band for that kind of attention,'' Bono added, ''but they seem intent on pursuing us. They seem to have gotten tired of the Duran Durans and so on. It's something we'll have to be careful of.''

The inevitable conclusion is a familiar one: don't believe what you read in the British tabloid press. It's something Marty Whelan might note. Because, happily, for the moment the news on Larry's hand is that there's no need to panic. ''We're recording the new album at the moment and I'm having very few problems with my hand,'' he confirmed.

Exactly when the finished work will hit the streets remains to be seen but enthusiasm is running high in the U2 camp. Both The Edge and Bono have separately expressed the kind of excitement about the work-in-progress which suggests that something very special is on the cards.

''We're hoping to finish recording the album by the end of the year,'' Bono revealed. ''There may be a single out before Christmas or it might just be into the New Year.'' But the last year's work is certainly rapidly coming to maturation...

U2 fans won't have to wait with baited breath for very much longer.

Larry: ''He can, he is and he will be playing drums.''

THE DRUMMER'S DISABILITY
September 1986

Larry behind the kit in 1984

OUT ON HIS OWN

**The Edge talks to Bill Graham
about his soundtrack album
"Captive" - and about
the hidden reservoirs the
band are charting in their
search for the follow-up to
"The Unforgettable Fire"**

IT'S HAPPENED so many times before. As a band gets big and frees itself from the early tour/album/ tour treadmill, its members find time weighing on their hands. Sooner or later, somebody fills the vacuum with a solo album and fans get worried it's the beginning of the end, the first symptom of a split, the first sign of the end of a beautiful affair.

So, with The Edge now releasing a soundtrack album for Paul Mayersberg's "Captive", there's reason to have a twinge of doubt even about the much-vaunted solidarity of U2. We can easily forget the band is almost a decade old, a long life in this game when nearly all of their contemporaries have fallen off the vine.

Am I unduly nervous? Almost certainly. Four cars parked outside The Edge's new South Dublin residence contradict that fear. Inside I find all four members of the band, sipping cups of tea and quietly contemplating the day's labour on their new album.

Work may be a means of withdrawing from the world's distractions, of rediscovering the reasons why U2 started — yet I'm still uncertain.

It isn't so much that they're in peril to the usual hazards of the decadent rock'n'roll lifestyle (though there have been some hilarious, untrue rumours about Bono that would have the over-imaginative believe that just because he's been seen to take an occasional drink in public, he's suddenly started to lead a lifestyle more suited to a member of The Pogues).

Stuff and balderdash, of course, but there are other reasons to check the current creative health of U2. Prosperity and fame can have other more insidious effects. Does comfort cause a slackening of the will, killing the hunger and stilling the incentive that motivates a group in the first place? This evening The Edge will, of course, say no — but it's his eyes not his words that will tell the truth. Normally, the most equable, the least animated member, it's hard to crack the reserve of U2's most masked man.

Tiredness does the job instead. As always, the answers are measured and sensible but after a day's studio slog, the habitual veil seems to have slipped from his eyes, revealing an intensity in his gaze that's usually carefully camouflaged. Yes, the eyes always

have it. The Edge still has his visions to express.

BUT THE official reason for the interview right now is The Edge's wish to talk about his soundtrack for "Captive". He's always hankered to compose music for films and once the whole "Unforgettable Fire" campaign was over, he took himself to London to write material.

But these were sketches without any specific project in mind. He found it easier to write them than to sell his talents to Hollywood. By his account, that was a more arduous process than winning even the first elusive record contract.

He seems to have started in all innocent over-ambition: "I got a list of my favourite directors and then got the office to ring them up but I got disillusioned very quickly. Because I soon realised that the sort of people I was ringing up, Stanley Kubrick, Polanski, Scorsese — they're even more protected than Prince."

Rock's still a junior sibling to the movies. Even when your group's won the cover and compliments of *Rolling Stone* that doesn't mean inevitable access to Hollywood's most charmed circles, as Edge learned. All he encountered were agents' assistants, the most junior, forbidding doorkeepers at the pyramid's base.

Instead his link came through London. Enter English producer, David Puttnam, godfather to many Irish talents. "Suddenly the English industry opened up," Edge recalls, "and it seemed to have a much more downbeat attitude."

The elements then quickly gelled. On Puttnam's introduction, he made contact with Don Boyd who was producing "Captive". Impressed with The Edge's portfolio, he and director Paul Mayersberg flew him to Paris, where he saw the rushes before beginning work.

The Edge happily says that they made few demands on him. Mayersberg didn't even come to the studio to monitor the work-in-progress, though he agrees that Boyd was hopeful of a hit single to sell the movie. "I was saying I can't promise it," Edge reflects. "I have no history of success in that area at all. All I can provide you with is music to fit your movie. Originally I think there was a little bit of readjustment that they had to make. But once they got my music and saw what I was doing, I think they were happy to give me that trust."

Nonetheless, there is one song, the theme tune "Heroine" which features Sinead O'Connor, a talent of tremendous potential, on lead vocals. Like much U2 output, it isn't so much a "song" as a piece of music whose attractions become more obvious with increased play. Ultimately radio exposure and other commercial considerations will determine its destiny but in the meantime, it's an effective opening gambit.

The experience has strengthened Edge's already firm opinions about film music. The recent past has seen an increasing tendency towards tie-ins between American youth movies and song collections which often have the barest relation to the action of the movie. An example is "Sid And Nancy" where the majority of the songs have the briefest, most subliminal presence in the film itself.

The Edge distrusts that policy. A follower of such classical soundtrack composers as Enrico Morricone, he fears such quality work is out of vogue. His own understanding of film-making has also changed. He isn't complimentary about the bureaucracies and power-structures involved.

"It's a nightmare of authorities. Ultimate control rests with — who? There is no control because there are so many people in there. First of all, the stakes are so much higher. A movie can make a fortune but it also costs a fortune. The number of people involved and the intricacy of the production itself is obviously hugely more complex than making the album — the cinematographers, the actors, the lights and sound people. And that's just on the creative side. Then you've got to bow down to the financiers and if you're a director you'll often fight with your producer. But the financial people are really the people who have the last word.

"So for me, I was on the far extreme of that sort of boardroom situation. You find that it has an influence on you, that sort of mentality. As soon as you're in the film world, you get this sort of feeling that there's a hell of a lot going on behind the scenes. It's like being on the tip of this great commercial iceberg where all you can see is the small tip around you — but you know it goes on and on, that it's a much larger thing."

He better understands directors' insecurities after the experience: "Having just seen that particular tip of the iceberg, I realise what an obstacle course it is. Also having met directors, I find that they survive on their wits and their ability to talk people with money into believing they can provide them with a good film. In other words, most of it is just the gift of the gab. And the rest of it is a do-or-die thing."

With Michael Brook on hand, the album reflects the non-rock elements in his musical personality. But will it satisfy the casual listener?

"That's a difficult question," he admits. "I would say 'yes' but it's definitely for a certain mood. The thing about soundtrack albums is that they fulfill your wish and provide what you're looking for only at certain times. Eno's ambient music is like that but this has more of a range than that."

Bono once described The Edge as the European of U2 and he doesn't deny that characterisation: "It's not conscious. It's just a taste thing. My ear as a musician has never found a great deal of

> "My ear as a musician has never found a great deal of solace in the blues scale. Instead I've been drawn to the sparse, melancholy European feel."

solace in the blues scale. I've never been drawn to it. Instead I've been drawn to sparse, melancholy feels that tend to be European.

"There are certain groups that span both — think of The Velvet Underground. They have a European-ness, John Cale, and an American-ness, Lou Reed. For myself, I don't know where it comes from but I'm always drawn to certain harmonies, feels and sounds and they tend not to be American. It doesn't mean I don't like the blues but there's a difference between loving and appreciating something and then bringing it into your own work."

Meanwhile, back at the band: U2's prominence meant that they were the leading recipients of flak, some personalised and rather hurtful, about their involvement in Self Aid. And yet their position was curiously ambivalent as should have been clear from their performance which, if it never claimed to be a politically perfect statement, on the day got closer to the bitterness and anger unemployment causes than any other act. For though U2 had placed their organisation at the service of Self Aid, they weren't full believers in every aspect of the event.

The Edge explains they were involved not because they necessarily endorsed "all practicalities or finer details of it but because we concurred with the sentiment behind it. And we just knew we couldn't turn our backs on it. It was a gestural thing that was all about hopes and aspirations and very little about real answers."

A similar continuing ambivalence runs through his reflections now: "If somebody asked us tomorrow to do it and we were in the same position, we'd do it — but that doesn't change the fact that we had deep reservations about the practical side. Like, what happens to the funds, did anyone really benefit in a job sense?

"Some positive energy came from it but there were also a lot of flaky aspects. But I think we decided we can't let those things get in the way of this day and what it will mean, not just in Ireland but elsewhere. And we thought — so what if it doesn't achieve that much? It's an important gesture."

Did their reservations affect the tone of the set, in particular the choice of Dylan's "Maggie's Farm"?

"I think we had to be honest and the set was maybe in response to some of the negative press the event was getting. Also we didn't want to go on there and say nothing. We wanted to comment. We were thinking of loads of covers — Patti Smith's "Free Money" was one. "Working Class Hero" was another we toyed with... In the end "Maggie's Farm" was right on the day because emigration is the most difficult underground problem in this society.

"I'VE A day-job as well," Edge had joked earlier when I enquired about the possibility of future soundtrack projects. And indeed he has! Right now, U2 are dab in the middle of work on their new album and still lack a full sense of its direction — but

The Edge: "I have a day-job as well!"

I'd be lacking in responsibility to *Hot Press* readers if I didn't quiz him on it.

Word around town is that it's a partial extension of "The Unforgettable Fire". Daniel Lanois is back at the controls while Brian Eno has been darting in to add treatments. Equally it's been recorded both in and outside Windmill — thus today's gathering at Edge's house.

"What I can say about it is that it's a complicated bitch to finish," The Edge laughs. "It's got more variation than anything we've ever done. It's an album of songs, an album of creating moods, an album of aggression... It's too early. We have all these hopes and fears for it but it's taken so much out of us. Ideally, it will be everything we have to offer: there's nothing to limit us in our situation."

The band's appearances on both *TV Ga Ga* and Self Aid set up strange expectations. On each occasion, U2 seemed to be cutting themselves adrift from their previous transcendental reputation and turning into some mutant blues band, almost treading on the turf of The Fall and The Birthday Party. Edge counsels caution in our interpretation of those forays. "Some of that was mischief," he reflects. "We were just fooling around a bit. There was a lot of experiment on the Amnesty tour where we were doing a lot of strange cover versions. Some of it was just seeing what we could do but some of it *will* be going to the album."

He's becoming more talkative: "This album is just going to be so wide. The influences on display are just so diverse. There's no sort of geographical location to it. But I don't want it to sound like a liquorice all-sorts. There is going to be a continuity to it."

Even in his more restrained tones, there's an undertow of passion to his explanations. More than anything else, artistic ambition can be the spur and The Edge still has sounds in his head he wants to express in the context of U2.

But those television performances also suggest the band were tired of being portrayed as rock's token goodie-goodies. Early in the year, Bono has talked of wanting to be "unreasonable". Has there been a shift of mood?

"I think what Bono meant," he interprets, "is that we want to be a little less easy to follow and predict. I think as a band we've suffered from a certain sound and because we've always been very open about our convictions in certain areas, people thought they knew U2 and could imagine what our next step would be. I think there's a great deal of anger in the group which has never previously been expressed in musical terms. I think it used to come through in performance but now it may be there in the material."

Interestingly, Edge mentions the author Kathy Acker. He may be more curious about her cut-up method than her sexual

"We never dropped the ball, we still have the same determination to create. All U2's goals are artistic ones."

message but these are references that aren't normally associated with the U2 camp. But then the fascination about U2 has always been about the tension between their polarities: between their initially unfashionable religious beliefs and rock decadence, between their professional business ethic and an increasingly deviant artistic ambition. It's also telling that, just as rock has become more monotonously conformist, U2 are raising their own increasingly individually subversive colours.

This isn't the band whose singer once worried about brazen underwear ads on the London Underground escalators. How does The Edge see the development of their beliefs?

"I would say that none of my fundamental beliefs have changed but they've broadened and matured and been tempered with a wider experience of (a) what's good about the rest of the world and (b) what's bad about religion everywhere. We have come to realise it's such a corruptible thing, that basically religion only works on an individual basis. That organised religion is so fragile and easily corrupted that you really can't trust it.

"I basically assume that every single group, or religious community, has a problem, is in some way screwed up. I don't believe that there is one single, perfect spiritual way and, in realising that, obviously you become a lot more open and that's generally what's changed."

The band's American experience of Moral Majority moguls like Jerry Falwell certainly forced one early re-examination of conscience. The Edge betrays anger when he says that Falwell preaches that "God dresses in a three-piece polyester suit, is white, speaks in a Southern accent, is from an Anglo-Saxon background and has a wife and children. And then you say, how does that relate to a Chinese peasant and you realise it doesn't relate at all.

"The principles must be universal to be understood and appreciated and if that's not the case, it's not worth a shit. And that's where I am," he finished — slightly laughing as if abashed by his audacity.

Did he ever worry they might be tempted into using their position, into issuing creeds and manifestos, become rock Jerry Falwells?

"God forbid," he answers, smiling again. "It's too complicated for one man to set himself up as knowing all the answers and we don't attempt to. There's certain very obvious things we're shouting our mouth about and that's as far as we're prepared to go."

HE QUOTES Brian Eno's adage that "possessions are a way of turning money into problems." I'm asking about money and success. The Edge remains unruffled.

Will-success-spoil-U2 questions are inevitable, particularly in

Ireland where their profile and significance is in highly visible contrast to the fortunes of their generation, all the school-leavers who got dumped on the dole or emigrated. Indeed the danger of U2 has never resided in the more publicised style of self-destruction, as per Boy George. Rather they must beware of a gradual and almost imperceptible dimming of artistic vision, the slowly-hardening arteries that the victim hardly recognises. U2's rebel streak in '86 may be a direct result of their conscious effort to ward off such an insidious condition.

On money, Edge comments that U2 have always "valued its potential but never it." He'll admit there could have been problems "if we had had an enormous first album." But of one thing he seems utterly convinced. "We never dropped the ball," he says. "We still have the same determination to create." And he adds, "all U2's goals are artistic ones."

Honestly, only the album will finally answer the questions. But in the meantime, the eyes inspire confidence. The windows to his soul don't need springcleaning.

OUT ON HIS OWN

October 1986

The Edge: the eyes inspire confidence

EMOTIONAL RESCUE

"The Joshua Tree" clarifies how U2's vocation has become the revival and renewal of rock and the recovery of its most romantic values. It also highlights the group's new commitment to the song.

Review by Bill Graham

WITH "THE Joshua Tree", the U2 pendulum swings back to America again. If "The Unforgettable Fire", partially through Brian Eno's guidance, was their most European record, this, their fifth studio album, turns their sights again on the Big Country, sometimes howling off in pursuit of the ghosts that possess the American soul. In time, it may be reckoned their most influential album to date.

It also clarifies how U2's vocation has become the revival and renewal of rock and the recovery of its most romantic values. Between the increasingly mercenary implosion of hard rock into a static vaudeville routine and the intervention of pop dance-floor values, rock has lost its lustre and mystique of genuinely redeeming passion. From one angle, "The Unforgettable Fire" can now seem a strategic retreat, to regroup, reassess the situation and gain new ammunition. But if that album necessarily circumvented some of the issues, "The Joshua Tree" returns to a frontal assault.

It is also the second successive album where U2 strip away the skins of their previous styles. Only the opening "Where The

Streets Have No Name", "In God's Country" and, possibly, elements of "One Tree Hill' preserve previously identifiable hallmarks. Otherwise, The Edge's guitar has developed its own military tendency, homing in on the legacy of Jimi Hendrix and Led Zeppelin, while the group's new commitment to songs finds both Bono and the rhythm section contending on dance-floors they never previously frequented, with complete confidence.

For, stylistically, the triumph of this album is that, like Prince, U2 prove an act can still be contemporarily commercial *and* also capture the higher ground. There's a host of unexpected influences here but they've been discriminatingly used, to release rather than imprison the band. The effect is to release rock also from its own self-imposed shackle, for, in the process of resetting their sights, U2 unravel a series of musical problems, other less resolute souls have abandoned for cliche.

Twice, they almost teeter on the brink. Both "Red Hill Mining Town" and "I Still Haven't Found What I'm Looking For" are more obviously singles than anything previously released bar "Pride", but the first is perilously close to Bon Jovi in its

scarf-waving melody, while the latter is destined to provoke comparisons with Rod Stewart — albeit before that singer's career became an endless audition for "Dynasty" and "Miami Vice".

Bon Jovi and Rod Stewart? To some, this will sound like I'm excusing a crude sell-out. That isn't true at all, for two reasons. First, because Bono has never before sung with such emotional accuracy. And secondly because this is a most deceptive album, simultaneously swimming into the mainstream and then recoiling from its most repellent values.

For if the music is pro-American, the message hardly is. For instance, if "Red Hill Mining Town" initially sounds like potential standard MTV fare, its lyric about an unemployed and dispossessed mining family definitely isn't. Thus "The Joshua Tree" consistently shifts targets and expectations.

> **" 'The Joshua Tree' is a most deceptive album, simultaneously swimming into the mainstream and recoiling from its most repellant values."**

But, then, U2's own perspectives have also shifted. "The Joshua Tree" may be the first album where U2 have dared to let the demons loose in the studio, the one where, ultimately all the issues of religious faith seem as complex and clouded as they really are. On "Exit", both the guitar and rhythms convey a brooding premonition, as Bono tells the tale of one of those psychotic saviours with warped interpretations of the Old Testament, a murderer slaying with *the hands of love."* Here, U2 finally confess their gradual recognition of the Anti-Christ in everybody.

For faith is no longer what once it seemed. "I Still Haven't Found What I'm Looking For" is all its title says, U2 gone soul and gospel but admitting doubt and restlessness. Elsewhere certainties become conundrums: *"Sleep comes like a drug... sad eyes crooked crosses... In God's Country"* (America not Ireland — foreign correspondents please copy) boasts a powerful ambiguity: "Bullet The Blue Sky", *"Plant a demon seed, you raise a flower of fire/See them burning crosses, see the flames, higher and higher."*

This last track is where U2 really cut the cable. The fourth track into the first side, on it The Edge releases a dirty, furious wall of sound under remorseless, lockstep rhythms, these musical dramatics in service to a scenario that's located somewhere in the killing fields of Central America. A key track, where U2 rubbish heavy metal conformity, it could also become this year's "Bad", the spontaneous combustion centrepiece of the tour as Bono lets fly with a rap about a tempter *"peeling off those dollar bills."*

Its violence also underscores the difference between this album and its predecessor. For if "The Unforgettable Fire" 's airier textures seemed to evoke the more celebratory, mystical aspects of belief, "The Joshua Tree" finds U2 as worried, even frightened, men grappling with the moral burdens of suffering,

culminating in the closing track, "Mothers Of The Disappeared", about the victims of state terrorism, and patently inspired by last summer's American benefit tour for Amnesty International.

Could and should their politics be more explicit? It depends on your perspective. U2 presently content themselves with a liberal moralism that's alert both to how planet pop limits local language and the fact that their potential American constituency cannot, by any stretch of the imagination, be equated with *NME* readers. But even if the sheer force of U2's music dramatizes their parables, as a lyric-writer, Bono may still be erring on the safe side of coded ambiguity.

Of course, there's more to "The Joshua Tree". "Trip Through Your Wires", once an unruly debutante on *TV Ga Ga*, has been disciplined into a Dylanesque stomp, with Bono let loose on harmonica, while another love song and possible single, "With Or Without You" has perhaps his most controlled vocal, building from an almost conversational first verse over a bare rhythm section to a soul-baring confession.

"And you give yourself away," he sings — a line which may be the key to the U2 ethos, to the heart of a band who have consistently preached their own brand of self-surrender. This album may be scattered with references to the desert but, in this

Without U3 — Bono during the making of the "With Or Without You" video.

dry and waterless place, U2 would also be at one with Al Green in singing "Take Me To The River"...

That river returns on "One Tree Hill". Dedicated to their Maori roadie, Greg Carroll, killed in last year's motorcycle accident, it starts with light, glistening, almost African guitar from The Edge, over Adam and Larry's own amendment of tribal rhythms, with the guitar becoming increasingly aggressive through the song. But "One Tree Hill" is hopeful, not grim. *"We run like a river to the sea,"* Bono sings, Mike Scott's metaphor recast in terms of eternal life and the Maori's own belief.

Once again, U2's religious romanticism becomes the source of positive values. More secularly-minded people may think this preposterous but U2's religious impulse — closer to Sufi lore, based on love not dogma, preferring the kernel to the shell of formalism — is curiously capable of reviving the old skin of dead rock ceremonies that, as a secular substitute for religion , have patently degenerated this decade.

Somehow they continue to evade the traps. "The Joshua Tree" rescues rock from its decay, bravely and unashamedly basing itself in the mainstream before very cleverly lifting off into several higher dimensions. They've been misunderstood occasionally, even by their committed supporters — but after "The Joshua Tree", with its skill, and the diversity of issues it touches, one thing is absolutely clear: U2 can no longer be patronized with faint and glib praise. They must be taken very seriously indeed after this revaluation of rock.

EMOTIONAL RESCUE

February 1987

U2: the four of us

THE WORLD ABOUT US

On the release of "The Joshua Tree", Niall Stokes and Bill Graham talk to Bono, Larry, Adam and The Edge about the making of U2's *tour de force*.

IF YOU'RE a decade older than U2 and recall their earliest steps — including that first chaotic demo session, a live half-hour take that was literally out of control, time and tune — your emotions mix justified Irish pride with an almost absurd sense of deja vu. You pinch yourself very hard. Have the fresh-faced makers of "Boy" really matured into such influential men, rock potentates on a scale we humbly refused to dream of then?

U2 remain familiar figures on the Dublin landscape, etched in familiar cameos: Adam drinking across from you in a Dublin nightclub, Larry slipping into the shadows to view some unknown local band, the Edge shopping with his pregnant wife Aisling on the street opposite the *Hot Press* office, or Bono swopping tall tales with an elderly working-man in his local bar.

Unlike earlier generations of Irish artists, U2 have resolutely refused to decamp to London, Paris or New York. Perhaps that's why we have yet to fully come to terms with the special nature of U2's appeal — or with the dawning realization that the torch has been passed to *them* as the lone remaining band of their generation to breathe new life into old rock ceremonies and revive abandoned dreams. It's much easier to call across the bar and ask Adam to pass the cigarettes.

Once, writing about the United States, Bono was pained about being a "Stranger In A Strange Land" but by now U2 are familiar figures in the Promised Land. And this provides much of the focus for their new and sometimes tempestuous offering "The Joshua Tree". While a song like "Red Hill Mining Town" is specifically about the trials and tribulations visited on working class people in the British miners' strike, the album as a whole represents the American side of U2's collective personality. And underpinning that musical emphasis, lyrically "The Joshua Tree" traverses an ethical and emotional journey across many different Americas.

Previous British rock tourists have made albums of their US sketch-books but this one is different. There's an unmistakable Irish tinge on "The Joshua Tree" that frees it of the condescension and detachment which so often characterises the UK rock perspective on the United States and its people. The Irish don't view America like the Brits. For one, the continuous tide of emigration by generations of Irish has created its own intimacies.

Equally, a natural evolution can be traced between the still vibrant Irish folk tradition and the original musical sources back of country. Indeed U2's own early and enthusiastic courting of an American audience — an attitude which contrasted sharply with the often defensive superiority of British bands of the same generation — had its own natural cultural roots. At bottom is a feeling of empathy and respect —not for American institutions but for the people of a vast and many-faceted continent.

This long-standing and mutual love affair has recently been shadowed by a new ambivalence on the Irish side. Remembering our centuries of suppression by Britain, we instinctively side with the underdog Nicaraguan government against the White House's destabilizing plans. In another small and vulnerable nation, Washington's Central American policies have touched a raw nerve. Released against the sordid backdrop of Irangate, "The Joshua Tree" is about articulating the sense of outrage which America's unique combination of arrogance and apathy inspires from an Irish pespective. But it is about more than that.

In a world where power is abused on a colossal scale and people are trampled into the dust without compunction by political and economic masters who have lost all sense of human dignity, U2 have sought and found the ultimate symbol of triumph over adversity. "The Joshua Tree" is about the belief that you cannot kill the human spirit. And it is about the final spark of optimism, that in spite of the arid wasteland of contemporary power politics, something beautiful and enduring can be forged out of human commitment and idealism in action.

"The Joshua Tree" is about refusing to lie down in the desert, to wait for the vultures to come and pick on our collective bones. It's about power in the darkness...

Not surprisingly it stands out like a beacon against the backdrop of musical murk which characterises rock'n'roll in the late eighties.

I N   T H E   restroom of U2's new rehearsal premises, an abandoned warehouse a mile from the band's Dublin Windmill Lane Studio headquarters, Larry Mullen patiently scans a tape to decipher the lyrics of a song U2 just might cover on their forthcoming world tour. His concentration isn't surprising but the object of his attention, Al Green's version of Curtis Mayfield's "People Get Ready", is.

Certainly such a soulful choice might have been deemed uncharacteristic of U2 in the past — but then, besides U2's artistic principles, they also have a mischievous habit of confounding expectations. After all, they've been boxed in before. In late '80 when U2 released their debut album, "Boy", many lumped them in with Liverpool groups, The Teardrop

Explodes and Echo And The Bunnymen as part of *that* year's neo-psychedelic movement. Later, after their third album, "War", they were slotted beside fellow-Celts, Simple Minds, Big Country, The Alarm and the more wilful Waterboys, as crusaders for an anthemic "Big Music". But by now, it's become transparent that U2 owe allegiance only to their own stylistic creed.

After "War", they resolutely broke loose. Following the final Dublin date and triumphant homecoming of that album's tour, Bono spoke symbolically of "breaking up the band" and starting afresh to re-invent U2 with the same four members. They refused to record any "Son Of War"-style sequel. The Stateside stadium pickings might have been tempting for an emergent group with an already intense following but U2 chose to enlist Brian Eno and his sorcerer's assistant, Daniel Lanois, to craft a new direction, the dreamscape that was "The Unforgettable Fire". They weren't to be trapped as a guitar anthem band.

"Without The Edge, Larry or Adam to assist, Bono suddenly felt musically naked and embarrassed."

"The Joshua Tree" is a further shift in the pattern. Bono has jokingly cast himself as the "American" of U2 and the Edge as the "European" but, though such polarities may be artificial in such a tightly-knit group, this graphic album's musical and lyrical pre-occupation with so many conflicting American ways contrasts vastly with its more impressionistic predecessor.

Thus, the immaculate conception of "People Get Ready" as a cover. It might not surface. At the end of a tiring rehearsal day, U2 were rather listlessly toying with the song but, nonetheless, its selection is an indicator of how they're finally closing in on soul. "The Joshua Tree" may contain its critiques of American policy but this Janus-faced album also draws on abiding American musics for its most positive values, as U2 display the abundant resources they have, by now, amassed.

It is also the U2 album to date that most palpably acknowledges that there was musical life before '76. Formed in the slip-stream of punk, U2's four members were like any independent teenagers of those years, fixated by the likes of Television, Patti Smith and The Ramones but distrusting such as The Rolling Stones as the play-things of an older generation. Yet Mick Jagger and Keith Richards are crucial to this story. The fathers proved they had much to teach their disputatious sons.

Bono calls it "The Night Of The Long Knives". With his wife Ali, he'd spent a month in Ethiopia, both working as volunteers for World Vision on an educational relief project —a visit he now only shyly and reluctantly discusses — and he'd immediately travelled to New York to add his vocals to the Artists Against Apartheid "Sun City" record. Then Peter Wolf took him off to meet The Stones.

In a New York studio, Mick and Keith were casually running

through some old blues standards for their personal entertainment and they inquired if Bono had any songs or party-pieces of his own. He didn't. Instead without the Edge, Larry or Adam to assist, he suddenly felt musically naked and embarrassed. But undeterred and inspired as if by an implicit challenge, he retired to his hotel bedroom for a sleepless night, writing the ghostly and chilling "Silver And Gold" in some seizure of spontaneous creative combustion.

The experience hastened a reassessment. To youngblood groups of U2's generation, the blues pardonably meant long hair bar bands filling up the Dublin dates they hungered for. Bono doesn't hide the fact that U2 inherited a skewed tradition. Already interested in gospel, he knew he must now finally check the blues, dredging the record collection of artist friend Charlie Whisker (also, incidentally, the hearse-driver in the ominous stovepipe hat featured on the Clannad "In A Lifetime" video). Those new insights and the prodding of friends like T-Bone Burnett and newly arrived Dublin resident, Waterboy Mike Scott, hardened his and the other members' convictions about the inadequacies of U2's previous songs.

"The music had to serve the songs," the Edge says of their new strategy and though the guitarist was initially hesitant about Bono's latest enthusiasm, as if it might capsize the band, they righted the ship as the Edge sailed in with his own incandescent contributions, notably to "Bullet The Blue Sky" and "Exit", that last track only routined and recorded on the final day of work on the album.

Of course, U2 weren't foolishly trying to recreate the doubtful glories of the British Blues Boom. Though there are hints in the guitar playing, in Bono's use of the harmonica and most obviously in "I Still Haven't Found", the new influences worked as a trace element, a presiding spirit beckoning them to simplify and focus their approach.

And though robust in spirit, "The Joshua Tree" doesn't shirk bleaker personal issues, partially reflecting a year when U2 shipped some heavy blows in Ireland. First and most crushingly Bono's PA, the personable New Zealand Maori, Greg Carroll, to whose memory the superb "One Tree Hill" is dedicated, died in a motor-bike accident when he crashed into an unlighted car. Then there was Self Aid, when U2 fell foul of our talent for selective criticism.

Every reputable Irish recording act still in business — from Van Morrison, Bob Geldof, and Rory Gallagher across to Paul Brady, De Danann, Moving Hearts and Christy Moore shared the bill on the day —but it was U2 who were singled out for a personally abusive cover and editorial in *In Dublin* which charged them with liberal hypocrisy. It was a grossly off balance and unfair attack, and it hurt, particularly since U2 had donated proceeds from their last Irish concert to the construction of the fledgling City Centre Arts building. U2 have made their commitment to

'What was that note, anyway?' Larry & the Edge in pensive mood.

their own environment manifest in very concrete, practical terms.

In the event what U2 delivered at Self Aid was the blackest and most ferocious set of their entire career, the highlight a sinister, gut-churning "Maggie's Farm" with a twist in its tail for the green tide of emigrants bound to work — or to look for work —in Maggie Thatcher's Britain. No longer could the band be put down, even by their most mean-spirited detractors, as purveyors of a soft-centred, blindly optimistic version of reality.

The controversy passed over like a summer squall. Besides, U2 lost no loyalty from their Irish legions. But it contains a paradox: that a band about to embark on the crusading "Conspiracy Of Hope" tour, should be so suspected by anyone in their homeland. Now, Bono gets angry if he's called a liberal.

It's a mark of the change that's come over U2 these past two years. It's also a measure of their growing maturity and depth. "The Joshua Tree" is both their most ambitious album and their most troubled. With a new emphasis on the poetic power of language, U2 place less reliance on faith. They are less buoyant in their celebration. Rather with "The Joshua Tree", they are asking questions of themselves and of their audience which might not have seemed within their scope until recently. There are no easy answers.

> "I thought, why can't U2 do blues or gospel," Bono recalls. "I began to see U2 in a strait-jacket we should break out from."

Hot Press: Can you explain the motivation behind the making of the album?

Edge: As with much U2 work , it's 'reactionary' in a sense. Whereas "War" was a reaction to the weak, placid music, we saw everywhere, I think this was, in a funny way, our reaction to "The Unforgettable Fire". We had experimented a lot in its making and done quite revolutionary things for us, like "Elvis Presley In America" and "4th Of July". We felt on this record that maybe, options were not such a good thing, that limitation might be very positive. So we decided to work within the limitations of the *song* as a starting-point. *Let's actually write songs.* We just wanted to leave the record less vague, open-ended, atmospheric and impressionistic. Make it more straightforward, focussed and concise.

Bono, before you went to New York for the "Sun City" sessions, had you any prior notion of what the new record would be like?

Bono: Before I went away the album I had in the back of my head is the album we've yet to make. It has been put aside for this. You see, I was starting to write songs and it was almost like I felt U2 can't do these songs. Like, U2 can't do blues or gospel. So I thought to myself, why can't U2 do these things? I started to see U2 in some strait-jacket we should break out from.

How did the other three respond to these new angles?

Bono: Adam has always been the roots man in the operation. On tour, it'll always be reggae, Aswad or Black Uhuru blasting out of his hotel room. Larry's more interested in the songs and simple structures. It's speak up or shut up. Write a song, three chords, say what you have to say. So he liked the directness of blues and something like "Trip Through Your Wires".

And the Edge?

Bono: *(Pause)*...How can I put this?... *(Further pause)*... Early on, Edge was less taken with it but later, he really came through when he saw that the songs were good. Put it this way: Edge didn't own a copy of "Blood On The Tracks". Edge's collection still started in '76 at the New Beginning. His interest was in European groups like Can and music back to Eno. So this was opening a new world or *(laughs)* a new can of worms. And yet the spontaneity of this new kind of music really excited him.

There's this idea of yourself as the American and him as the European.

Bono: Yeah and Ireland's right in the middle. There's a tension between the two but it's the right kind of tension. And it's funny because at the end of the record, I was arguing for the more atmospheric songs and he was going for the rock'n'roll. We'd swopped places somewhere along the way, much to our amusement.

Edge: We approached arranging and producing each song like it was unique. We just hoped the album would have a sonic cohesiveness based on the idea that *we* were playing it. There was definitely a strong direction but equally we were prepared to sacrifice some continuity to get the rewards of following each song to a conclusion. I hate comparisons — but like The Beatles at their height, in terms of unusual production techniques, we wanted to do what was right for the song.

Adam: I think we've come up with songs where there was a whole process of music inspiring lyrics and lyrics then feeding back on the music and the whole thing becoming intense. And we found that because Bono had enough time to produce lyrics that really did work, it was much more satisfying.

Bono: I used to think that writing words was old-fashioned, so I sketched. I wrote words on the microphone. For "The Joshua Tree", I felt the time had come to write words that meant something, out of my experience.

To what extent did writing a bleaker album reflect personal experiences?

Edge: Well, there's still hope... I think this record's bleak because that's what we're seeing but there's also that positive side to it.

Bono: You could say this is forbidden ground for U2 because we're the 'optimistic' group. But to be an optimist, you mustn't be blind or deaf to the world around you. "Running To Stand

Still'' is based on a real story while ''Exit'', I don't even know what the act is in that song. Some see it as a murder, others a suicide — and I don't mind. But the rhythm of the words is nearly as important in conveying the state of mind... If I can be objective and of course I can't, the album's real strength is that though you travel through deep tunnels and bleak landscapes, there's a joy at the heart of it.

How then did Greg Carroll's death affect you – being confronted with something tragic, completely outside the band's control?

Adam: For me, it inspired the awareness that there are more important things than rock'n'roll. That your family, your friends, and indeed, the other members of the band — you don't know how much time you've got with them. I'd rather go home early than stay up all night mixing a track.

Bono: *(quietly)* I feel the same.

Adam: For a long time, we did deny those simple things that give you pleasure, to keep the band going. Seeing your brothers, sisters, wives, children.

Bono: The emphasis among family and friends, when we had a number one record and were a big band, is how much you've got and I'm not talking about money. Not how much you've lost. The sense of loss came home through losing Greg Carroll. But the sense of loss has continued — I feel it even now, having made a record and not seen friends and family for the last three months and now, not being able to see them again because of the tour and so on. Because U2 work on everything. Like Larry is working his butt off on the merchandising, making sure the t-shirts — and this might sound insignificant — are made out of cotton and at an affordable price. So we're sitting on all these things. For the first time, I'm beginning to see the value of being irresponsible, of not giving a shit. Because giving a shit costs a lot. That's serious.

To dwell on the positive side, how does somebody from New Zealand get involved with an Irish band?

Bono: To do him justice, you can't talk about him the way we felt. We met him in Auckland and there are five volcanic islands which make up Auckland and the tallest is One Tree Hill. And my first night in New Zealand, Greg took me to One Tree Hill. He'd worked around the music and media scene and Paul McGuinness thought this guy's so smart, we can't leave him here, let's take him with us to Australia. He'd been doing front of house for the promoter... Greg Carroll's funeral was beyond belief. He was buried in his tribal homeland as a Maori, by the chiefs and elders. And there was a three day and three night wake and your head could be completely turned around and ours were again and again.

Regarding two other tracks, "With Or Without You" and "I Still Haven't Found What I'm Looking For" – there was a time when U2 wouldn't have been remotely considered a dance band.

Edge: We never thought about that side. They used to say about U2 that we had an anti-dance stance, music to fall over to — which I thought was funny. I remember in an American club on an early tour, Bono, after a few bevvies was persuaded to go on the floor and the DJ put on ''Out Of Control'' and not only did everybody leave the floor but *he* couldn't dance to it either.

A track like "Bullet The Blue Sky" is of interest in the context of how heavy metal has become so stylised. Late Sixties hard rock was much freer. How do you think a contemporary HM fan would take it?

Edge: It's an idiom reminiscent of an earlier era of rock but I don't think it's metal. When Jimi Hendrix was playing, it meant so much more than the post-blues yawn when guitar players rehashed something that once was potent and became a total cliche. My background is much more Tom Verlaine and John McGeoch but, in this case I thought there should be no limitations. I wasn't going to hem myself in because it might be controversial.

Bono, how have your attitudes to singing changed?

Bono: For those years when I didn't really know if there was a

Bono: ''I suppose I'm happy to be unhappy.''

place in rock for U2, or whether I wanted a place in U2, I think I was quite uptight. Sometimes people saw in the songs a self-righteousness because I was like the scared rat in the corner who attacks. As I worked out where we wanted to be, I loosened up and loosening up, discovered other voices. I became interested in singing — whereas before if it was in tune and in the right time, that was enough. And this is the same guy who was thrown out of U2 in 1977 because he couldn't sing! I find it hard to listen to the first three records because of my singing.

There's now a greater sensuality, which relates to the maturing of U2.

Bono: Yeah, you just stretch it out and realise a whisper can be louder than a scream. You learn that there's a time for letting go and a time for holding back.

To what extent does that come from being more at home with yourself?

Bono: I suppose I'm happy to be unhappy. Anyone who really knows me knows that, as they say, I'm never going to be at peace with my pipe (laughs).

How does this process of personal maturation relate to the artistic vision of U2?

Bono: We grew in an odd way as people. From 18 or 19, we were pushing the van to Killarney and then on a bus in America and then it's a plane to Australia and Japan. And we were completely occupied with things spiritual. After "Boy", the next two albums were almost made in our spare time. We weren't even sure we wanted to be in a band. So we were interested in growing on spiritual levels but actually quite retarded on other levels.

And even musically: our musical life began again with "Unforgettable Fire". It wasn't even a priority. I think we must own up to that. For two years, we were writing songs and going to the studio for "October" and "War" but that wasn't where we were at. We came through that and we realised we *are* musicians and we want to be in this band, U2.

Edge: And after this album, I'm more interested in playing guitar than I have been for the last three years. I'm having to learn because I've forgotten how a bit, honestly.

On a personal level, do you get annoyed by the newspaper gossip that celebrity seems automatically to bring? The local papers seem to be searching for you in every nightclub in town.

Bono: My father, who I love very much, is one of these guys who believes what he reads. He'll say to me: I hear you were throwing your weight around in some record store when they hadn't what you wanted and you were telling them you were Bono and they'd better have it. And I was laughing, wondering where this one had come from. So I sort of told him off and said: 'Da, you cannot believe what you read.' Then one night we were talking and he said: 'Yes, you can't believe what you read. I'll tell you a funny thing I read and even I didn't believe it. Apparently some fella's going around saying you own a hearse and you were driving around Donegal in it.' *(Laughs).* Fact and fiction just get blurred in a city like this. *(Bono does indeed own a hearse, which he drove in the Clannad video)*

Adam: You just can't fight it. It just gets worse and it's going to happen much more in the next year or so.

Bono: I live in Bray but the people in Bray are protective about myself and Ali. They don't bother us. But we get hassled by people from abroad, calling to the house. Some of it is okay but it's also a place where, as Ali likes to put it, she lives also. She says: 'I don't want you watching me put the washing on the line.' I've got to back her up. I don't mind inviting people into the house but I've got to honour her. But we get some amazing things. I remember a whole party of French people who applauded me outside the door. I'd just got out of bed and *(laughs)* I said: 'No thank you, I'm the wrong guy.'

I don't know how this will sound — but there was this one girl in the bushes. She was Italian, 18, very beautiful, sitting there in the flowers. And she said: 'I just wanted to come to Dublin and meet U2 before I die.' And I thought: 'they always come up with a good angle but this really *is* a good one.' I didn't know whether to laugh, just in case. So I talked to her, didn't take it too seriously and went off. But the next day, two BMWs came along and out came these Italian men in designer suits with flowers and flowers, presenting them to me because we had looked after this man's daughter who had some incurable illness. And that was almost shocking. How could I live up to that responsibility? God Almighty. I just can't come to terms with that. The bottom line is that music means a lot but what they haven't separated is the music from the musician. Because the musicians are only ordinary people. It's the music which is extraordinary if you like.

Adam: There's a weird process which I've just begun to understand. Particularly when you get the letters from 15 year olds. And they're asking questions as if you're the second line of defence for their heads. They've become disillusioned with their parents and they think their teachers are assholes now.

Bono: And they haven't yet found out we're assholes *(laughs)*.

But the pressure of celebrity – is it more than you can cope with?

Bono: It's one of my feelings that if you're around Dublin long enough, people just won't even notice. I love this city. I love it and I hate it and I love it and and I hate it. What I hate is to see how much they have destroyed Dublin — to see them pulling

"If you don't like what Bono's doing," says Adam, "you put your instruments down and walk off-stage. That's your choice."

down the buildings. The closest I came to throwing a large brick through the window in the last two years was outside the Royal Hibernian Way. I had to be dragged away. I mean, the rage I feel inside me when I see the pill-boxes they have planted outside Christchurch Cathedral. Well Larry just says to me: 'Come on, when you're worried about the way a city looks like, you know you're okay.' You know, there's a lot of people out there who can't afford to worry about what the city looks like.

At Live Aid, when Bono scrambled off the stage, you must have thought: jaysus, what's he up to?

Adam: If you don't like it, you put down your instruments and walk off stage. That's your choice *(laughter).*

Bono: Live Aid could've been a classic example of shooting ourselves in the foot. I was as high as a kite after Live Aid because, you know, Linda McCartney kissed me. And I was sharing a microphone with Paul McCartney! But when I got home and watched a video of Live Aid, I was so desperate and depressed. I really believed I had made a big mistake. I couldn't sleep. And I drove down the South East and I met a sculptor who was actually making a bronze piece which was meant to be the Spirit of Live Aid, a naked figure and it was called The Leap. I talked with him and he said he'd called it The Leap because I had left the stage and this image connected with him. The figure wasn't me. It was meant to be the whole spirit of it. But I felt, if he understood what I was trying to do and he was a man in his late fifties, outside of rock'n'roll... But there's no question about it, I'm not doing that again. And I still don't understand why I did it.

What were the emotions you felt when you were going on stage at Self Aid?

Bono: That's a bit of a can of worms, isn't it?

Adam: Humble, I guess.

Bono: There was a very interesting reaction afterwards. The people who believe in U2 are very ordinary people, working-class people. The only flak we get for being in a privileged position is from the middle-class. I felt how can I write a song about being unemployed when I am fully employed? How can I stand on stage at an unemployed benefit when I know U2 are not short of cash?

But one guy came up to me afterwards and said: 'I'm really pissed off about what you said on stage.' And I said what do you mean? And he said: 'You said you don't know what it's like to be unemployed. We didn't want to hear that — because we know you know what it's like, even if you *don't.*' It was amazing, the last thing I expected to hear. And then I heard all these stories about people singing "Maggie's Farm" on the dole queue on the Monday morning, which I found funny. I don't know whether they were slagging us off or just enjoying the song.

There was a blackness to that performance which marked it out from the rest of your live work.

Bono: There's a side to U2 in Ireland, where the mammies and daddies are proud that U2 are an Irish group doing well in America — like Barry McGuigan. And there is a sense too that maybe some politicians had pigeonholed us like *(mimics rural hack's insincere sing-song accent),* 'there's U2 now, a good example of young people. Playing their *music*' — when getting off their lazy backsides is what they really mean. And I just wanted to say: Look Mister. Because I knew there'd be certain politicians watching the programme and I didn't want to let them off the hook. Because the truth of it was that a lot of people were *on* the hook because of their policies. I just wanted to *be* that

Larry Mullen and Bono

anger. I allowed that anger to be a part of the performance.

How did you feel about the political impact of the "Sun City" project? It seemed to start strongly but then fizzled out somewhat.

Adam: I'm sure the actual success of the record was politically interfered with. There were a lot of radio stations that wouldn't play it because of advertisers. In certain places, it wasn't released. But I think it's part of a movement that began with Live Aid.

Bono: Many people don't know it but the Dunnes Stores Strikers actually sang on that record. In the background. If not quite in tune, certainly close to it!

Were you happier with the practical impact of the Amnesty International "Conspiracy Of Hope" tour?

Bono: Well, Amnesty doubled their membership in America. But the best news I had all year was a letter from one of the U2 fanzines telling me that all over America now they're setting up these U2 clubs. But they're not exclusive to U2. They're also an appreciation of Peter Gabriel, The Waterboys and groups that, for whatever reason, they've linked together. And I was looking at this U2 fan club poster and it had an entrance fee of 3 dollars. At first, I felt — what's this about, charging to hear U2 records? But then I discovered this money was going to Third World concerns. And that, all over America, they had set up these clubs where they listen to U2 records and actually write cards for Amnesty. And if you can inspire something on that small scale, that's just everything I could ever ask for. All, in fact, I would ask for.

Where do you think you'd be now if U2 weren't formed?

Bono: Hmmm, that's an interesting one. God almighty. Whoo! Get me another beer!

Adam: I think Dublin wouldn't have contained you. I think you would have been off somewhere.

Bono: I don't know. To be honest, U2 saved my life in a way because I am literally unemployable. There's nothing else I can do.

There was a time when you talked about a streak of delinquency there.

Bono: Not delinquency. I think I would have imploded, as distinct from exploding in my musical life. I mean I worked as a petrol pump attendant. Can you imagine me as a petrol pump attendant?

You've seen people who were friends turning to drugs as one sort of escape route – as people in Dublin have done in increasing numbers recently. Would that ever have been a possibility?

Bono: I really understand the attraction...I don't come from the viewpoint of someone who is completely unsympathetic to drug users. I understood it then and I understand it even more now because of, for instance, being onstage for two hours and then not being able to sleep for six or seven or eight hours.

What was the impact personally of seeing people going through the ordeal of drug abuse?

Bono: Ah, I wrote the song, didn't I? I just wrote "Bad".

The point is Dublin is rife with a particular problem which people have to come to grips with in their personal lives. To understand the background to the song might help people.

"There's the America of Ronald Reagan," The Edge comments, "but there's also the America of Bobby Kennedy, Abraham Lincoln and George Washington."

Adam: In its simplest form, I've always seen heroin as a very evil thing. Consequently that's always inspired a great fear of it in me so I can assume that anyone who takes it has a similar fear. To actually have their back so much against the wall, to be controlled by it, is something I can't understand. I haven't been that close to the edge. I've certainly been near it a few times in one way or another but to imagine that next stage is pretty much impossible.

Bono: *(referring to "Running To Stand Still")* I heard of a couple both of whom were addicted and such was their addiction that they had no money, no rent, so that the guy risked it all on a run. All of it. He went and smuggled into Dublin a serious quantity of heroin strapped to his body so that there was on one hand, life imprisonment, on the other hand, riches. Apart from the morality of that, what interested me was what put him in that place. *(Quotes the lyric)* *"You know I took the poison from the poison stream/Then I floated out of here."* Because for a lot of people, there are no physical doors open anymore. And so if you can't change the world you're living in, seeing through different eyes is the only alternative. And heroin gives you heroin eyes to see the world with; and the thing about heroin is that you think that's the way it really is. That the old you, who worries about paying the rent, the old you who just worries, is not the real you.

How did you feel about losing Phil Lynott?

Bono: A thing that really bothers me personally is that for two years, myself and Ali lived in Howth, on the same road as Phil, in a little cottage that we rented at the time. And I would see him everywhere else *but* on that street. Every time I saw him, he'd say 'Why don't you come down for dinner? You know, you have to come down for a bite.' And I would say 'you have to come up for a bite. You have to drop up.' Every single time. And I never did call down and he never did call up. That's what came back to me. I never did call up.

Sexually, U2 have a very clean image. How have you reacted to gender-bending pop and glam rock games?

Bono: I am interested in that aspect of sexuality. When I look at my lyrics, I'm obsessed with borders, be they political, sexual or spiritual. It's not a subject I've broached yet but I wouldn't rule it out. I'm also interested about the New Victorian era because of AIDS. I know a lot of homosexual men and most of them I get on with. Some overtly camp men I don't get on with.

But it all comes down to love. How can anyone attack love? That doesn't specifically condemn or condone homosexuality or any kind of sexuality. I could never attack love.

Sexuality was and is traditionally associated with rock 'n' roll rebellion. But how does it relate to U2's idea of subversion?

Bono: I think there's nothing more radical or revolutionary than two people loving each other because it's so hard to do it and to keep those feelings going. In a sense, U2 are owning up to those feelings and emotions that have been swept under the carpet of rock'n'roll in favour of these cartoon things.

Edge: One thing about the gay question is that in America, gay rights and gay liberation has suddenly been put back ten years because AIDS has suddenly become an excuse for anti-gay feelings. I think that's a very unfortunate development.

You were in Nicaragua during the year. What do you remember most about it?

Bono: The funny thing about it was Somoza's house, the house of this great ugly dictator. I was expecting a palatial residence but it was all falling down — and they just *left* it falling down. Then the theatre, the arts centre in Managua, is bombed out and they left it bombed out and just placed the stage in the middle of a gutted building. People come through holes in the wall to watch the plays and they leave it there as a testament to the earthquake. So you sit in this bombed out building watching a performance and somebody like Daniel Ortega comes in and it's no big deal. I said to somebody: this is the sexiest revolution I ever saw, you know the women in their khaki greens, they've got smiles stuck on their faces. They're not at all malevolent like the troops in Salvador...

They must be finding it hard to keep smiling in the face of the US blockade.

Bono: The spirit of the people in Nicaragua is being beaten down. They've no food, they've no supplies and I was actually at a rally of Daniel Ortega's and just the look in the people's eyes, they wanted so much to believe in their revolution. People think with their pockets a lot of the time and you can't blame them for it, women trying to bring up children and fellas with no work. It's just very sad to see the stranglehold America has on Central America in practice. When you go into a restaurant and they give you a menu, there's 15 items on the menu and they don't tell you at first they've only got one. You have to ask 14 times before they tell you, no, we just have rice.

But now you're about to tour America, Reagan's America.

Bono takes the lead

Edge: It's a very different America from the one we've seen over the last couple of years. People were so behind everything Ronald Reagan stood for but now I think when we go back, we'll be seeing a broken country in a sense. Either that or people refusing to look — which is a more frightening prospect. I've been talking to some Americans since Irangate. People's faith in the Administration, and therefore their faith in politics generally, is shattered.

Bono: I believe you. I really believe in America. I really believe in Americans, I should say.

Edge: There's the America of Ronald Reagan but there's also the America of Bobby Kennedy, of Abraham Lincoln and George Washington.

Bono: And of Werner Von Braun. I mean, there's a right-wing vein running through America at the moment and it's made of steel and with all the will in the world, it seems almost impossible to break or bend that. It lies dormant for maybe a few years and it comes out with its cold steely grip on America. Dick Gregory, for instance — there's no question in his mind but that Lenny Bruce was escorted to death's door by this right-wing America. There's no doubt in his mind that Martin Luther King was escorted to the same door. He's a conspiracy theorist, he believes that heroin was introduced to white America only when white America began to wake up and speak out in the early Sixties on campus. I'm not a conspiracy theorist but there is no question: there is this iron hand.

Edge: Whether it's official or not.

Bono: Well, the paper-clip conspiracy — it's quite clear now that America became a haven for nearly 300 Nazis and war criminals. That Nazis helped to put the first man on the moon is now a fact. But, that said, I still believe in Americans. I think they're a very open people. It's their openness that leads them to trust a man as dangerous as Ronald Reagan. They want to believe he's a good guy. They want to believe that he's in the cavalry, coming to rescue America's reputation after the Seventies. But he was only an actor. It was only a movie. I think the picture's ended now and Americans are leaving the cinema feeling a little down in the mouth.

Edge: David Lee Roth should be the next President. He'd scare the shit out of the Russians *(laughs)*.

From here, you wonder just how much, or how little, many Americans know about what their government's doing.

Bono: Just give me the truth. I always think of that line: just give me the truth. Because in America, the media is so important in deciding what is and what isn't the truth...I must say I'm still really stuck with my memory of our first trip to the US. We were just so wide-eyed. We really embraced America and indeed America embraced us. And over the last few years we've had to re-evaluate our impression of America because of that fact that we walk onto a stage every night. When we're in America playing to 20,000 people and that's a lot of people, we have to ask ourselves the question: what can rock 'n' roll music do? Go round in circles? But I think on this record there are questions asked, if not answered, about America.

Edge: Awkward questions.

Bono: And insofar as we are Irishmen, on one level we have no duty to speak out against America or bite the hand that feeds us,

as they would say. And I think we *have* bitten the hand that feeds us but we do so from a position that, as I say, we have belief in Americans. We're not anti-Americans or anti-America, we're anti-Ameri-kay. It's still a thrill to be there. I mean, America is the promised land for a lot of Irish people. It really is.

Adam: And I suppose there's a serious sort of Irish influence in America, when you think of the family links.

Bono: Try the Kennedys. The Kennedys made poteen. I mean they were bootleggers in the days of prohibition. I'm sure there was some potato wine involved there *(laughs)*.

But is there some real hope of penetrating, of denting, the apathy?

Bono: Well, I think, first of all, it's not your first reason for being on stage, to effect change in the political climate of a country. I don't know what the first reason is but it's not the first reason. But I like to think that U2 have already contributed to a turnaround in thinking.

Edge: And if we have, it's not even the point, is it really? You don't write a song because you think it's going to change somebody. You write a song because that's the way you feel.

Adam: You write a song because something hurts. I mean if you look at social change within America, that came from the Delta areas, the plantations or wherever. A lot of the change in America is rooted in blues music; that was what people listened to. It was the protest music of the time.

Bono: I don't think it's up to bands to have their politics and point of view worked out. I don't think it's up to me as a singer to have answers. I just think it's important that you put questions. I

> "I told you in a nightclub a year ago that I was sick of being reasonable," says Bono. "I learnt to come out as an unreasonable man."

The Edge grins and bears it

don't know of a rock'n'roll band that ever offered up answers and I think it's wrong for pop-stars to be politicians. I like the idea of Jim Morrison who called the Doors "erotic politicians" *(laughs)*. I thought that was kind of funny. Because you're put in a position where, because you have made music that means something to people, your politics or point of view is given far too much importance. What comes to mind is Elvis Presley who meets with Nixon and he's made an anti-drug marshall — and the man is loaded, out of his brains, with the badge on. I've said it before: Elvis Presley's genius was the way he held the microphone, the way he sang into it.

You know, Bill, there's a question I'd be interested in asking you. People expect that if you don't come through with a very strong point of view that you're therefore a liberal and personally I share with everyone — it seems everyone else in my generation — an apathy with regard to Irish party politics. The questons I ask are deeper than that. But why are there only these three choices in Ireland, left and right and middle?

Or middle, middle, and middle.

Bono: Yeah in this country, it's middle, middle and middle or right, right and right, depending on your point of view. I ask myself why I have to make a choice, left and right. I wonder how ideologies born at the turn of the century can ever be hoped to apply to the 1980s. Reaganomics or Thatcher's England — they reflect old, old ideologies. Old ideologies on the left, old ideologies on the right and if you don't like either of them, your're supposed to be a liberal. And I don't like the liberal point of view — least of all... I just picked up your review, Bill, this idea of U2 enjoying the middle ground.

Hold on, I didn't write "enjoying"...

Bono: Well, we might sit on the fence politically at times, and because, for instance, there's a picture of myself and Garret Fitzgerald in the paper, people think maybe my politics are the same as his party. But I've stressed that my interest in him is much more as a man than in his party or their politics. What's the alternative? I don't know what the alternative is in Ireland. Ireland seems politically so absurd, that the main parties have all the same policies and the Labour Party which is my own background — my Dad voted Labour most of the time and I would generally vote Labour — yet if we go by the elections, the Labour party doesn't mean anything at this point. I just look around and I see grey.

The term "liberalism" isn't necessarily a word of rebuke. It's more a word of description.

Bono: It is to me... I don't feel liberal at all and I don't think anyone who knows me would call me liberal.

Obviously, there's a question of what one means by liberal.

Bono: I know. It's just that I'm more interested in the man as opposed to men, one man as opposed to a crowd of men. And that

Adam Clayton: a pint of plain is your only man!

explains the spiritual side of my writing because I think in a funny way the country almost gets the party it deserves, that it has choices... I know I had a row with Paul Weller about that at Band Aid — about the old argument that it's the system. I just don't go: "It's the system." I think men choose the system they live under in our age...

But if the choice is so absurd, where do you turn?

Bono: It's just that I suppose I'm more interested in what you might call a revolution of love. I believe that if you want to start a revolution you better start a revolution in your own home and your own way of thinking and of relating to the men and women around you. I'm *trying* to come to terms with global ideas like Live Aid, Artists Against Apartheid, Amnesty International and the "Conspiracy Of Hope" tour. These ideas are great ideas. We believe in and belong to them yet, for me, the future lies in small scale activity. For instance, commitment to a community, like U2 are committed to Dublin, commitment to the people in your place of work, commitment to relationships and the ones you love. I find that the people often with the big ideas and the big mouths, you know — it's like the old story that Lennon beat his wife...

Stalin probably did! *(laughs).*

Bono: Okay, Stalin probably did beat his wife and definitely other people's wives and their husbands. And let's say that's when I start these questions, the more fundamental questions, those big black and white issues I'm more interested in as I get older.

I told you in a nightclub about a year ago I was sick of being reasonable. I learnt to come out as an unreasonable man *(laughs).* I know what you're getting at and I know what other people are going to get at. "Red Hill Mining Town" is a song about the miners' strike and the only reference to Ian McGregor (The British Coal Board Chairman) is *"through hand of steel and heart of stone/our labour day is come and gone."* People beat me with a stick for that but what I'm interested in is, seeing in the newspapers or on television that another thousand people have lost their jobs. Now what you *don't* read about is that those people go home and they have families and they're trying to bring up children. And those relationships broke up under the pressure of the miners' strike. Those men and women lost pride in themselves and that affects their sex lives, literally... *(quotes again)... "the glass is cut, the bottle run dry, our love runs cold in the cabins in the night/We're wounded by fear, injured in doubt/I can lose myself but you I can't live without/Cos you keep me holding on."* I'm more interested in the relationship at this point in time because I feel other people are more qualified to comment on the miners' strike. That enraged me — but I feel more qualified to write about relationships because I understand them more than what it's like to work in a pit.

Both water images and the notion of surrender stand out very strongly in the lyrics.

Bono: I used what I thought were very classical and therefore accessible images and symbols. Almost biblical. Really simple things, so that whatever culture you come from, they mean something.

What's the implication of the notion of surrender?

Bono: Surrender is not what it used to be.

What is it?

Bono: In "With Or Without You" when it says *"and you give yourself away and you give yourself away"* —everybody else in the group knows what that means. It's about how I feel in U2 at times — exposed. I know the group think I'm exposed and the group feel that I give myself away. And funny enough, Lou Reed said to me, 'what you've got is a real gift: don't give it away because people might not place upon it the right value.' And I think that if I do any damage to the group, it's that I'm too open. For instance, in an interview, I don't hold the cards there and play the right one because I either have to do it or not do it. That's why I'm not going to do many interviews this year. Because there's a cost to my personal life and a cost to the group as well.

But there is a spiritual value about giving yourself, your ego, away?

Bono: That goes back to the song "Surrender". I always believed in the Biblical idea that unless the seed dies, is almost crushed into the ground, it won't bear fruit. Again Lou Reed was telling me how he grew up in the 50's when machismo was a way of life and you did not give yourself away, in fact the

opposite, and he said he found the fifties idea of Cool a real strait-jacket in his life.

Why is it that you've become more closely linked with figures from the previous rock era than most if not all the bands from your generation?

Bono: Well, this boy from Ballymun was actually on tour with Lou Reed and he used to stand every night on the side of the stage and watch U2. He seems to care so much about U2 and I learned so much from him. And one night, I said to him *(adopts conspiratorial whisper)* "Berlin's my favourite album" and he said "It's mine too." He thinks it's the only one he got right. But it's true: we're attracted to people like Frank Barsalona who brought The Beatles and The Who to the States and Chris Blackwell who was there with Bob Marley. Our record collection began in 1976. We weren't there when rock'n'roll began. So we're attracted to people who have the perspective we don't have. Like Pete Townshend is a guy you can ring up.

Larry: Why don't you give everyone his telephone number? *(general laughter).*

> "Pete Townshend is a guy you can ring up," Bono asserts. Larry has a bright idea: "Why don't you give everyone his telephone number?"

THE WORLD ABOUT US
March 1987

Larry: the last word

U2

ROCKIN' ALL OVER THE STATES

As "With Or Without You"

hits No. 1 in the

US singles charts,

Liam Mackey joins U2

on their biggest

- and most successful -

American tour to date.

IN AMERICA you don't take the lift, you ride the elevator and in all of the Big Country there can be no more deliciously spine-tingling, stomach-heaving and literally ear-popping an ascent than that which takes you, at a top speed of 600 feet per minute, from the crowded pavements of 5th Avenue and 34th Street to the 102nd floor of the Empire State Building, where, at an altitude of 1,250 feet above sea level, you stand beneath a red neon-tube sign proclaiming 'The Top Of The Big Apple' and — deep breath —take in the dizzying panorama that made King Kong swoon. (Apologies Fay Wray!).

On the way up, you have to change elevators at the 80th floor and join the long queue where ticket stubs are presented to the checker before proceeding skywards on your journey. It's here your correspondent does a double-take, for fastened with sellotape to the turnstile is a sheet of white paper bearing the hand-printed inscription: 'Wanted U2 Tix'.

Well, signs of the times and all that symbolism, but, really, is this ever a long way from another day and another wanted notice, one that was pinned to a bulletin board in a Dublin secondary school ten years ago by a fifteen year old who played the drums and wondered if anyone else shared his enthusiasm for forming a rock'n'roll band. For a millisecond, all the gigs, songs, words, labours, travels, traumas and thrills of a decade in the life of four young Dubliners, crash, collide and resolve into this corny but irresistible metaphor for U2 in America as of May 11th 1987. "Wanted U2 Tix" — a small sign with a big plea, 1,000 feet above New York City. This is top of the tops, higher than higher — and right now, U2 are up there with the world at their feet.

A LOFTY perch but a downcast mood — the girl checking the tickets in the Empire State Building knows her chances of seeing U2 live this time around are slim to nothing. "Friends of mine were raving about U2 from the very first time they came here, saying 'you just have to see this band'," she tells me. "But I never did. Then last year I saw the Amnesty tour on TV and decided 'right I'm not going to miss them again'. But when I went to get the tickets I couldn't believe it — they were gone just like that."

Bono on-stage at Meadowlands, New Jersey, May 12, 1987

She's not alone in her disappointment. Such has been the excess demand right across America, that scalpers at the concert in Hartford, Connecticut, for example, were asking $115 for tickets with a face-value of $15. And in New York, the shock to the system of Aiken Promotions man Peter Aiken upon receiving a dental bill for $600 was outweighed only by his utter astonishment at the dentist's suggestion that he'd waive the fee if Peter could get him two tickets for one of the five sold-out 20,000 seater concerts in New Jersey. Re-write the script — an eye for an eye and a tooth for a U2 ticket.

To borrow from Americanese, the bottom-line is that at least for the duration of this first leg of their US tour, which began in Tempe Arizona on April 1, U2 are the biggest thing in rock in America, triggering off a mass-media landslide in the process. By the time they've finished up in Meadowlands, New Jersey on May 16, the band will have topped both albums and singles charts, seen all their elpees re-enter the Billboard Hot 100, appeared on the covers of *Time* and *Rolling Stone,* been featured on the major TV networks, become the top grossing live act in the country and played to a pocket-calculator knows how many people while thousands more rued their misfortune at missing out on a certified highlight of the 1987 touring calendar.

But then that's not the bottom-line at all. The real bottom-line is that the four people who make up U2 have still to do what they've been doing an awful lot for the last ten years, albeit now against a backdrop of staggering dimensions —they've got to walk on-stage, pick up their instruments, and for around one hundred minutes, show committed fans and first-timers — and perhaps even remind each other — just what it is they've got that's raising all the fuss an' holler.

THE VETERAN'S Memorial Coliseum in the multi-purpose Civic Centre of Hartford, Connecticut is packed for the last of U2's three concerts in the Constitution State. This summer the band may well be one of the biggest things to roll through, what the Lord Mayor of Hartford not inaccurately calls "this green and pleasant corner of Southern New England" but even U2 must on occasion play second-fiddle to the attractions of other leisure pursuits. Thus their three concert stint was interrupted for one night so that the Coliseum could accommodate an ice hockey play-off. It sounds like a major logistical headache but these American arenas are nothing if not adaptable — and, so, inside 24 hours they simply took out the stage, installed the ice rink, took out the ice rink and reinstalled the stage. QED. In fact, it's an ideal venue for a rock concert on this scale — big but not gargantuan. Positioned three-quarters way down the arena, the stage, with the PA suspended in circular formation above it, is

completely enclosed by seating that rises tier upon tier, offering perfect sound and vision to every member of the capacity 16,500 crowd. Looking down on the scene tonight you begin to suspect that, for promoter Jim Aiken, over here to finalise arrangements for the U2 and David Bowie concerts in Ireland, this kind of American concert arena comes close to his concept of professional heaven.

U2's arrival on-stage is so low-key and almost casual that it momentarily catches the audience by surprise. For the past minute and a half they've been singing and swaying to the sound of "Stand By Me" coming over the PA when, without fanfare, U2 are on-stage, seamlessly taking up from where John Lennon's "Rock 'n'Roll" cover of the Ben E King song left off.

Performed with the houselights on full, the opening says two things — one that there are effective (albeit, in this case, ingenious) alternatives to the standard curtain-raising theatrics of Stadium rock and, two, that as Irish fans discovered at Self-Aid, U2 are no longer the world's worst cover band.

" 'Stand By Me' proves that, as Irish fans discovered at Self Aid, U2 are no longer the world's worst cover band."

But the time for such reflections comes later, as with the houselights still up — and paradoxically heightening rather than detracting from the drama — The Edge rings out an instantly familiar intro and both band and audience are surging into "Pride In The Name Of Love". After that there's a first pause for breath, the houselights dim, and the emotional temperature is re-adjusted completely with the serene and quietly dignified "MLK".

In the course of a twenty song set, ranging in mood from rage ("Bullet The Blue Sky") through sadness ("Running To Stand Still") to boisterous good humour ("Trip Through Your Wires" with Bono blowing a raspberry of a harmonica solo), and which embraces the band's history from "Electric Co" (The Edge strapping on his Explorer as of yore) to their brand new no. 1 American single, "With Or Without You", U2 play with confidence and conviction, only Bono's occasional but obvious throat-weariness, cutting up rough. Yet while in itself sufficient to confirm the band's stunning mastery of the medium, it's doubtful that the show will be remembered among the tour highlights. Invariably, there's more to the memorable concert experience than a band's performance alone, and while the missing part of the equation in Hartford might have been the unfamiliar spectacle to Irish eyes of a rock audience — albeit a noisy and upstanding one — staying right where their tickets told them to stay, or simply something as subjective and mundane as my own creeping exhaustion after a long haul by air and road, either way, as I head backstage to the sound of a cast of thousands singing the refrain from "40", I'm already relishing a second chance to see them again two days later in New Jersey.

U2 and Paul McGuinness at their press conference in New York, May, 1987

But first it's time to unwind and cool down with a beer. Backstage a hospitality room has been set aside where the band can mingle with friends, industry figures and the visiting Irish press corps. I recognise Carter Allen from his appearance on *Today Tonight's* U2 report earlier in the week. A Boston dee-jay, he was the first person in America to spin a U2 record on radio and remains a firm friend and fan of the band.

So too does fellow Bostonian Peter Wolf, formerly lead singer with J. Geils (whom U2 supported on one of their earliest US forays): apparently Wolf had come to the show on the previous Thursday and passed on a compilation tape of country songs to Bono, whose interest in American roots music appears to grow daily. Robert Johnson, Hank Williams and Luke The Drifter are just three of the names he'll later tell me have "become part of the record collection." Carter Allen, for his part, has brought along a tape of vintage blues he's promised to give the singer.

Poring over schedules and lists with Chris Roche and Jim Aiken is Alvinia Bridges, who's in charge of press publicity for the tour. A tall, striking black woman for whom the word 'statuesque' could have been coined, she's previously worked in a similar capacity with The Rolling Stones and was at Slane Castle for their concert in 1982. How does working with U2 compare with the Stones job? "When there's greatness there," she says diplomatically, "it's all great."

The band wander in and fan out into separate conversations. The Edge is well pleased with life. "We're really into the swing of things," he says of their string of shows to date. "Once it would have taken us a month — now it's happening in a week."

As highlights of the tour so far he selects gigs in Los Angeles and Boston, as well as the single going to number one. "I really

didn't think it would do that," he reflects. "I just didn't think it was an obvious song for radio at all."Then there was Bob Dylan's joining them on-stage in L.A. As Edge tells it, the performance was improvised on the spot. The band suggested doing "Knocking On Heaven's Door" to which Dylan replied he wasn't sure if he remembered all the words. Finally agreeing on the song, they all then huddled in a knot onstage trying to decide on the key, while 20,000 people screamed themselves hoarse. In the end they performed both "Knockin'..." and "I Shall Be Released" and another little piece of rock history was written. I suggest that, after tonight, a further collaboration might see Dylan giving harmonica lessons to Bono. "Ah, that's all part of the act — Bono's really a great harmonica player," replies The Edge deadpan.

The Demon Harper himself was in a more pensive mood, concerned about all the attention the financial aspect of the tour was getting. All this emphasis on what he called "The Money Tree", when he would rather talk about the music. As he did so his mood brightened. "We're already writing new songs, and The Edge is just brilliant right now," he enthused. "Y'know, I feel like we're really entering our hey-day."

He discounted reports that Bruce Springsteen would duet with him in New Jersey as "a total fabrication" and on the general subject of media attention, was obviously concerned at how the British press had sensationalised some comments he'd made in America about his relationship with his wife Ali. But if the fibs are getting bigger they're not entirely a new thing. "Remember the one about Maire Ní Bhraonáin," he laughed, "first Adam was supposed to be having an affair with her, then me — in the end we thought we should have a picture taken of all four of us in bed with Maire. *That* would've confused them.''

Ah yes, bed. It's time to go our separate ways — the band in a fleet of stretch limos accompanied by a wailing motor-cycle police escort to Bradley Airport where the Viscount they've chartered for the tour awaits to take them to New York; and *mise* and the rest of the Irish press contingent back to our Hartford hotel, where the porter, who hasn't seen his native Waterford in 40 years, points to a ghettoblaster and tells me: 'You know what we call those boom-boxes over here? We call them third world briefcases.' It's time to rest my weary head.

ON THIS humid Sunday afternoon in Manhattan, Tommy Makem's Irish Pavilion is playing host to a throng of media people from Ireland, Europe and America, who occupy themselves at the free bar and munch on such classic Emerald Isle delicacies as green, white and gold vegetable pate crackers, until the arrival of U2 and manager Paul McGuinness, amid a hailstorm of camera clicking, signals the start of what's billed as a pre-European tour press conference.

As the CBS and NBC television cameras roll, an Italian journalist rises to address the first question to the five gentlemen seated behind individual mics placed on a long linen-covered table. She requires a basic point of information about the concert in Rome and Bono having duly obliged regains her seat. A long, embarrassed silence ensues. ''Is that it then?'' quips Paul McGuinness. ''What are you doing for your birthday?'' an American voice calls out — for today does indeed mark the beginning of Mr. Hewson's twenty-seventh year on the planet.

''Well,'' says Bono, ''my wife got me drunk this morning *(laughter)*. I was supposed to get up early and think about all the things I'd like to say to the European press. But we've had a few cups of coffee and I'm feeling well on the way to having the best birthday I've ever had actually — No. 1 single, No. 1 LP, what more can you say?''

(Ali's arrival overnight was apparently by way of an unexpected birthday surprise and I hear later about the scam which had the other members of the group calling Bono from his hotel room to open the large, cardboard box — actually a fridge container —standing upright in the corridor, and which contained his human 'present').

The conference gathers momentum but little coherence, as for close on an hour and a half, questions and answers ricochet around the room, the subject matter careering from the trivial all the way through to the absurd — at one end of the scale, a question about why The Edge wears grey shirts, and at the other, the unanswerable 'when is the Northern Ireland conflict going to be resolved?' In between there are moments of humour and

modest revelation.

Bono on his harmonica playing: ''I play it *so badly* at these concerts *(general laughter)* and I keep meeting people afterwards, all these fans, and they just say 'Hey, y'know I really enjoyed the concert and everything — but listen, my brother, he knows how to play harmonica, perhaps I could introduce you to him.' *(More laughter)*. In fact *(produces harp from pocket)*, a member of the crew actually handed me the harmonica as I was leaving and said, 'y'know, maybe you'd like to practice... ' ''

On the problems with his voice in Arizona that forced them to cancel a show for the first time ever:

''A very important man came and looked down at my throat and told me that no, this wasn't just hoarseness — I had actually lost my voice. It's the first time it ever happened to me and it gave me a real fright actually. It really scared me. But it's okay now, sure.''

The Edge on Bruce Springsteen:

''I think what he shares with us is an understanding of live performance, probably because like us he spent many years traipsing up and down North America and Europe in transit vans doing clubs and theatres. He paid his dues in that way, so he really does understand an audience and I'd like to think we do so as well. Bono: *(leaning into the mic and grinning)* ''I think his wife's fantastic too.'' *(Cheers and jeers from the floor)*.

Bono on the need for a good rock venue in Dublin:

''That would be something it would be nice to find a solution to, it's something we would be interested in getting involved in, but not something we should talk about until we've worked out how we could do it.''

Bono interrupting a rambling question that appears to be straying onto familiar territory:

''Is this going to be a religious question? Because as you know we're all members of the Frisbeetarian Order. Just signed up since we've come to America. We believe that when you die your soul goes up on a roof and you can't get it down *(general hilarity)*.

Bono on the music he grew up with:

''My older brother had a lot of tapes — The Jimi Hendrix Experience, The Who, The Beatles...''

Bono on the music Larry grew up with:

''The Sweet and Showaddywaddy.'' Larry: ''And Abba, they were a big influence on my musical career.''

Bono on the post-''Joshua Tree'' U2 audience:

''There's a new audience there for U2 but the old audience is also there — the real fight is who's getting the tickets. But we never wanted to be an elitist group, we always wanted to play to as many people as we could. We set out to do that. I must say as we end this, that this has been some year for U2. We started off in 1977, I think it was September or October, just four people who

> "Religion? We're all members of the Frisbeetarian Order. We believe that when you die your soul goes up on a roof and you can't get it down."

Larry Mullen: "Fair play to me!"

couldn't play, just plugging into Adam's amp and I'm just amazed to see that ten years later, so much has happened to us that's been so good. So, thanks a lot for everything."

But perhaps the final quote from this press conference should go to Larry Mullen, whose well-timed quips throughout the afternoon had both band and audience in stitches. Towards the end, asked if he was worried that U2 might not sell out their second Croke Park concert, the drummer paused for a moment of sober reflection. "The fact that we would like it to sell out is not the reason we're doing it. We're playing America, and we're doing a lot of gigs in England so when the question of Irish gigs in Cork and Belfast came up and the first Dublin gig sold out, we just felt why should we underplay the country in which we started out. So if it doesn't sell out it doesn't make any difference. It's the fact that we do it, that's what we're here for — to play to the people."

After this, perhaps the longest public speech he's ever made, Larry sits back into his seat and says: "Fair play to me." The other band members lead the applause.

IT'S MONDAY May the 11th and tonight U2 play the first of five concerts in the Brendan Byrne Arena, better-known as Meadowlands, New Jersey. Though they don't officially play New York until the return leg of their American tour in the Autumn, this is a real acid test, as near to the core of the Big Apple as makes no difference. The media build-up has been running at full-tilt for the past 48 hours. K-Rock Radio Station, whom one local journalist and long-time U2 fan claims are just recent band-wagon jumpers, have followed up yesterday's six hour A to Z of U2 — well A to W actually, beginning with "A Day Without Me" and ending with "With Or Without You" —by reporting live this afternoon from the *soundcheck*. "That's The Edge you hear tuning up behind me..." By six o'clock both NBC and CBS evening news have screened extracts from the press-conference, and as one presenter puts it, "The young Irish band are all set to rock New Jersey."

Tonight we take a ride, cross the river to the Jersey side, and with the Manhattan skyline behind us, darkening against the pale orange of the setting sun, swing left off the New Jersey Turnpike and draw up outside Meadowlands, a solitary, gleaming white super-structure rising like some huge, sci-fi apparition from a broad expanse of desolate wasteland.

The selling of beer may have been banned here since a riot at a recent Iron Maiden gig, but inside Meadowlands tonight, long before U2 take the stage, a crowd of 20,000 are already soaring on a natural high, whipping up their own DIY fervour, as the Mexican Wave travels in huge ripples around the stadium. The lively blues and country-based rock of support band Lone Justice earns them a generous reception and while the electricity continues to crackle in anticipation of the imminent emergence from the tunnel of The Main Act, I learn that the girl sitting on my right is seeing U2 live for the first time. A seventeen year old New Yorker, her concert diary thus far in 1987 has been of the standard American FM variety: Bon Jovi (twice), Journey and AC/DC —though the latter she didn't "rate at all". She's only just bought "The Joshua Tree", knows some of the earlier material and is looking to be impressed.

She is. For tonight, U2 move beyond excellence and into the realms of greatness. From the opening "Where The Streets Have No Name", with The Edge's guitar riff scything across the moody organ intro before the band arrive in force, to the traditional denouement of "40" with Larry rapping out the beat and leaving the people's choir to do the rest, this is a U2 performance full of hunger, fire, artistry and surprise.

It's the constant innovation, the squaring up to new challenges, from a band who could easily play it by the book and still inspire a frenzied response that impresses most.

"You'll have to all keep quiet for this one," says Bono at one point introducing "Springhill Mining Disaster", the extraordinary Peggy Seeger ballad that's become synonymous with Luke Kelly. I'd been told that the band had faced problems performing it to a screaming audience at least once already on the tour, but tonight twenty thousand people sit enraptured as, with controlled passion in his voice, Bono sings of bone and blood being the price of coal. It's an utterly compelling and convincing performance — and even the singer himself appears taken aback by the impact it makes.

"I've never seen people sitting down at a U2 concert before," Bono tells the crowd after the song — "and I'm not sure that I like it!" Cue: the opening notes of "New Year's Day" and it's as if small explosions have gone off under every seat in the house.

The song over, Bono runs up a ramp stage right and begins gesticulating up at the balcony. Within seconds there's a rush of bodies down the aisle, and eventually two girls are helped onstage where they proudly hold an Amnesty International banner throughout a soaring "Pride In The Name Of Love".

"This is a song that nearly didn't make it to the record but I'm glad that it did," shouts Bono introducing "I Trip Through Your Wires" during which he flips The Edge's hat over the guitarist's eyes as the band manifestly enjoy this hearty dose of down-home rock'n'roll. They maintain the fun mood for "C'mon Everybody", Bono borrowing a denim jacket from somebody near the front of the stage, and throwing shapes all over the place. "U2 trash another classic," he tells the crowd.

"I Still Haven't Found What I'm Looking For", "Bad", "In God's Country", "I Will Follow", "Homecoming" — this is a concert bursting with a wealth of great songs, a testament to a body of work that leaves the band almost spoiled for choice these days. The most indelible mark however is left by "Bullet The Blue Sky". Played with scalding intensity, its sound evokes a vision of hell, as angry red searchlights scan the stage and arena, Bono spits out the lyrics with venom and The Edge summons up the ghost of Jimi Hendrix, searing into the "Star Spangled Banner".

A deafening noise rocks the stadium when U2 leave the stage, a combination of cheering and screaming, unlike anything I've ever heard before at a rock concert, and which, incredibly, continues to rise in volume until the band return for encores that include "With Or Without You", post-scripted by a quote from "Love Will Tear Us Apart Again", "Gloria" and finally "40" when for the first time in my U2-watching career I notice that The Edge and Adam swop lead and bass guitars, even though the guitarist convinces me afterwards that they've been doing it ever since the song was recorded. It was one of those nights — a U2 champagne gig, even if these days, they might forget to bring the bubbly onstage.

AFTERWARDS, I get a word in Edge-ways in the backstage bar that seems 99% populated with faces from home.

"My legs were like jelly going on there," the guitarist cheerfully admits, before letting his mind wander back to an early gig in the Arcadia, Cork, when on another night of challenge, with prestigious British rock critics in the audience, U2 pulled the fat from the fire.

"I've never seen people sitting down at a U2 concert before," Bono tells the crowd after the song, "and I'm not sure that I like it."

Now that they've so magnificently claimed the higher ground, it might seem ironic or naive to be talking about challenge and risk and adventure, and even of gigs long past, but on a hot night in New Jersey, this famous four showed that they've still got everything to play for.

U2 are running to avoid standing still. Catch them if you can.

ROCKIN' ALL OVER THE STATES
June 1987

ALL IRELAND WAS THERE

It's a double home-coming, as U2 return from their odyssey 'round the globe to bring "The Joshua Tree" tour to their fanatical Irish supporters in Dublin and Cork. Bill Graham reports.

"**I F I** *could stick my hand in my heart/And spill it all over the stage/ Would that be enough for your teenage lust?/Would that help to ease the pain?*"

– "It's Only Rock 'n' Roll" (The Rolling Stones)

"It's Larry's fault. He *did* start it... The way he hits the bass drum is the thing that makes this group still a rock'n'roll group... People will talk about U2 being a 'live group' or 'the only live group' and they'll talk about me as the singer because Bono will jump off the balcony to make a point — but it's not me at all. It's Larry's bass drum."

– Bono to Liam Mackey, August '83

IT REALLY *is* Larry's drums. This past month, U2 must have received enough coverage to waste all the oak plantations in Coolatin Woods but watching a sea of pale, sun-starved fists pummelling the air to the blonde one's beat, it almost seemed conceivable that the whole point of their ten year career, in all its heartache, endeavour and triumphs, was to compensate for Larry Mullen's rejection by those other regular occupants of Croke

Park on big match occasions, The Artane Boys Band.

I jest, of course. But all the recent soul-searching coverage of the world's best bad-weather band rarely isolated that bass drum and in failing to do so equally often forgot — they still haven't found what they're looking for — that U2 are, after all, a rock band. So let's say it now, one more time with feeling: even if they bullet the grey skies above Croke Park with anthems of a momentary Eden while denimed youths drink cider in the drizzle at Drumcondra bridge, spending their youth before their call to the Auld Triangle in Mountjoy above, running, running to stand still, this, most fundamentally, is what U2 are: *a rock band.*

The prelude to Dublin U2 dates always makes me a trifle uneasy and uncomfortable, that somehow, somebody will spoil the party; it's impossible to avoid becoming nervously fearful of the vast burden, the bundle of contrary Irish expectations — we still haven't found what *we're* looking for — thrust on U2's shoulders, almost as if we believe them single-handedly capable of redressing the National Debt, inaugurating a reign of peace and prosperity in a land of hormone-free milk and honey and

Introducing: The singer!

The drummer!

The bassist!

abolishing "Dallas" from our television screens, when really it would take just one guy to fall off the roof of the Cusack Stand to capture the headlines and smash all our cherished, if contradictory dreams about this band, thereby letting pundits galore devastate another forest, inevitably scripting a further mordant chapter in Ireland's newly-discovered sociological soap.

Sometime on Saturday afternoon, a slightly drunken Simon Carmody, of Dublin trash psychedelic outfit The Golden Horde, was reciting the lyrics of "It's Only Rock'n'Roll" in my ear. He had a point. And yet U2 might consider it a sign of defeat to sing The Stones' song. Even now, they still prefer "Imagine"...

ON SATURDAY, Ronnie Drew leads the community singing on the Dublin anthem "Molly Malone"; the Jacks are definitely back, a confirmation of U2's influence, as The Dubliners, in their 25th year, make their debut on the Northside's most Holy Ground, the headquarters of the Gaelic Athletic Association of Ireland. Yet it is also a sign of how the band have widened their musical agenda that Ronnie Drew and his band of benevolently bearded folkies can share this bill with Lou Reed.

Those sea-removed Gaels, The Pogues, effectively span the gap between generations. At their first Celtic chords, the audience erupts like it's Shea Stadium, and when The Dubliners return, joining The Pogues for "The Irish Rover", Drew gets drowned out in the din for probably the first time in his life! In between, Shane MacGowan and Co suffer from sound problems as the drums and bass overwhelm the acoustic instruments, almost as if someone had left a couple of aircraft engines running on stage. In parts, people are responding to the ideal not the fact of The Pogues — though both "A Pair Of Brown Eyes" and "Dirty Old Town" would have lifted the rafters, if there'd been any at Croke Park.

Lou Reed's set also takes the low road, greasy basement rock that lets the backbeat lead the stadium Service. This means a less stark version of "Street Hassle" and a respectful reception from an audience who realise he has some symbolic importance in the day's scheme of things, but don't really know the songs. After all, hardly any of this audience were even conceived before the Velvet Underground were founded and Neil Blaney was planning the seven towers, for an Irish version of "Walk On The Wild Side", in Ballymun. Still Uncle Lou really fights it through with "Video Violence" and then on "The Original Rapping" makes the persuasive case that rap was invented by Lenny Bruce.

He exits to muffled applause, making way for the day's main attraction.

AND NOW the city prepares to conduct its own symphony.

This must be a much younger crowd than U2 get elsewhere, here to reshape this day for *their* celebration. Above the Hogan Stand, the advertising hoardings unwittingly predict the agenda, with three traditional Irish themes highlighted, the Allied Irish Banks ad planted between Gaelsport, Féile na nGael Óg Sport and an exhortation to 'Travel to Britain with B & I' — reminding us of fifties realities that long predate rock'n'roll.

And so we enter an Eden where "The Streets Have No Name", a promised land beneath a slate sky where for two hours, all petty restrictions to paradise are abolished, where reason can be trampled beneath the beat of a big bass drum and where all everyday Irish identities are dissolved, as U2 are swallowed whole by their audience. Is it any wonder that some guy will climb *his* highest mountain, invoke James Cagney, replaying the climactic scene from "White Heat" on the roof of the Cusack Stand? But even as you refuse to look and Bono appeals to him to quit his eyrie, you also know that this is the point where rock reveals its secret desires, an almost inevitable outcome as electric co's play "Break On Through To The Other Side".

"The gig reveals some stress between the old and new U2's, between the hypnotic, ecstatic drone band and the one now digging for roots'n'roll."

It is an Event, Ireland's bi-annual opportunity to be awestruck and I'm not entirely certain set details count. Still the gig reveals some stress between the old and new U2's, between the hypnotic, ecstatic drone band and the one now digging for roots'n'roll, between the one still sweeping over "God's Country" and the one that binds together "People Get Ready", "Help" and "Springhill Mining Disaster". The nagging feeling is that U2 may not yet have achieved complete integration of these diverse strands.

"Pride" however is stunning, so powerful that it probably causes another small earthquake in Brussels while, at the first encore, amid the strengthening darkness, "Bullet The Blue Sky" finally lets the lighting crew loose as The Edge brutalises his guitar and Bono angrily reworks its lyrics for those who run into brick walls, Irish-style. Then for "Party Girl", Ali enters stage left with a bottle of champagne, and the day's work is done. You depart feeling some sense of relief that they've successfully survived the first date of their residency. This has been the audience's show.

SUNDAY SEEMS more relaxed, intimate and musical, as if everybody's more conditioned to the environment. The support acts set the tone effectively. Featuring just vocals and guitar, and therefore being immune to any sound gremlins, Christy Moore is an ideal choice for the occasion. With his back to the banks of the Royal Canal, "The Auld Triangle" is perfect, though beneath the glowering skies, he tempts the meterological fates with his hilarious tale of festival muck-savagery, "Lisdoonvarna". This

The guitarist!

The crowd at Pairc Uí Chaoimh in Cork Pic: B.L. Mac Gill

year's Kildare team definitely shows promise for the All-Ireland!

Then The Pretenders deliver the best support set of the two days. I can't understand the continuing charges of heavy-handedness laid against them, unless their critics would prefer them to play, like The Weather Prophets, before twenty sainted souls in Wigan. Chrissie Hynde has a luscious voice and pens the most delicate songs, but more than that, she also knows both where to implant the guitar solos for stadium dynamics, and that r'n'b aggression can't be excluded from rock.

While they storm through ''Mystery Achievement'' and ''In The Middle Of The Road'', The Pretenders retain the interlaced guitar symmetry of ''Message Of Love'', ''Back On The Chain Gang'' and ''Kid'', the last dedicated to the late Peter Farndon and James Honeyman-Scott. But they're met with partial indifference from an audience who seem to recognise only the latest singles, ''Don't Get Me Wrong'' and ''Hymn To Her'' and so don't get the encore they deserve.

U2's set gets a thorough revision from its previous day's shape. Out go ''Springhill Mining Disaster'' and ''People Get Ready''. At the start ''C'mon Everybody'' follows ''Stand By Me'', both played like it's encore time. With ''October'' and ''Running To Stand Still'' also included, they balance their lyricism with their rock'n'roll assault-course more effectively and, as a special treat, Lou Reed comes aboard for ''Bad'' as he and Bono rap the riff back to its origins in ''Walk On The Wild Side''. It all seems less hectic, with U2 more in control.

It may also be the U2 I prefer, a U2 of greater levity and healing. Maybe, for their own self-protection that's the band they must be here, if they're not to be impaled by impossibly conflicting demands, if they're to effectively manage those

politics of ecstasy that can sometimes border on rock'n'roll chaos. Both sets had magnificent moments and certainly the flawed perspective of the 200 yards distance from the stand to the stage doesn't help but on the first day, it didn't quite cohere. On the second it did, without ever ultimately setting hearts on fire.

Perhaps that is inevitable in a group undergoing its most fundamental musical change, at the exact point it hits the celebrity stratosphere. And how can U2 hope to replay the spontaneous combustion of that white hot inner-city Sean MacDermott Street free gig of aeons past in front of 60,000 people with a guest list that includes a coalition of Garret Fitzgerald, Eamonn McCann, Frank Feely and the Waterford Hell's Angels?

Maybe this makes me another pundit as proprietor but I think Bono should be laughing. And beware. As yet, in Ireland, we're still blind to the blast in the bass drum.

A T L A S T their return to Cork provided the U2 Irish date I've been looking for. Till Pairc Uí Chaoimh, I've always preferred them abroad. Maybe that's insider bias: certainly on the road, you get wrapped up in the band's own crusade, sharing experiences with an intimacy that can't be available in Ireland.

Yet since their first major headlining outdoor appearance at Phoenix Park in 1983, I've always gone to a U2 Dublin performance with a vague sense of foreboding, aware of something stessed and forced in the atmosphere about them. Those concerts have always been over-obliged to be an Event with an Irish capital E, almost a reproduction of the Second Coming.

Where do they stop being a rock'n'roll band and start being a hologram of the cover of *Time*, an icon to be revered and profaned? Under those strains, the music can take second billing. In Dublin, U2's ideals of an Irish rock community are under constant challenge. Politically, socially and creatively, this is excellent — it prevents complacency. But despite so many riveting, quixotic, dramatic, compassionate, dangerous and triumphant moments, U2 — and especially Bono — don't always seem at ease.

But at Pairc Uí Chaoimh, U2 lost any tension as this Irish audience — a lighter shade of Gael — finally awarded them their right to party. At last, after over five years, U2 played a genuinely informal and *happy* major concert in their homeland. For once U2 were let breathe fresh Irish air and thrived on it.

"At last, after over five years, U2 played a genuinely informal and happy major concert in their homeland."

C O R K   was a homelier sort of homecoming, in complete contrast to Croke Park. Instead of apathetic, slate skies, a salmon sunset. Instead of mean, inner city streets with ciderheads legless in the drizzle, launches ferried the crowd up the Lee beneath the tree-lined Montenotte hills. Instead of a hospitality marquee with full buffet and a cast of Dublin socialites, here there were sandwiches, and friends of the Cork crew.

I may exaggerate some but Act and Audience achieved an easy-going harmony and balance here that was absent in Dublin. And playing long past dusk, U2 could use their lighting, with complete control of their effects.

They also had a special if unbilled support. The warm-up Beatles' tapes were an event in themselves. Everyone sang along to "All You Need Is Love" while empty, plastic bottles wheeled and skimmed through the air. All quite marvellously daft for this was a day of high, exultant spirits, a hooley not a hazard. All this prologue lacked was a Mexican wave.

From the start with "Stand By Me" and "C'mon Everybody", there was a natural exchange of affection. By the fifth song, "I Still Haven't Found What I'm Looking For", Bono was quipping "it's great to be back in Los Angeles" and recalling their earliest Cork dates at the Arcadia "when I saw the queues around the block — and for the first time, it felt good to be in a rock'n'roll band." It was only the first in a flow of frequent compliments.

At the first Croke Park date, "Exit", "People Get Ready" and "Help" all seemed weak links in the mid-set chain but here, each gained from U2's relaxed command. Where "Exit" had slammed furiously and senselessly against a brick-wall, now it kicked the set into a higher gear, Bono and The Edge's violent guitar cohering in this parable of "a religious man who became a dangerous man" that's also taken as a form of personal confession and exorcism.

And if at Croke Park, you could doubt U2's rock'n'roll aspirations and worry that they might be making a false move away from their mastery of hypnotic dramas, here again, "Help" and especially, "People Get Ready" had the authority to calm those fears.

"Sunday Bloody Sunday" was special and offered another contrast. In Dublin, Bono can get existential, prowling the stage to arouse and redirect the passions of the hour. But in Cork, there was no need for incitement or Bono's stick of gelignite. He needed only to turn the microphone to the audience to let them sing the chorus, as the band floated on the swell of the massed voices.

This was symptomatic. U2 had only to request — not plead for — "Help". And when by "New Year's Day", Bono was mischievously playing Tarzan and hoisting the girl from the audience over his shoulders, you could sense in the ritual a lightness of spirit absent from previous Irish concerts. For once, they weren't watching their backs, guarding against the party-crashers and being their own best security-men on stage. For once, they could concentrate on the music and let it flow. And it flowed...

T H I S   C O N T I N U I T Y   of tone, this sense of a community enjoying itself for all the reasons rock'n'roll was originally invented, let "Pride In The Name Of Love" be a real joyous fusion, let "Running To Stand Still" attain a truly intimate poignancy and finally let the line, *"you give yourself away"* in "With Or Without You", be generous, thankful, gracious and perfectly felt. Perhaps "Bullet The Blue Sky" was less raging but this was one Irish concert when U2 were buoyed not buffeted by the waves, where the band found a haven they've long deserved.

Of course, it was an end-of-tour party. Of course, it was The Edge's birthday, and his wife Aisling emerged from a white cardboard birthday cake in the middle of "Party Girl". Of course, this was the band's repayment of past favours to the Cork mafia. But these weren't the only contributing factors. Away from the Dublin battleground, U2 were finally let play a self-renewing, self-redeeming set.

For once band and audience were on the same level. For once, U2 weren't refracting impossibly contradictory expectations. And when at the closing anthem of "40", Bono crooned *"I will sing you a Lee song",* he was doing no more and no less than returning a favour.

ALL IRELAND WAS THERE

July 1987

Neil McCormick, a friend of

THE UNBELIEVABLE BOOK

U2 in their earliest days, who,

as a writer, has closely

monitored their progress

since then, analyses Eamon

Dunphy's much-touted

'authorised' biography

"Unforgettable Fire" – and

can't quite believe

what he reads

IN AUTUMN 1976, my younger brother Ivan, then a 2nd year pupil in Mount Temple Comprehensive School, was the proud possessor of a Teisco Strat copy electric guitar. He was asked by Peter Martin, a pupil from the year ahead, to bring his guitar along to a meeting in Peter's friend Larry Mullen's house. They were thinking of forming a group. Larry had put a note up on the school notice-board about it. Peter had an expensive guitar and amp but couldn't play. He was going to be manager.

On the big day, four other Mount Temple pupils came along, Paul Hewson, Adam Clayton, Dave and Dick Evans. All crowded into the Mullens' kitchen to discuss music. Names like Led Zeppelin, Deep Purple, Fleetwood Mac were bandied about. The meeting ended with a chaotic jam session. Nobody really knew what was going on — there were too many guitarists, not enough amplification and no concensus as to the correct sequences of the songs being played.

Ivan attended a couple more rehearsals, which were held in a Mount Temple classroom. Paul Hewson quickly took things over and began organising everyone, playing little himself but expending considerable energy attempting to almost magically summon, cajole and exhort music from the others' instruments. Ivan remembers an almost endless jam of "Smoke On The Water", a song he was hearing for the first time.

At 14 he was the youngest person present and was way out of his depth. He was tolerated at first however because of his guitar, which Dave Evans would liberate him of for the duration of the rehearsals, leaving Ivan to strum almost inaudibly on Dave's cheap acoustic. Peter Martin was quickly phased out and Ivan bought his amplifier from him.

The evening he arrived home with his proud new purchase, Adam rang him. He wanted to know if Ivan had bought Peter's amp because of the group. When Ivan replied in the affirmative Adam, improvising wildly, told him the band had got this gig in a pub but Ivan wouldn't be able to play because he was too young to get in. Even at 14, Ivan knew when he was being given the elbow, however diplomatically. (Dick Evans, at 17 the eldest of the would-be rock stars, was apparently not so sensitive and resisted repeated attempts to ease him out of the fledgling band with too

Contemplating the future: Bono in 1980

Eamon Dunphy

Neil McCormick

many guitartists, simply by continuing to attend rehearsals until he had established himself as a member).

The band, of course, became U2 (when Dick was finally —amicably — phased out) and the rest is, if not quite history, at least the makings of a best-selling biography...

I V A N ' S   R O L E in the U2 story is not, as we have seen, a major one, though his recollections provide telling insights in their own way: into the leadership qualities of Bono's character, in an image of The Edge that is perhaps not quite as meek and mild mannered as is often suggested, in Adam's early display of managerial diplomacy. Any hurt Ivan felt was soon forgotten and relationships patched up when he formed his own group (with me and Frank Kearns, now of Cactus World News) which the young U2 generously helped out, extending loans of equipment, rehearsal rooms, support slots, advice. The Edge wrote out the chords to The Ramones' "Shock Treatment" for us — though we later discovered he had them in completely the wrong order, thus throwing an interesting slant on the oft-remarked originality of his guitar playing.

Larry sat in on drums for one gig (though, considering himself a pro compared to us, he refrained from attending any rehearsals, resulting in an even more excessively chaotic performance than usual, with the drums starting and ending at least a bar behind everything else). Not all their help was so altruistic: Adam, easily the most pragmatic member, off-loaded his cheap Ibanez-copy bass on me at the inflated price of £70 by preying upon my ignorance (and my unwillingness to admit it). "It's got good action," he murmured nonchalantly, plonking out a riff. "Yeah, it sure has," I agreed, wondering what and where the action was and if there was a switch to control it.

Ivan recalls his early involvement with the boys-who-would-be-*Rolling Stone's* band-of-the-80's with amusement. It has provided him with the opportunity to cap acquaintances' eulogies of the band with an off-hand "Yeah, I was in the original line-up." He can no longer claim this with any authority however. But I can.

In Eamon Dunphy's "Unforgettable Fire: The Story Of U2", he recounts how, at that first meeting, "Paul Hewson had turned up with another Mount Temple pupil, Neil McCormick, who, like everyone else present except Larry, fancied being lead guitarist in the new group." I'm flattered to be in a best seller. I'm mentioned on three separate occasions — an interview I conducted and an album review I wrote are quoted from (accurately). But each mention harkens back to that first, fateful band meeting.

Well, let me put the record straight. I did not fancy being lead

guitarist. It would be strange if I had. I wasn't there, I didn't even own a guitar and much less play one. A minor, minor detail in the *grand* U2 design perhaps, but let's not stop there. Ivan was certainly under no illusions about being a lead guitarist, he simply wanted to be involved. Similarly Peter Martin, who is not mentioned in the book, could not have coveted any role since he had not yet even mastered the basics of his instrument. And it would appear highly unlikely that Adam, who arrived with his bass guitar slung over his shoulder, would have been entertaining any thought of playing lead. That leaves Paul, Dave and Dick, not quite 'everyone else present.' The statement is extraneous and inaccurate, like so much else in this ill-conceived book, one of a succession of minor fallacies, which cumulatively throw the entire project distinctly off-centre.

> **"Adam Clayton's musical bluff is part of the U2 story, an integral part, a vital part. But it is not part of this U2 story."**

Dunphy continues his account of that first meeting by listing the bands and music discussed. Bowie, The Stones, David Essex, The Sweet, Elvis, Rory Gallagher, The Beatles and more are listed. "And of course the punks," Dunphy writes. This was a bunch of young, suburban Dubliners in Autumn '76. The Sex Pistols had yet to release a record. Punk had only a low profile in England and it certainly did not raise its snarling head in Larry's kitchen. Early set lists included Bay City Rollers songs — it was still a long way from Anarchy in Artane.

The musical tastes listed — far more tasteful than accurate I fear — were apparently agreed by the main protagonists, while I did not express "any contrary preferences". (Hardly surprising under the circumstances). "The first meeting," Dunphy continues, "revealed important truths. Larry and Dave could play. Paul and Adam were less accomplished. Dick could play... Neil decided to bale out."

In truth, unfortunately truth not being quite as succinct as fiction, nothing of the sort was revealed at the first meeting. It took a long time for the various abilities of the principals to emerge, Adam in particular bluffing everyone out with his equipment and his jargon. Adam's musical bluff is part of the U2 story, an integral part, a *vital* part. But it is not part of this U2 story.

"U N F O R G E T T A B L E   F I R E" is an impressive looking tome. With its elegant cover and quality printing, this officially sanctioned biography of one of the most important, exciting, influential and successful rock acts of our time has the appearance and presentation of a major work. It was not written by some blindly enthusiastic fan nor an anonymous hack but by an established and (sometimes) respected journalist, famous in his and U2's native land — albeit in the field of sports commentary, far removed from the world of music. In the context I approached

...and in '87

Larry Mullen Jnr. in 1982

this book with anticipation but read it with growing disappointment and dismay.

From my vantage point, as a friend and early fan and supporter of the band, I was faced with inaccuracy at the kind of level I have just pointed out — *in every chapter where I was personally acquainted with the truth.* I filled 18 pages of a small notebook with Dunphy's errors, misrepresentations, misunderstandings and misinformed comment.

Often they are small things, barely worth commenting on in isolation: Bono's small community of friends, many of whom went on to form The Virgin Prunes, was actually known as Lypton Village and not simply The Village, as Dunphy reports (why they chose to call themselves Lypton Village is another story, though I clearly recall Bono turning up in school with a Lypton Village badge, which he claimed had mysteriously appeared on his jacket during the night). Similarly The Edge was named just that by members of Lypton Village, and not simply Edge as Dunphy informs us — in fact for a long while he would be addressed teasingly as The Edge, as if that were his whole Christian name, as in "Pass the salt The Edge if you don't mind." (And, on the subject of names, no mention is made of the fact that the young Paul Hewson was not at all happy with the appellation Bono Vox that Guggi landed him with, and didn't really come to terms with it until he discovered it was pidgin Latin for Good Voice).

Bill Graham was in the same year as Bob Geldof in Blackrock College, not the year ahead of him. Niall and Dermot Stokes went to Synge Street CBS and not Terenure College. They did not start Scene magazine — it was already in existence when they worked for it, purely as hired hands. *Hot Press* was Niall's venture, not a

joint Stokes brothers project. Simple facts, all easily checked, all reported inaccurately in Dunphy's book — begging the question why? Why include a mention of where somebody went to school in the first place? Presumably any background material is meant to provide insight into their character, some kind of sociological comment on them for anyone who understands the area of reference. For Niall and Dermot, school is virtually the only background material Dunphy supplies. It stands out, handpicked from their lives, ostensibly illuminating them in some way for the reader. But there is a world of difference between the privilege of Terenure College and the tough, essentially working class, Christian Brothers discipline of Synge Street. Thus, Eamon Dunphy not only insults the people involved, he throws an entirely false light on the picture, with a simple fact that, if he was not certain of it, he need never have included in the first place. It suggests a lack of knowledge, a lack of research — and ultimately a lack of care — which together are at the heart of this book's gross inadequacies.

THE PETTINESS of each of these errors does not mean that they can be simply disregarded. The truth is that they combine to distort the big picture. Dunphy comments on Larry that "the cool, leather-clad look he cultivated set him apart from the adolescent pseudo-sophisticates who occupied much territory in Mount Temple." Larry was a schoolboy, as *gauche* as any other, if already strikingly good looking. I have photos of Larry bearing no resemblance whatsoever to James Dean. It would be almost the mid-80s before the cool, leather-clad look made its first appearance.

We are informed that for the band's second live appearance

"word of mouth around the Northside ensured a good crowd... The talk was of a new band that was going places." What talk? They were a support band for Chrissakes, whose only previous appearance had been playing Bay City Rollers songs (and not as Dunphy reports "a parody of the Bay City Rollers") at a school talent contest. Nobody went to see them, they went to see the headliners, a Northside R'n'B band whose name I can't recall and whose presence Dunphy fails to even acknowledge.

The way he writes it, the crowd was won over by Bono's 'bleeding passion'. He fails to recount that on this particular occasion the band, then trading as The Hype, played an exceedingly ramshackle version of The Moody Blues' "Nights In White Satin" featuring my sister Stella and her hippy friend Orla Dunne on backing vocals and flute, with Bono holding his mike up to them because theirs broke down half way through. "They'd had all kinds of bands at St Fintan's," Dunphy writes, "but never one like The Hype." For once he may be right, though for all the wrong reasons. (According to Bono the two backing girls thought the band could be good apart from him and tried to persuade The Edge to kick him out. My sister, however, denies this. She says she *never* thought they could be good).

There are more substantial errors: the role of Jackie Hayden (then Marketing Manager of CBS Ireland) in the release and promotion of U2's first single is entirely undervalued, his marketing ideas being exclusively credited to Paul McGuinness and Ian Wilson. Dunphy also fails to mention that that single was actually recorded as a demo, a vital piece of information not just from a musical standpoint but also in the chronology of their efforts to secure a deal and their rejection by CBS. On another subject entirely, and one on which he should at least be on more familiar ground, Dunphy gets the date of Bloody Sunday wrong, locating that fateful and murderous episode in 1971 rather than 1972.

And there are absurdly inaccurate anecdotes, such as Bono's supposed run-in with The Stranglers when U2 supported them at the Top Hat Ballroom. As Dunphy recounts it, Bono burst into their dressing room to find them indulging in various rock'n'roll vices (the worst of which seem to be 'sprawling around' and 'drinking wine').

" 'Fuck you,' Bono raged (writes Dunphy), 'I thought it was about no fucking heroes.' 'What's the problem, man, help yourself,' a mocking Strangler offered. 'Stick it up your arse,' Bono raged as he banged the door behind him." That's an awful lot of rage for a support band depending on the goodwill of the headliners.

In truth, Bono merely spent some time fruitlessly trying to persuade Stranglers' leader Hugh Cornwell to wear a U2 badge on

stage, using the "No More Heroes" line to apply pressure. The presentation of this scene in the book is simply laughable.

The catalogue of errors piles up until it's impossible to see beyond it. If what I know firsthand is so inaccurately represented (and these are *not* all the errors of which I'm aware, not by a long shot), then I can have no faith in any of the rest of Dunphy's storytelling. There is simply nothing I can take at face value in this book.

DUNPHY IS not only guilty of outrageous inaccuracy, he is also grossly ill-informed on the subject that should be at the story's core: music. His lack of understanding of what he is writing about leads him not only to make major mistakes in detail but also, crucially, in the *spirit* of what he is writing. It is there in the recounting of the St Fintan's gig, in The Stranglers' anecdote and in the whole of Chapter 5 of this book, The Punk.

Sometime in Autumn '77 Bono came into school with a tight haircut, snappy sixties-style clothes and wearing a chain that stretched from an ear-ring to a safety pin in his mouth. He caused a minor riot in the school corridors, as young kids burst into tears and ran away from him. His girlfriend, Ali, would not go near him and broke off their romance (to be patched up later in the day). Teachers were not amused. But Bono was. In the prefects' room (neither of us were prefects, but it was a place to hang out), he winked at me and removed the safety pin, demonstrating how you didn't actually have to pierce your cheek to keep it in place. He seemed mightily pleased with the response his appearance had

"Dunphy is not only guilty of outrageous inaccuracy, he is also grossly ill-informed on the subject that should be at the story's core: music."

Early stardom: Bono, Larry and Adam make a charity appearance in Dublin

provoked.

"Unforgettable Fire" misses the humorous element to this anecdote, as well as misplacing it entirely. For a start Dunphy reports it as occuring in Autumn '76, a whole year out. If Paul Hewson was a punk in '76, he'd have been virtually the first punk in Ireland. But the fact is that Bono was *never* a punk. He played at it for a day or so, certainly brought elements of its vision to his music, and observed it all with fascination. (I remember him coming in raving about bands he'd seen on *The Old Grey Whistle Test*, knocked out by how The Jam had moved like jerky silent movie stars). But the safety pin and chain never made another appearance. Bono and his band became part of a new wave, but Dunphy doesn't understand this distinction because he doesn't understand punk.

His essay on its origins reads like schoolboy sociology, treating it as a political movement instead of a sporadic and spontaneous musical phenomenon. Sid Vicious is elevated to the same level as Johnny Rotten, the same mistake that was made by the tabloids and the second generation punks on the basis of his name and his death — but Dunphy is writing of punk's origins and Vicious had no relevance there. He writes of punk being for the disenfranchised who "drifted on a sea of concrete." The equation is: bulldozers + urban ghettoes + tower blocks = Punk Rock. Dunphy simply has no level of musical insight to see through the almost comically simplistic imagery that punk built around itself. "Good Golly Miss Molly!", Dunphy writes, "Punk was a disgusting, disgusted, anarchic kick in the balls for all those who didn't live on Concrete Way." That may be the way it seemed to a sports correspondent but, 10 years on no music magazine would publish such a cringe-inducingly juvenile assessment of the phenomenon, except perhaps *Smash Hits* — as a joke.

Dunphy's misplacing of the punk incident makes a fallacy of U2's musical development. If Bono had discovered punk prior to joining the band, what would he have been doing singing Peter Frampton's "Show Me The Way" and other aforementioned delights from the band's early sets? But there is no sense of musical development in this book, no reflection of the shift from covering The Moody Blues to covering David Bowie's "Suffragette City", and from there to "Anarchy In The UK" (always a ludicrous song for a Dublin band to play). There is no mention of the first, live-in-Mount-Temple-rehearsal-room demo they recorded of a (now forgotten by the band) slightly countryish song. No analysis of their early numbers: "Street Mission" — a rock epic of spiritual longing that would end their sets — "Life On A Distant Planet", "The Fool", "Cartoon World", "Speed Of Life", "Concentration Cramp", "So Sad", "In Your Hands" — songs in which they first got to grips with their music and Bono defined the two characters that would dominate his early lyrics, The Boy and The Fool (only one of whom ever made it

onto vinyl).

Edge's originality as a guitarist is often mentioned but nowhere defined. Its roots are never traced — clearly because Eamon Dunphy doesn't really have a clue whether he's original or not. Similarly Bono is always dominating the stage but Dunphy never paints a clear picture of his evolving stagecraft. Bono was exciting in those early days, always trying out new routines like his Boy In A Box act, where he would mime opening a box to find himself in another, then another, then another... talking all the time, agitatedly, about this predicament. Bono gabbed constantly, over and between songs, never knowing when to shut up: his current stage persona is virtually reserved in comparison.

The reality, of course, is that Dunphy fails to trace U2's development simply because he has no grounding with which to understand or comprehend it. His incidental comments on music are always absurdly misinformed — thus Manchester's Buzzcocks become 'another local band'; The Atrix have the 'The' removed from their name, thus robbing it of its theatrical pun; Television become 'one of the better punk groups'; Stone The Crows' Les Harvey becomes 'father of the famous blues musician, Alex' (there's little likelihood of a paternity suit given that both of them are dead but Alex is probably turning in his grave right now at the thought of his Brechtian theatrics being described as 'blues').

Dunphy's musical ignorance results in farce at times, as he recounts anecdotes which he patently does not understand. Much fuss is made at one stage of an incident in The Baggot Inn during a sound check: "Normally the monitors on stage, the sound boxes, were turned towards the audience. Here Bono, Edge and Adam had reversed the process, turning the monitors towards themselves. Larry wanted his turned as well."

Adam strikes a pose

The anecdote is meant to reflect U2's constantly questing minds — they took nothing for granted. Unfortunately for Dunphy, monitors are exactly what their name suggests, they monitor the sound for the band. They are, of necessity, pointed away from the audience, towards the group. Only an idiot would set them up otherwise. U2's innovation could be claimed by (and must be shared with) every group and every sound man since monitors were first introduced. Sometimes, reading this book, I get the feeling somebody's been pulling Dunphy's leg.

"UNFORGETTABLE FIRE" is a story of a rock'n'roll band written by someone who refers to the phrase 'be bop a lu la' as 'be bop a loo loo'. Dunphy's lack of understanding of rock'n'roll, his apparent lack of interest in it, his possible dislike for it, leads him inexorably to a vision of U2 as being *entirely separate* from the rest of popular music culture. It is an assumption which is as stupidly wrongheaded and sloppy as it will be misleading for those who come to the book wondering what it *is* that distinguishes U2 and makes them great.

Such a facile notion could barely be entertained by anyone with the slightest grounding in music, but for Dunphy it is there from the word go, from the first school talent contest performance and in his recounting of the St Fintan's support gig. "Boy" is referred to as "true and real in a way rock'n'roll had rarely been before" instantly writing off 25 years of great music that cut to the very hearts of its listeners. His simplistic reviews of U2's albums always set them aside from a world of rock'n'roll that for Dunphy 'was mostly fantasy', his greatest conceit being his presumptuous elevation of the "Unforgettable Fire" LP. He badly misinterprets (and misrepresents) U2's most subconscious, instinctive and atmospheric work as an album of social protest and nuclear holocaust, claiming on its behalf that "the idiom of rock'n'roll had never been so comprehensively challenged before."

The statement is grand, eloquent — and utterly meaningless. Coming from someone who patently knows so little about the idiom of rock'n'roll it's a display of unforgivably pompous ignorance. How many records do you have in your collection, Mr Dunphy? Can you define the limits of rock'n'roll? Map the area that, thus far in its history, has been covered by the startling diversity of acts that have grouped together, however loosely, under its name? Do you have any comprehension of what it was that had been so "comprehensively challenged"?

It's the kind of ludicrous posing implicit in this pretence at a critical perspective which will insult the intelligence of anyone who reads "Unforgettable Fire" who *does* care about rock'n'roll. For Dunphy the song "Pride" helped "rock'n'roll grow up, won

it respect and self-respect." Rock'n'Roll has been growing up a long time — a litany of artists who had already won it respect and self-respect long before "Pride" would be as pointless as it would be long (and as impossible for any two genuine critics to agree upon). U2 would certainly be in most people's current lists, along with Bob Dylan, John Lennon, Talking Heads... I don't even want to begin. And then there are all the artists for whom 'growing up' and 'respect' are *not* what it's all about.

Dunphy takes the view of *Rolling Stone* critic Dave Marsh (and like many non-music writers Dunphy apparently acts on the assumption that *Rolling Stone* is the pinnacle of rock commentary) that rock was "a voice and a face for the forgotten and disenfranchised." This is valid up to a point and certainly reflects some aspects of rock's magnetism but Dunphy takes it too literally, assuming that it encompasses the whole of rock culture, before he laboriously describes how U2 were redefining it.

> " 'Unforgettable Fire' is a story of a rock'n'roll band written by someone who refers to the phrase 'be bop a lu la' as 'be bop a loo loo'."

In what amounts to virtually a mini-essay in itself, Dunphy contrasts the affluent optimism of the 60's with the despairing austerity of the 80's. It is an entertaining read but its conclusion, that U2 are the band of the 80's because they respond to a need for social realism, "legitimising suburban existence, identifying its concerns and expressing them vividly and powerfully through rock'n'roll", is ridiculous. Bruce Springsteen could, perhaps, be seen in this role but U2 have never been about social realism —their songs, especially on "The Unforgettable Fire", are far too interior for that, too unspecific. When Dunphy writes of "Bad" being a song about heroin, and "The Unforgettable Fire" about nuclear war, he makes U2 sound like The Specials, crusaders for social justice. U2 could be said to be responding to a spiritual need, filling a gap engendered in a time of widespread uncertainty and insecurity — but not in the manner Dunphy suggests, and certainly not alone.

This episode quite clearly demonstrates Dunphy's strengths and weaknesses as a writer. His analysis of the mood of our times can be informed and wittily opinionated but his musical conclusions are inevitably sadly inappropriate and ill-informed. The book is inflated with background details and author-opinionation whenever Dunphy has a chance to get to grips with something he knows. Thus the first chapter, Bono's Story, is both the most complex and the most readable as Dunphy places him in the context of Northside Dublin and of his family (there are 11 pages dealing with life in the Hewson household *before* he was born!). He deals well with the contradictions and conflicts innate in Irish religious attitudes, and how these conflicts brought Bono steadily towards his own Christian beliefs, and there is interesting Irish political background material, including one of the most concise essays on the IRA that I've ever read. But ultimately these 'sociological' passages are as irritating as the rest of his writing because they are so unbalanced.

Bono's parents and Larry's parents are treated in exhausting detail — Dunphy's on home ground here, he's got the ball and he's going to run with it, even going so far as to throw in entirely irrelevant detail (such as the anecdote about deported communist Jim Gralton who hailed from the same *general area* as Larry's mother). Had he been capable of sketching the same level of detail on all areas of the U2 story it would have been a fascinating, absorbing (if probably eccentric) document. However Adam and Edge's parents are lightly sketched at best — they're British and Dunphy either can't get to grips with them or didn't put in the necessary research to do so. As in so many other areas of this book, it's a case of what might have been...

FAR TOO often throughout "Unforgettable Fire" Dunphy is clearly out of his depth and resorts to writing that is fatuous in its uneducated opinion. He constantly betrays his own interests with sudden bursts of eloquence: the only time he actually gets agitated is on the subject of sport — not exactly central to the U2 story — when he describes the people who ban soccer from Croke Park as having "damaged minds". Describing the "essence of Irishness", Dunphy puts sport first, quickly adding culture and music, as if suddenly remembering where he was.

The crazily uneven nature of the book is not only an indication of Dunphy's bias but of his weakness as a biographical journalist. The two week Amnesty International Conspiracy Of Hope Tour in July '85 takes up 18 pages and is dealt with in far greater detail than anything else in the U2 story. This is not a reflection of its *importance* but of the simple fact that Dunphy was, quite obviously, present with his notebook out. While the early gigs, far more fascinating and vital in U2's development, are scantily covered, the Conspiracy Tour passage is over-abundant in gig details, backstage meetings and after-hours behaviour. Two paragraphs are spent on an analysis of comedian Robin Williams' performance in Chicago, there is over a page on U2's backstage encounter with black political comic Dick Gregory and another on Muhammed Ali. These encounters are reported solely because of Dunphy's first-hand presence — a presence that the writer does not openly concede, and which is entirely irrelevant to the U2 story. What of Bono's meetings with Bruce Springsteen, Pete Townshend, Bob Dylan, Frank Sinatra and a host of other

Bono and Ali in 1981

fascinating characters, who Bono will often comment on with wit and a fan's excitement but who never make it into the book?

The issue of what should be included and excluded in a biography is a complex one. There is simply no way any one book could entirely encompass one life, never mind four. But Dunphy's omissions are inexcusable, particularly in the light of the weight he attributes to something as brief as the Amnesty Tour. There is no mention of Mother Records (and the accompanying link into the Dublin scene which that would have provided). There is no mention of Bono and Ali's visit to do volunteer work in Ethiopia, or of their visit to Central America, which obviously made such a big impression on the singer. Greg Carroll's death which wounded Bono and the band very badly, is just briefly and unemotionally dealt with.

Characters like Pod and Dick Evans, meanwhile, disappear from the story with little explanation. Wives and girlfriends, at best, are treated as sketchy appendages to the central characters. Many crucial songs don't even warrant a mention. Chas De Whalley and Martin Hannett, U2's first producers, are not dealt with in even a remotely convincing way. We hear that U2 want Brian Eno to produce their fourth studio album, but it is never explained *why* (and, of equal relevance, why *not* Steve Lillywhite who had produced the first three and was evidently still on good terms with the band). No mention is made of what must have been a crucial incident in Adam's life (and which received extensive national newspaper coverage), when on January 10th 1985, he knocked down a policeman and dragged him for 40 yards behind his car. (Clayton, who according to the Irish *Evening Press* told the Garda to "stop messing and fuck off", was disqualified from driving for two years).

Although this book was written with the co-operation and blessing (since apparently at least partially withdrawn) of U2 it was never an 'official' biography — Dunphy made it clear that he owed no allegiance to the band, he had no special duties to cover up unsavoury episodes in their lives. Yet the absence of the policeman incident suggests either that Dunphy took it upon himself to do so — or that his research was so flimsy that he never heard of it in the first place.

Adam would be the first to admit that this episode was part of his 'wild years', when his rock'n'roll behaviour reached an unacceptable level — particularly for a member of a band who aspired to better things. But while Dunphy addresses the issue of Adam's alienation from the others and gently alludes to the seamier side of his lifestyle, he never confronts the issue head on.

He writes with an almost puritanical scorn of the 'rock'n'roll lifestyle' and its victims (usually the stars themselves, in Dunphy's worldview), yet he seems to give a nodding approval to

Adam's behaviour on the basis of nothing more than Adam's easy-going, civilised nature. "His tastes in *apres* concert diversion were more traditional than those of his U2 colleagues... he usually slept late the next day, sometimes waking up in his own bed", Dunphy comments on Adam's private life. In the previous paragraph he had baldly stated: " 'It didn't make you happy' might have been the epitaph for sex-alcohol-drug-sated heroes who'd got lost among the carnal delights of being a Rock Star." It is typical of the wooliness of the book that he makes no attempt to reconcile his contradictory attitude to the two statements...

Negative comment is reserved for the essays by other journalists which Dunphy has chosen to include at the end of his book (and of course for the interviews he's subsequently done to publicise "Unforgettable Fire", posing all sorts of questions about his 'moral integrity' — but that's another story).

Not quite an appendix, these pieces (three from *In Dublin*, plus one entirely irrelevant piece on Phil Lynott from *Magill*) represent the reverse side of the coin — by and large they're witty, entertaining and reasonably informed essays on the non-deification of U2. The fact that these articles are better written and more informed than anything else in the book does not however justify their inclusion. If Dunphy had felt the issues they broached to be valid, he should have made room for them within his story, embraced them and dealt with them as part of the big picture. To add them as appendages is to avoid his own responsibilities as a biographer. As if saying, "this is the way it was, but these guys disagree", Dunphy reflects his own lack of commitment to the project.

> "It is time to turn that famously abrasive voice upon himself. Dunphy may have been a first-class footballer but this is a fourth division book."

IT IS this lack of commitment which is so galling. Eamon Dunphy has been quoted as saying that he received a six-figure advance for the book. He could quite conceivably earn up to £250,000 (or more!) for the two years' work involved.

This earning potential has little or nothing to do with Eamon Dunphy himself — it is money which will be generated on the back of U2's success and drawn from the mass of fans, who have shown U2 such loyalty and support over the years. It is shameful to see such a lucrative job so badly done and the ordinary people who will finally pay Mr Dunphy's wages for the work involved, so utterly shortchanged.

As a biography, "Unforgettable Fire — The Story Of U2" is shoddy. As a musical biography, it is a travesty. And Dunphy has no one to blame but himself. In his sports writing he constantly espouses the pursuit of excellence and is caustically contemptuous of anyone who does not meet his 'exacting' standards. Well, it is time to turn that famously abrasive voice upon himself. He may have been a first class footballer, but this is a fourth division book.

Dunphy has repeatedly ridiculed soccer writers who have not themselves been involved in the game, calling their professional competence into question and suggesting that their judgements and responses count for nothing alongside those of John Giles and himself. It is all the more ironic then that, from the outset of "Unforgettable Fire", his lack of musical knowledge and empathy tell us that he has bitten off more than he can chew.

That much was foolish. What is unforgivable, however, is the lazy and sloppy manner in which he put the book together. The cornerstone of any biography is *research*. For "Alias David Bowie", Peter and Lenie Gillman conducted approximately 150 interviews. For "His Way", a biography of Frank Sinatra, Kitty Kelley undertook over 857. In neither case were the stakes any higher than in Dunphy's, nor the potential returns greater — yet Dunphy's credits acknowledge less than 60 (possible) interviews.

He interviewed only one pupil, Maeve O'Regan, from the band's Mount Temple days. He spoke only briefly to Steve Averill who was intimately involved with the band from the outset and who has a vast wealth of knowledge of music, and of the local scene. He never spoke to Jackie Hayden, who was effectively responsible for the release of their first single. Neither did he speak to either Jim Aiken or Denis Desmond, two promoters who could have given an insight into what it was like dealing with the U2 organisation, the praises of which are sung in the book, from the *other* side. Nor did he talk to Niall Shortall, a former sound engineer with the group, who is mercilessly shafted in a description of an incident from an early British tour. It is by thus spreading the net, and talking to people who have come into conflict with the subject, that a biography achieves balance and ultimately real insight. But apparently that would have been too much trouble.

I say that Eamon Dunphy conducted less than 60 *possible* interviews for a reason.

"I never met Neil McCormick," Dunphy writes, "but I picked his brains all the same."

Eamon Dunphy did not pick my brains. Had he done so, I would have picked the thinking behind this ill-conceived book apart.

THE UNBELIEVABLE BOOK
December 1987

The Edge picks his brains

U2

BAND ON THE RUN

**Bill Graham travels to
Louisiana to discover that U2
are once more in the throes
of a re-birth.**

I N A recent interview with America's *Musician* magazine, Larry Mullen sought to restore the balance: "Isn't it incredible that, when you reach a certain stage, everything (you do) suddenly becomes *important*? Everybody has been talking about the U2 phenomenon and not so much about the music."

It's a common complaint, after a sudden introduction to the fame game. Frequently the instinctive and self-protective reaction amongst musicians is to re-emphasise the mundane and deflate the myth. This is particularly so in the case of the drummer, who is U2's most tenacious guardian of practical musical values.

And yet Larry Mullen's comment does effectively set the agenda. In '87, U2 entered that twilight zone where the accessories of phenomenon tend to overwhelm the essentials of the music, in which all the fictive U2's of the millions' imaginations begin to swamp the core U2 the four in the hot seat hope they can still control.

As The Edge puts it: "Until 'The Joshua Tree', U2 were the biggest underground band in the world." This year, however, they became the New Kids on the celebrity block, the fresh faces

of fame who weren't abusing their status as a short-cut to endorsing carbonated water and coca leaves, ideal icons to be elevated into the mass media mythic. This year they became larger than life, perhaps also learning along the way that Christ's press agents, St. Paul and the four Gospellers, may just have been more powerful than the Messiah himself.

Conflict one, then — between the phenomenon and the music. But there is also a second tension between American and Irish perceptions of them. After all, U2 both live in and leave the land of their birth.

They export themselves (first and foremost) to a country where success is venerated and taken for granted. They live in a society still keyed to post-colonial failure and a supporting role in the celebrity stakes. Before U2, only Barry Fitzgerald went to Hollywood.

Thus, their success has amounted almost to a shock to the collective Irish cultural imagination. Usually, the odd swallow, a Stephen Roche, makes our summer. But U2's triumphs this year went far beyond even our most ambitious expectations. As a

result, both in the responses to the Croke Park concerts and to Eamon Dunphy's biography, the non-music pundits (especially) seemed to be refitting U2 out for a contradictory array of causes, conveniently concentrating on the Bono Vox amplifier up front — but, equally conveniently, forgetting that there are also, drums, bass, guitar and vocals in the mix. By year's end, U2 were often publicly misconceived as being both impossibly larger (the social significance squad) and begrudgingly smaller (all the gossip that's fit to print) than they most adequately are. For Ireland, U2 represented a real problem of scale.

So, let's get back to basics: U2 are a rock band. Continue the basics: U2 might even concede they partially achieved their primacy because the competition, with the shadowy guerilla exception of REM had collapsed. As now occurs with laughable regularity, U2 got tagged as this year's New Beatles — previous members of that exclusive club: The Police, The Bangles, The Raspberries and... um... The Knack! — but unlike the Sixties, there were no counterparts like The Rolling Stones, Dylan, The Byrds and The Beach Boys to grapple for supremacy with them. In '87, as both Pink Floyd and The Grateful Dead betrayed rock's wrinkles and middle-aged flab, U2 were the only white and verifiably young rock group of equally verifiable substance about whom columnists could raze the Oregon forests, penning significant, generational essays.

But forget the rind, there's also a new seed. I fly to America with some inkling of new developments, of a concert film and a live album. What I haven't anticipated is a creative re-birth and a song-writing surge that together amounts to yet another new U2 being born.

These changes went latent in "The Joshua Tree" but suddenly I seem to be meeting the members of some born-again post-punk, post-blues, post-country, post-gospel, post-Everything Bar The Apocalypse band. Larry Mullen comes out of the closet as a country fan. Bono writes songs for B.B. King and Roy Orbison. They record demos in Sun Studios and adopt the alter ego of The Dalton Brothers. "Actually," says The Edge tellingly, "we've fallen in love with music again."

BUT THIS weekend, America may have other priorities. At Thanksgiving, America closes down for outside examination as planes and boats and trains bear prodigal sons and daughters home for their turkey, cranberry sauce, sweet potatoes and a binge of American football, making this interloping Irishman feel like a Hindu at Eastertime. And in Baton Rouge, the state capital of Louisiana, beside Robbie Robertson's "Crazy River", the vast inscrutable Mississippi, the sleeping South is sleepier still and the efficiency of — successively — my airline, hotel and local

"You become an icon," Bono reflects, "and the iconoclasts of the world will take the piss and throw pot-shots at you."

taxi-driver make Irish tourist ways and laws seem positively teutonic in comparison.

It doesn't seem the most immediately stimulating time and place to explore the love affair between U2 and America. Baton Rouge is a new city for the band. They've previously played New Orleans, a hundred miles downriver but as with the following Nashville/Murfreesboro' date, Baton Rouge has been tacked onto the end of the tour. Or, "the giddy part", in Paul McGuinness' cautionary words. U2 have twice traversed America, passed the peaks of New York and Los Angeles and are now in freefall, experiencing that combination of road-weariness and disorientation that induced the Seventies sport of hotel re-decoration.

To the concert, then, on the campus of the city's university, to find tour publicist Regine Moylett being pestered by a Texas freelance who claims he's writing an in-depth, socio-political feature for *The Sun* — a notable if naively original scheme to get free tickets. Inside, it's an ideal American auditorium, a purpose-built basketball arena that seats 12,000 in the round in comfort and intimacy.

The audience is apparently classless, essentially costumeless. Away from the coasts, Americans don't practice the dedicated tribal segregation of the Brit, the only slight eccentricity amid the jeans and leisurewear being a discreet sprinkling of Madonna/Goth frills'n'lace, the most tangible signs of their veneration being a few tricolours and banners, even including one dyed "Bono For President".

Certainly U2 arrive to the sort of lung-busting tumult that elsewhere greets a presidential nomination yet, at times, the Baton Rouge crowd seem almost to be smothering the four in their circle of affection and Southern hospitality. Possibly too, they're partly representative of the more pop-orientated audience U2 have landed with "The Joshua Tree".

They don't always get their cues. Before "Sunday Bloody Sunday" Bono talks about how it's wrong "to bully small countries the *size* of Ireland" (grand cheer) "or Nicaragua" but the second example gets a more confused, muted response so he misses full impact.

It is a practised, enjoyable and sometimes playful set but one inevitably less headlong and incisively intense than their Irish summer performances, as if these veterans are playing within themselves — like a Liverpool 2-0 cakewalk at Oxford — which is more instructive for those telltale moments when consummation doesn't quite occur.

The new earthed roots-rock U2 doesn't always mesh with the old, skydiving approach, "Exit" segues into "Silver And Gold" as if the only common denominator is the Edge's clanging guitar. At times on "Exit" and on the quote from "Sympathy For The

A drummer's moment of reflection

Devil'' in ''Bad'' — *''pleased to meet you, hope you guessed my name''* — it seems as if Bono wants to temporarily escape those enveloping sunshine smiles. Even kindness can kill a band.

''THE ORGANISATION is fraying at the edges. The real story of 1987 concerns five people first — but also Anne-Louise Kelly, Ossie Kilkenny and all those people who've committed so much time and energy to the band — just trying to stay head above water in a tidal wave of a year. As John Lennon wrote so well: 'Nobody told us, there'd be days like these'.''

Next evening, on their free day in Nashville, Bono sits in a corner of the hotel dining-room, reflecting on the year's star-crossed activity, his pride mixed with some rueful tinctures, acknowledging that U2's relationship with their native country wasn't always comfortable.

''We had this idea in our heads that here we were, this Irish group in Ireland, and we thought we could literally back out of Ireland into the rest of the world with our armour up. And the idea that we would ever have to turn around and face a rearguard action from our own kind was something we hadn't quite planned on and literally took us aback.''

He snatches a laugh. Bono knows well these are problems 99.99% of bands in Ireland, and the world, would sell their grannies into white slavery for. Nonetheless, he's irked by certain coverage of Eamon Dunphy's biography and criticisms of the band's Mother label by both Sinead O'Connor and the Dublin band Aslan.

He continues: ''Like bands who attempt to help out, and maybe get it wrong, will actually get space by saying you're like any other record company. Or people you've met along the way all believe that their own version of U2 is what the world needs to hear.''

For any sins of omission, he pleads disorganisation: ''When those phone calls are ringing every day of the week twelve hours a day, it's a madhouse... U2 a corporation? It's much more like 5 Go Down To The Sea and can't swim. Ruthless bastards, no. Inept sometimes, yes. We made a lot of mistakes this year in the planning of our own tour and our own lives. Sometimes, our planning of other people's lives has been 10 on a list of 100 when it should have been first.''

But he acknowledges the near inevitability of it all. ''You become an icon and the iconoclasts of the world will take the piss and throw pot-shots at you. And if I were on the other side, maybe I'd have reacted the very same way.''

Over-sensitive and regularly prone to gestures of over-spontaneous generosity, Bono can cause overload when, as sometimes happens, he hasn't fully thought through how his promises can become flesh. Now he's stepping back from Mother.

One reason, though he still champions The Subterraneans, Hothouse Flowers and The Real Wild West, is a sense of disillusionment with imitative Irish music. But another is that ''Larry and Adam are taking over Mother because they're people who find it very easy to say 'No' and if people get pissed off with them, they don't mind — whereas I get pissed off too.''

He recounts Pete Townshend's advice: ''He took me aside. About Mother, he said, you're making a big mistake. He said, with The Who, we went down many side-roads and back-roads and lost sight of Main Street. We set up this, that and the other. And often, he said, if you attempt to help people, they'll hate you for it in the end. And I said, no. No. But, he said, really they will.

"And in 1987, in Ireland, I see that maybe rock'n'roll bands might be better off if Mother didn't exist."

His doubts may be the result of U2 ending up as the only game in town. Significantly Bono now speaks of being more comfortable with people like Christy Moore, Makem And Clancy, Ronnie Drew and Clannad than his near-contemporaries.

In '87, nobody's yet threatening to rival them, even as a medium-scale attraction. Besides Mother may have fulfilled its original purpose as a launch-pad, now that In Tua Nua, Cactus World News, Tuesday Blue and Hothouse Flowers have flown the nest. Without redefinition of its function, Mother could become a source of spoon-fed dependency far from any name of pride.

That's not much stimulus. Meanwhile outside is America. Exiles off main street, The Dalton Brothers enter its arms. There's nowhere else to go.

"I know it's bizarre," says The Edge, "but what we're now playing with is as new to our audience as it is to ourselves."

BONO MUST always be romantic. If, on "The Joshua Tree", U2 set their sights on American authoritarianism, now they're looking for stars in bars. Now Bono runs that voodoo down.

"I actually find it hard to go asleep over here, to blink in case I miss something. I find, for instance, the language very accessible. American writers, from Tennessee Williams through the Black and American Indian poets I'm reading, they seem to be 'sexier'. Sexuality and spirituality co-exist in American music, in a way they don't in Irish or British music.

"Music and words are falling off the buildings here. In the red-light districts. In the neon signs. In the down-town areas. Even in the jive, the names of the roads."

He speaks of mysteries. Mightn't there be a public America that's fearful of them?

"Sure. That isn't an America I see a lot of — but generally, it's the other side that interests me anyway. The late-night bars. The fall of America interests me as much as the rise of America."

So, later that night, we check out Nashville's own neon blur. A small tour party including Bono, Ali and the Edge venture out. But it ain't so lyrical. We pass a club featuring Donna Mead, the well-known singing Northside shopping centre. Bono's pun, for it is his, must be sub-conscious. Because despite its association with the folksy values of country music, downtown Nashville is a gloomy monument to the entombing architecture of institutional America. Not unlike environment commentator Frank McDonald's vision of Hell, the centre is ringed by freeways and cluttered to suffocation by massive office blocks. The developers tore the country from Nashville's heart, long ago. They probably held a hoedown to announce their plans.

At night, most human life has fled. Typical is Tootsie's. Once this bar was Nashville in the rare oul' times, where the country stars regularly relaxed after-hours. But now, as we walk in, the signed photographs on the wall are starting to fade and curl. When the studios moved out of town, Tootsie's was condemned to be a back-water.

Now as two guitarists play Hank Williams for tips and we buy our Buds, our only company on lonely street is another party of tourists. A restless Bono prowls to the bar across the street but that joint ain't jumpin' either. Here, the only outlaw the Dalton Brothers meet is a lone panhandler begging for dimes as we leave.

Another bar has more warmth and custom. A six-piece band slips easily between country, blue-eyed soul and rock'n'roll, the celebrity guests gag on free, sugary, sparkling wine and the guitarist sings the only folk song he knows: Van Morrison's magnificent and moody "Brown Eyed Girl".

But Bono and the Edge don't notice. Instead they're talking to a topless dancer from the next-door club. "She told me they only last six months," Bono relates. "Because the guys prefer them nervous and vulnerable. Once they look experienced, they're sacked." Turns out herself and her boyfriend claim they're Christians, only paying the rent, living out the small-change of American contradictions, in this concrete'n'western town.

Such distractions keep a band sane. Sometimes that social pan-handling finds a nugget of a song line. As The Edge later remarks, "You really have to *look* in this country to find out what's happening. When we first came here, America was like walking into an episode of Starsky And Hutch. Everybody would talk the same. I used to think TV America was exaggerated. It wasn't. Miami Vice goes on every day in every major American city. But once we were here two or three times, we were able to refine. We were like prospectors, coming here to find the gold. It wasn't easy. It was like finding the right people, radio stations and obscure record stores — and eventually finding the source of this thing."

The Edge talks of a renewed "love affair". Suddenly it seems U2 have become wide-eyed, though penetrating, fans of music they'd never reckoned with. Bono will speak of jazz and a recognition of horns — instruments which he used to deplore — with genuine enthusiasm. "I'm overpowered by the likes of Miles Davis. Suddenly at 27, listening to 'Bitches' Brew'. Discovering Gil Evans, seeing the sense jazz makes in cities like New York and Chicago. Seeing, for the first time, the poetry of folk music, of country. The release of gospel music."

What's potentially most intriguing is that U2 may be arriving at their enthusiasm from a position outside the institutionalized history of American popular music. Bono somewhat delightedly

Bono where the streets have names

says: "Most people I've met who've turned me onto the blues are jealous because I'm getting into it for the first time. And they remember the time they got into it."

As the Edge astutely remarks: "Most average Americans don't really know about the heritage on their own doorstep. The music that's big in America is the Top 40 album, whatever's on radio. Our contemporaries and younger bands, have a very patchy understanding. So what we're finding, and I know it's bizarre, is that what we're now playing with is as new to our audience as it is to ourselves. We're not playing this music to people who know this stuff, although it's on their own doorstep, under their very noses."

He readily confesses he was the band's most reluctant convert. As a teenage guitarist, he'd reacted intensely against the older generation of Dublin players, with their squalling, posturing, hard rock vulgarization of the blues. "All that shit was like dirt. I'd purged myself of all that," he says. "So, coming back to that now was like visiting something laid and buried. It was like opening the coffin and I resisted a little. For instance, we disagreed vehemently about what songs should go on the album. If Bono had his way, 'The Joshua Tree' would have been more American and bluesy and I was trying to pull it back."

That compromise led to the later flood of new B-side tracks.

Bono will argue that "the album is almost incomplete. 'With Or Without You' doesn't really make sense without 'Walk To The Water' or 'Luminous Times'. And 'Trip Through Your Wires' don't make that much sense without 'Sweetest Thing'."

Live, there hasn't always been such a neat resolution of the band's inner conflicts either. Last night in Baton Rouge, Bono admits "was a bad show. Not so much the band as myself. I completely lost myself. Being on a stage for me doesn't get any easier. Even in the Middle of 'Pride', the oddest thoughts come across me. I just want to pack up and go home.

"We're a snake who hasn't fully shed its skin," he believes, accepting that the creative U2 of '87 is co-existing uneasily with the U2 the fans want to hear. "That preys on me a lot. I don't know how to sing 'New Year's Day' now."

He looks up and laughs: "Now you're talking. All the other stuff, they aren't problems. This is the problem and what a problem!"

What a problem indeed!

NEXT NIGHT the soundcheck is almost as instructive as the concert. U2 chisel away at their new material and I hear their real aural testimony. Most songs are unfamiliar but "When Love Comes To Town", Bono's song for BB King, has put on musical muscle as well as two additional verses taking it far beyond its original lyrical simplicities since I heard its skeleton on an acoustic last spring.

It's neither a self-conscious pastiche nor a profane HM holler, U2 managing to enforce their own personality on the music, refusing to be drowned in the blues. Probably surprised, the local Southern staff give them the compliment of their applause.

Then veteran Irish guitarist and sometime Nashville resident, Philip Donnelly arrives to pick. The Daltons mutate into the (sm)Allman Bros, as The Edge forgets his teenage reluctance to copy an older generation of Irish players. The song itself reflects his observation: "I'm writing songs I can't describe. Some of them are blues, some of them are country, some of them are folky like the Byrds."

The show is also better. In Murfreesboro', the audience is more boisterous, less prone to shower U2 with amorphous affection than in Baton Rouge. Consequently, Bono has a more confident sense of what he's looking for.

Devils and angels interchange as the preacher takes his tale through a sequence of the killing hands of love and "Exit", Manson's favourite, "Helter Skelter", Lennon's plea for "Help" and a version of "Bad" which yet again includes *"pleased to meet you, hope you guess my name"* from "Sympathy For The Devil", with only a brief verse from "Silver And Gold". The persona isn't quite finished or even fully understood yet but you do recognise work in progress.

For U2 are no longer the wide-eyed Irish idealists of yore. By their profession, world citizens, they're finally admitting the deceptive imprecision of adult motivations, recognising now that their own experiences can't be adequately expressed in the primary colour of old. Comment on "The Joshua Tree" often centred on its critique of public political morality but my hunch is that U2 are now really facing into the slippery choices of private morality, pulled through the paradoxes of a door marked "Exit".

The public mask can protect their private searching. Next year, a live record will accompany their concert film but they also want this double album to float off new material, a strategy that will allow them to both experiment and guide their audience.

Back in that Nashville hotel, Bono summed up the real deal: "If we can't play the old songs, then write new songs. It's our only way of surviving and getting through the tour. I actually don't care if people don't like it, though how many songs will be put on this album is not decided... you may not like it, U2 fans may not like it — but we need it."

BAND ON THE RUN

December 1987

All the world's a stage

Edge: beret good

Adam: The horror. The horror.

SHAKE, RATTLE AND HUM

Sprawling across four restless, angry and sometimes contradictory sides, "Rattle And Hum" is nothing less than U2's most ambitious album yet.

Review by Bill Graham

SO HOW do you start pinning down this often angry, always argumentative, absolutely restless, sometimes sprawling and curiously contradictory hybrid of an album that — it should go without saying — is the most ambitious record U2 have yet released?

Could I suggest it concerns George Bush's — no, sorry — his handlers' opinions of Bruce Springsteen's "Born In The USA" and Jimi Hendrix's Woodstock pledge of allegiance; Jimmy Swaggart and the broadcasting "Towers Of Steel" where "Belief goes on and on"; U2's allergy to Levi's commercials and every record executive guilty of stonewashing spontaneous human imperfection out of the recording process; Heaven and the art of rock'n'roll motor-cycle maintenance; the mouth-to-mouth resuscitation of the ailing body of rock history that even they sometimes nightmarishly fear may revive as Frankenstein with a Fender; their own special American edition of *The Crane Bag*, Christ at Harlem's Apollo Theatre or The Confessions Of a Cedarwood Road Soul Singer; a desperate attempt to ward off the touring hazards of delinquency, boredom and the redecoration of hotel bedrooms; their own Irish emigrant's letter from America

— a post-graduate thesis; a collective two fingers to Albert Goldman; the absolutely vital distinction between a blindman's cane and a sheet-stain; and finally, the moment in which U2 don't so much just trust their instincts as recover, exercise and learn from them — as if they feared those faculties could be emasculated by disuse — by exploring beyond "Bullet The Blue Sky" to fall into (and sometimes recoil from) the arms of America, an embrace that finds them simultaneously blinded, liberated and fixated by the myths they wrestle with?

Among other things. Including the humour behind Adam Clayton's chuckle when film director, Phil Joanou, pretends to be a long-winded interviewer, inquiring about the gestation and birth of this rough beast. Because, since "Rattle And Hum" is one of the kaleidoscopically self-referential album of the tour of the book of the film species (Consumer warning: this review probably will be subject to revision once I see the movie), it's all too easy to stumble down blind alleys or be trapped into false conclusions on first acquaintance. Double-albums are always unwieldy affairs but U2 dare further hazards of misinterpretation

The light sees Bono

by segmenting the live tracks with new material that not only takes up 60% of the running time but also exposes an entirely new re-orientation, breaking up — and making up — the band again but, this time in full and potentially unforgiving public glare.

The first three tracks are the introductions, to ease the listener into "Rattle And Hum"'s challenging diversity of moods and styles. "Helter Skelter", never performed live by The Beatles, can be heard as a metaphor for the re-creation of personality on the concert stage but it's also the first clue that among this album's themes will be ecstasy, and its attendant hangovers and *tristesse*; "Van Diemen's Land", sung by Edge as a sparse folk ballad, sets up a separate theme of travel, displacement and emigration; and "Desire", grounded on a Bo Diddley/Rolling Stones' "Not Fade Away" riff, and smeared by a cheesy organ that could have been sampled from any Tommy James And The Shondells' record, further widens the stylistic terms.

> **"And yes, of course, 'Rattle And Hum' is populist, a stance highly unfashionable among those who fastidiously despair of popular culture... "**

But, after these foothills, "Hawkmoon 269" is the first assault on the summit. With the assistance of timpani and percussion, Larry Mullen's drumming is elementally studio-shaking, as Bono amplifies the themes of love's possession and compulsiveness first aired in "Desire", on a performance where producer, Jimmy Iovine, once a John Lennon collaborator, seems to be urging U2 on, to outsmart and outreach Phil Spector's muffled Plastic Ono Band productions.

For "Rattle And Hum" also concerns idols. Lennon is one whose influence will re-emerge later but a second is Bob Dylan, whose organ underpins "Hawkmoon 269" and whose "All Along The Watchtower" launches side two — a live version from the San Francisco "Save The Yuppie" free concert. *"All I've a got is a red guitar, three chords and the truth,"* shouts Bono. Overblown rhetoric? We'll also return to that issue later.

By now, it's abundantly clear that this is no longer the U2 U U(sed) 2 know. The band, who once glided and cruised in the fluent jetstream of The Edge's almost orchestral vibrations, now rattle and hum, acting as if they're on a dune buggy or express train, greedily scanning the sights out of the windows, gesturing to each other since they can't talk for the R'n'B radio blaring out at full volume, overloaded with the accumulated static of history.

Retro-romance? That's another issue since the live version of "I Still Haven't Found What I'm Looking For" follows, as the next attack on the peak. Recorded in New York with a gospel choir, the New Voices Of Freedom, this version fearlessly, ferociously and yet upliftingly pumps up the emotional volume inherent in the song's dilemma, a performance that affirms the absolute life-giving necessity of honest inadequacy and doubt, over death by dogma and spiritual pride.

Among other things again. Because, by now, it's also abundantly clear that U2 are struggling to clean not only the windows of any heavenly mansions on the hill but also those of Graceland, whilst only haunted by the suspicion that if they ever truly espied the Pearly Gates, they'd find St Peter and Elvis Presley negotiating a Pepsi sponsorship deal with Jim and Tammi Bakker (who've definitely found what *they're* looking for).

But not with Martin Luther King, who increasingly becomes this live side's guiding light. U2 don't approach black music with those London clubland values that can both equate community with conspicuous consumption, and tend to screen out both the politics and spirituality in Sixties soul. Indeed, it's almost as if they've unconsciously happened on the Washington civil rights march, and not Woodstock, as the touchstone of stadium rock.

So they drop in 38 seconds of black street singers, Sterling Magee and Adam Gusson's "Freedom For My People", invoke Martin Luther King's name on "Pride (In The Name Of Love)" and unleash the first political punch on "Silver And Gold" with an Afrikaaner-accented diatribe against apartheid from Bono — though I confess that all later versions pale for me after the solo original.

But on side three, the public ego is put aside. "Angel Of Harlem" is a beaut. Almost as if the colours of all traditions do sometimes bleed into one, an Irish band ventures into Sun Studios to collaborate with the Memphis Horns and Cowboy Jack Clement on a song for Billie Holliday. And by the final verse, Bono the empathizer and enthusiast is so immersed in her, you almost believe he'd use the whole side if not the complete album to sing her praises — except that he spent all the previous night in a Memphis bar in infatuated talk about the subject and, besides, probably forgot all the paper napkins he's littered with his notes. I'd say there's a second there, sir, 'cept "Angel Of Harlem" is so ace.

Bob Dylan then returns as co-author of "Love Rescue Me". Definitely a song that can get neglected on early hearings, this country-soul ballad — it would have been ideal for William Bell or Percy Sledge — casts a cold, private eye on fame with its key lines, *"Many lost who seek to find themselves in me/They ask me to reveal/The very thoughts they would conceal,"* as Bono wails sufficient to greet the ghost of Otis Redding on the close.

By now Love has become the face of salvation, they emphasise. And when the next guest, B.B. King duets on "When Love Comes To Town", the traditional scheme gets reverted as the bluesman, the devil's musician, sings the verses of Christian redemption.

But then as "Heartland" closes the album's most impressive side, U2 suddenly double back (or is it forward?), Brian Eno and Daniel Lanois re-emerging as aides. We're still in America, in

"Mississippi and the cotton wool heat" but this is a gauzy, heat-dazed, impressionistic track, almost as if they're showing how they'd rewrite "The Unforgettable Fire" in '88.

You also become aware now, listening to "Rattle And Hum", what U2 select from America — the ecstatic, the incantatory, the inarticulate speech of soul-searching American hearts rather than a country'n'western strain of story-telling realism. These songs switch from public ceremony to private doubt, from the stadium to the studio, generalising experience through the first person, and are usually unpeopled, except when U2 cast themselves in the role of fans, as in the case of "Angel Of Harlem".

Or in the angry, argumentative "God Part II", their tribute to John Lennon which again doubles back as Bono screams *"I don't believe in the 60's, in the golden age of pop/you glorify the past when the future dries up."*

This, even as they use Jimi Hendrix's "The Star Spangled Banner" to preface "Bullet The Blue Sky". What's more, they seem to confuse the issue even further with the last track, "All I Want Is You" which follows "Heartland" in reference back to "The Unforgettable Fire", thus ending "Rattle And Hum"'s excavation of rock's roots with a full minute of Van Dyke Parks' uneasy strings.

Too much confusion... all along their watchtower? No. At the last moment, U2 sway back from the jaws of revivalism. Spirit will always win over style for them and they really should have dedicated this album to Levi's for inspiring them to cut through the crap that has latterly domesticated the history of American music. Ultimately "Rattle And Hum" is their mission to rescue, re-energise *and* recast lost and dying spirits from those media homes where they'd ultimately be patronised and pensioned off.

Because "Rattle And Hum" is also a defiantly American and populist album. The point of U2 is that they are fired by an unshakable conviction that someone must still fight for that vast, unclaimed territory of popular culture between George Bush and the hardcore, lest nothing be heard beyond the hissing of summer lawns and Whitney Houston albums. But if they double-back, as they regularly do towards the close of "Rattle And Hum", it's to escape the triple demons of pastiche, dogma and any form of renewed rock tribalism.

And yes, of course, "Rattle And Hum" is populist, a stance highly unfashionable among those who fastidiously despair of popular culture, who, in their secret treason see the only useful remaining creative activity as the preserve of those marginalised dandies of the soul, who refine emotions and experiences untranslatable to the public arena.

Meanwhile, I'm left pondering just one of its multifarious conundrums — what's the connection between a blindman's cane and a sheetstain? Now And Zen you might profitably ponder that.

U2 by 2: Edge and Bono...

... and Adam and Larry

SHAKE, RATTLE AND HUM

October 1988

HUM'S THE WORD

And after the album, there's
the movie. *Hot Press* film
critic Graham Linehan
delivers the verdict on the
celluloid "Rattle And Hum"

SO HOW does one review "Rattle And Hum", the movie? As a 'journey into the heart of America'? No, because I can see no way in which that claim could conceivably be justified. How about as a particularly fine live film, to rival "Stop Making Sense"? Yes, because not since that film have I seen something catch the exhilaration and sheer force of a good live gig so completely.

As a documentary, "Rattle And Hum" often falls flat due to its haphazard logic; an interview here, some live footage there, a bit of colour scattered about near the end, bam, bam... no real form to it. But this is what makes it work so *well* as a rock'n'roll movie. Just when you might be getting exhausted from the live sequences, an interview comes in and gives you time to breathe. Black-and-white film has been chosen for no other apparent reason than that it looks good (which is no bad thing) and the effect when the colour comes in is of a part of your brain you never knew existed suddenly coming into play. Holy Gorrrrd!...

So this is a film mostly concerned with surface appearances (the interviews reveal little except how the individual band members might sit on an amp or whatever) and since this is what pop music is basically about (surfaces, pure emotion, cool-lookin' bands) the film is fully able to embrace and *become* its subject... warts and all.

There are some golden moments off-stage: the Gospel choir joining in on 'I Still Haven't Found...' is lovely (you can only imagine how Bono must be feeling while listening to this... the smile on his face gives you a good idea); the scene with B.B. King learning and singing "When Loves Comes To Town" with the band is a memorable one, even though it's marred by the showy cutting that goes from performance to rehearsal to BB talking about the song. It has continuity, but it's irritating not to see the song straight through, uninterrupted.

The worst moment comes during the band's visit to Gracelands, which is pretty cringe-inducing. Phil Joanou states in the book of the movie that he loves films about intensity, like "Taxi Driver" and "Apocalypse Now", but he seems to have forgotten another, fairly important, piece of work considering the circumstances — the ultra-intense "Spinal Tap". Walking around the house, staring at the various artefacts, I half expected them to plunge fingers into their ears and launch into a scuttered version of

An army of U2 fans throng O'Connell St on the night of "Rattle And Hum"'s Dublin premiere

The Edge, Adam, Bono and Larry deliver an impromptu set from a platform erected outside the cinema

"Heartbreak Hotel". There are also some contrived shots of the band looking moody beside the Mississippi, displaying the cautious embarrassment of a family faced with a new home-movie camera, and the film would have been tighter, better, if these moments had been left out.

The film's live sequences, however, are, by turn, electric, exhausting, violent, vital, moving, exhilarating, sexy, passionate, visually *unbelievable* and emotionally draining. From the pure noise of "Helter Skelter" to the hollowed-out music and imagery of "Bullet The Blue Sky", the film keeps you tense and itching to get out into the aisles and make a complete arsehole of yourself. Several times I had to restrain myself from clapping after a particular song.

Even Bono's speeches are concise and worthwhile, especially when he speaks of the Irish-Americans sending money to aid the 'revolution', so-called. "Fuck the revolution!", he yells. It's an old story, but maybe one Americans will finally catch onto with this film.

Phil Joanou's cameras ditch the Jonathan Demme approach (slow, steady panning and concentration on incidentals) and jerk, spin and cruise all over the fucking place, matching the band's energy note-for-note. The lighting is simple but effective, giving the band an undeniably heroic look that doubtless some will sneer at. But pop music is theatre... and it's part of a band's *job* to look cool. You know yourselves: who wants to zoom in on a bunch of sheep farmers?

Whether it's The Edge crouching over his guitar and persuading it to scream melodies like several instruments all at once, or Adam Clayton looking like an intellectual thug (a compliment, I promise) or Larry Mullen whacking the drums with the expression of a man who is literally and metaphysically on the job, or Bono just being Bono, they are truly an impressive sight. Bono especially acts as a focus for the music's emotion, bowing with weariness after yelling his heart out during "Helter Skelter" or crooning softly, head down, during "Bad". He is utterly compulsive to watch, and a star in almost every sense of the word. Also, something that has never quite registered till now: the man is an astounding singer.

All this leads to another reservation. I don't quite understand U2's pursuit of some vague idea of rock'n'roll roots. In the case of "Angel Of Harlem", this seems to mean that you have to sound like Springsteen circa 1979. As "Rattle And Hum", the movie, confirms, their music (and I'm talking about what began with "The Unforgettable Fire" and led to "The Joshua Tree") is as bleak, beautiful and *particular to them* as you could wish for. Their objective should be to keep it that way.

"Rattle And Hum" is an event, one hell of a rock film, the only rock film of recent memory to actually *move* me.

I love it; consider me a fan.

November 1988

The band plus director Phil Joanou (2nd from left) in the Radio 2 studios, with DJ Dave Fanning (headphones)

The businessman and the rock star: U2 manager and Executive Producer of "Rattle & Hum", Paul McGuinness, with Bono.

U2

Nearly a decade after the

A MIGHTY LONG WAY DOWN ROCK'N'ROLL

release of their debut single, U2 are widely regarded as the No. 1 rock band in the world. But the album and the film "Rattle And Hum" depict another kind of reality entirely. Larry, Adam and The Edge talk to Niall Stokes.

THE UNFORGETTABLE Five are at the gate of Windmill Studios, continuing the year-round vigil they keep, watching and waiting for a sighting of any one of the Unforgettable Four. The September skies are darkening early as I pull into the carpark, and head upstairs to pick up an advance copy of U2's latest, sprawling meisterwork, "Rattle And Hum".

It's late on Friday evening but the Principle Management offices are still abuzz with hyper-activity. Someone from Paramount Pictures is on the phone to see if the package from New York should be sent by special courier. Inside her office, Ann Louise Kelly has just opened the first batch of "Rattle And Hum" sleeves, handing me the by-now familiar gatefold package, along with a couple of inner 'bags', inscribed with lyrical trailers to the last year's labours. Locust wind or no locust wind, even at this initial encounter there's no mistaking the epic nature of the undertaking.

Larry is the only band member on the premises. "I hope you like it," he nods at the tape. "It'll probably take a while. It took me a while *(laughs)* — but I think it's a good record."

It's certainly the most complicated musical baby U2 have collectively been involved in giving birth to. Originally conceived as a live concert album, it comes with what might have been an albatross around its neck in the shape of the film — "U2: Rattle And Hum".

In the context, the obvious strategy would have been to go for a kind of greatest hits live package, getting down in definitive form, both visual and musical, the material which by "The Joshua Tree" tour had elevated U2 to that plateau reserved for the few major, enduring rock'n'roll talents. The band rejected that option before it had even been considered, however, going about the project in hand with their customary and somewhat idiosyncratic unwillingness to be limited by popular expectations.

The word initially was that the album would contain a few new songs, interspersed with familiar live material. Then that it would contain one full album of new material, with a live companion making up the anticipated double. Then that there would be very few of U2's live standards on board, this last piece of intelligence throwing expectations of a monumental "U2: Live And Dangerous"-style offering right out the window...

In a sense the album is inseparable from the film, which is inseparable from the album. Larry explains, however, that at all times the music took priority. Pressure to change the live production set-up to suit the demands of the movie was at all times resisted. "There was one occasion they asked us to shift the monitors," Larry recalls, "and I just said no — there's no way we're going to jeopardise the gig for the people who paid in. That was the basic criterion. They asked me to move the cymbals and I said no. In a situation like that you have to make a decision whether you're going to let the fact that the cameras are following you around affect you or not, and very early on I decided that I wasn't. It was up to them to work around us."

It's a reassuring thought to take home with the tape. Because the history of rock'n'roll has been littered with so many instances where bands have come a cropper on the big screen, any

"We all have our own demons," Adam observes, "and Bono's are bigger than everyone else's."

gesture in the direction of Hollywood must inevitably be viewed with that hoary old cocktail, fear and trepidation: the grisly spectre of Led Zeppelin's "The Song Remains The Same" will dog the concept of celluloid rock for years to come.

It's black outside now but the Unforgettable Five are still hoping for a glimpse. "Will Larry be much longer?", one of them asks. I haven't got a clue.

Pulling out of the gates of Windmill, "Rattle And Hum" snaps into the cassette player and the first notes of "Helter Skelter" cascade from the speakers: *When I get to the bottom I go back to the top of the slide... I'm coming down fast but I'm miles above you... Helter Skelter.*"

Nobody said this trip would be an easy one.

RATHFARNHAM, WHERE Adam Clayton has set up home, is at the foot of the Dublin mountains. The band have just gone to No. 1 in the singles charts in Britain for the first time ever with "Desire" when we meet in a quiet hill bar, but having celebrated the night before, Adam is now in a reflective mood. "I love it around here," he says with relish, "it's so quiet and the view of the city is beautiful." Later on, night lights will shimmer below like a tantalising treasure trove but for now the scene is one of calm and tranquility. It's a long way from stadia packed with 60,000 fans hanging on your every note, hungry at least for a piece of musical magic and often for so much more...

"Dublin is brilliant," Adam adds. "I don't want to get philosophical here but for a long time being in a band like U2 and living in Dublin didn't really make sense. In many ways you're an outsider — and it's scarey. But what's happened to us now in terms of international success, the fame vibe and all that, is even scarier *(laughs)*. So, like, the only people that really know you and that you feel really comfortable with are the people who've been

telling you to fuck off for the last ten years!

"When you're away from home, in the States or wherever, all they know about you is the records or the press, so they come to you with all these false pre-conceptions. You're this image of Bono or Adam Clayton or whatever — and while you can try and make them relaxed, they don't really hear you. Whereas here, you can get pissed — and people have seen you pissed before. You can meet them and they don't have expectations of you being able to cure their blind granny, whereas that's kind of what happens in the States."

At the same time, the 'healing' power of U2's music has doubtless been central to their appeal.

"It's great if people get comfort from what we do," Adam agrees. "Great. What more could you ask for from a pair of shoes? But that's what we *do*. It's not what we *are*.

"I mean we're pretty crazy," he elaborates by way of confirming the point. "The Bono I know is a lot crazier than the Bono people see on stage or whatever. We all have our own demons and his ones are bigger than everyone else's."

Adam has a few little garden gnomes of his own, which have driven him into the odd compromising position in his time. There was one infamous occasion which involved being tired, emotional and somewhat abusive to an officer of the law at three in the morning somewhere in Dublin, as a result of which he landed in court on a charge of driving while under the influence.

"I was an asshole," he says firmly. "I was drunk. But it was pretty embarrassing to see it spread all over the papers."

In this respect, there is a significant downside to celebrity in Ireland. In a small pool, where so-called superstars are relatively rare fish, the media tends to become easily obsessed with their activities — as do the authorities.

"In America they're not interested in going through your underwear," Adam argues. "There isn't this attitude that if he's a musician he must have drugs, which still pervades here a lot. You know, they put you through shite here basically — the customs, coming into the country and all that kind of stuff. And it's *rude*, basically. You want to be treated reasonably, like anyone else, whereas they tend to — the red light goes up and they think 'We're gonna get promotion'... "

The continuing rise of the British tabloid papers in Ireland and the scurrilous reporting style which is their trademark represents a further threat to the liberties people have traditionally taken for granted here. The *Star's* vilification of Christy Dignam, in which the former lead singer with the Dublin band Aslan was crudely accused of dealing heroin, Adam responds to with a combination of anger and contempt.

"I think it's disgraceful," he says. "No one deserves that kind

Adam sees the light

of treatment. Increasingly the press seem to print something and don't care whether it's true or not. They don't seem to realise that they're hitting you hard — and *you've* got to face your family and friends the next day. And whether it's true or not, people believe what they read, or some of it sticks. It really distorts the public's perception of things."

In this respect, U2 have recently been the focus for a series of vitriolic attacks in print by Sinead O'Connor, in which the band have been depicted as hypocritical and patronising frauds, abusing their position of prestige and power by stifling any possibility of adverse comment or criticism, while maintaining a pretence of helping to cultivate Irish talent.

"I think the people who know us can read between the lines," Adam reflects. "The people who listen to our records —they're not fooled by it. The fact of the matter is that we went to a lot of trouble to help Sinead's career in the early days. And that's what you do, if you can. Now, for some reason, she cannot accept that and has had to lash out. But Bono in particular pioneered Sinead. He went to a lot of trouble encouraging her; the Edge used her on the soundtrack for 'Captive'; there were various negotiations with Ensign Records that Ossie Kilkenny was involved in — so she's talking crap. I don't know why she's doing it — but I don't think people believe it.

"It's stupid. It's immature. She'll learn. But I know damn well that she won't be making records in ten years. I was interested in her because I thought she was a great talent and I thought she had a future. That's why you support people. Now I'm not so sure that she has what it takes to last."

Is there anyone else in Ireland right now who has? "I haven't been back long enough to know what's going on but I've a lot of

faith in the Flowers. I know they're moving very fast but I'm sure they can cope with it. And I'm really happy to see them being successful because that is something you miss in Ireland — the companionship of people who are going through the same kind of experiences we are. You need your mates which is one of the reasons why I miss Phil Lynott, a lot. I don't mean to be self-pitying but it can be hard trying to stay on top of what's happening and coming to terms with it all, and in that respect it was great having Phil Lynott around.

"It's ten years since Lizzy released 'Live And Dangerous'. I don't want to end up going the way he did, ten years after 'Rattle And Hum'. Or any of the rest of the band either... "

IN THE event, the album couldn't be further from Lizzy's most compelling vinyl testament. A live collection which ostensibly captured the band at the height of their performing powers, aficionados were later to learn that much doctoring of "Live And Dangerous" had taken place in the studios — what Jim Kerr referred to as 'the fixing and mixing' in relation to Simple Minds' "Live In The City Of Light". In contrast U2 have gone for a sound that's determinedly raw and abrasive.

"We didn't deliberately leave in mistakes," says Edge between sips of beer, "but what we went for above, shall we say, a 'perfect' performance from each musician was *feel*. For example, when we went to Sun Studios, during the Joshua Tree tour, that was billed as a demo session — yet we ended up with three backing tracks that appear on the album. The same with 'Desire' — that was cut at STS in Dublin, and it was the first time we'd ever played the song. We then re-cut it at A & M Studios in Los Angeles and it was a much tighter, more accurate performance but it lacked feel. And no one was in any doubt what to do — we just went back to the demo backing tracks. As far as we're concerned the feel is the most important thing, not tightness or accuracy."

It's a preference which runs counter to the prevailing values of international rock'n'roll as the 80's roll to a close and U2 know it.

"Music's become too scientific y'know," Edge elaborates, "it's lost that spunk and energy that it had in the 50s and 60s. When I listen to most modern records I hear a producer, I don't hear musicians inter-acting. And that quality, that missing quality, is something we were trying to get back to in our own music. What I like about 'Desire' is that if there's ever been a cool No. 1 to have in the UK, that's it because it's totally *not* what people are listening to or what's in the charts at the moment. Instead, it's going in exactly the opposite direction. It's a rock'n'roll record — in *no* way is it a pop song.

"Like, there's one guy who came up to me last week in a bar and he said (adopts broad Dublin accent) 'See you're No. 3 in England, Edge. Very good. Not much of a bleedin' tune though, izzit? Can't really hum it, can ya?'. There was something he liked about it but, y'know people don't...rock'n'roll has not been in the charts for *years*. We all forget because we grew up with great rock'n'roll, but now it hasn't been around. And that song is, I suppose, our statement. It's throwaway, it's instant, it's a vibe, it's got that groove going. Sure, you can draw a lot of comparisons with, say, the Stones. Well, they're all drawing from the same well, the same well we are drawing from for that song, and it all goes back to Bo Diddley..."

In a similar spirit, U2 refused point blank to tart up the live material for the album.

"We had very little to do with the live tracks," Adam says, "'cos we were up to our eyes working on the studio cuts. Jimmy Iovine got the live tracks sorted out, we were working on the studio stuff and then there were film mixes going on in another room. It was quite a tangle to fit it all together but Shelly Yakus did most of the live mixes and we were happy with them."

"I had to do the first thirty seconds of the guitar on 'Watchtower' because it wasn't recorded on the day, but that's it," Edge adds. "Everything else is as it was performed live. Nothing's changed."

The approach, as it happens, is utterly appropriate to a project which gradually transformed itself into an American odyssey, with U2 searching for and exploring both spiritual and musical roots. It's a mighty long way down rock'n'roll...

"The whole Memphis thing is based on the river," Adam says, "If you think about growing up in Dublin, you have the river and

the sea and England is over here and America's over there and, it's like there's *hope*. In a similar way, being in Memphis, sitting by the river, there's so much that goes up and down the Mississippi — it's your hope, it's your dreams, it's your fantasies, so you can understand why rock'n'roll happened there.

"You go into the Sun room and it's a modest room. It's got the old acoustic tiles on the wall and the pictures of Elvis and Roy Orbison and Jerry Lee and Carl Perkins — it's just history. You don't take a lot of technology into a studio like that —just the smallest amount of equipment you can do with. And you try to get back to that feeling of making rock'n'roll *without* having huge banks of Marshalls, or whatever. Just strip it back and play the simplest thing you can."

On "Rattle And Hum" U2 grapple with rock'n'roll, r'n'b, gospel and soul influences before emerging with a wild and sometimes anarchic brew that's entirely their own. One of the albums great moments is Bono's r'n'b soaked tribute to Billie Holliday, "Angel Of Harlem". For good measure, the spiky "God Part II" is dedicated to John Lennon.

"We're not trying to pretend that we're not influenced on this record," Edge says, "but at the same time we don't want it to be perceived as some kind of revivalist thing. It's *our* music — it just so happens that this is what we're listening to right now so it's obviously going to come out in our songs and our songwriting."

It adds somewhat to the ambience, no doubt, when you're surrounded by luminaries like Bob Dylan, B.B. King and the Memphis Horns. Dylan contributes a suitably contrary Hammond organ intro to the oceanically epic "Hawkmoon 269".

"Hawkmoon is a place in Rapid City, North Dakota," Edge explains, "we passed by it on the Amnesty tour and Bono, ever a man with a notebook handy, thought 'that sounds good.' So he used that as a point of departure for the song."

"Hawkmoon 269" is a powerful, poetic cry of unbridled need that digs deep into the listener's emotional reserves; one of the band's finest achievements to date.

"Bono's writing is, for me, startlingly good at the moment," Edge affirms. "He's blowing my mind all the time. I think he's still very much caught up, not just in where America is *now*, but also where it's come from since the 50's, that whole journey which Elvis' demise is some kind of metaphor for. So things like "Hawkmoon" and even "Heartland", that's the kind of writing Bono's really turned onto at the moment."

"It comes back to rock'n'roll," Adam adds. "It's an American form, it started there. And if your thing is rock'n'roll, you do end up having to go there and do it because it's not a European form of expression. European music is different and we feel much more a part of the craziness that there is in America. Europe is very

> "We feel that in becoming a big band, you can lose touch with the one thing that actually makes you feel alive - music."

The Edge: roof-raising with a Rickenbacker

that is the strange paradox and contradiction of U2 — that we were a very successful band, selling millions of records across the world, but what always turned us on was the music. We have, as Robbie calls it, 'the fever'. We've caught the fever and now we're looking, trying to put our finger on that thing.''

Was Dylan overawed at the prospect of working with U2 (he jested)?

''He seems to be into what we do, I don't know why. I think maybe he sees something in Bono which he identifies with himself when he was younger. But I've met him three or four times now and he's a man of few words in the studio, I'll say that much. The great thing about Dylan is that whenever he does talk, it's about music, y'know. That's really his heart and soul still. He just said (adopts nasal whine) 'hey, do you mind if I play some organ?' and we said sure, no problem.''

''But it's interesting,'' Adam adds, ''we have felt that, because we've become a big band, you can actually lose touch with the one thing that makes you feel alive, which is music...because you get caught up in the whole celebrity thing, the business trip and all that stuff. And we need people around us who keep us grounded to music, and we go after those people and Dylan is one of them. Robbie Robertson, Keith Richards, T-Bone Burnett —there's a gang of people that you feel comfortable with and that keep it all in perspective. It is the *music* that you keep getting up in the morning for. If it was doing a photo-session for *Smash Hits* or something, you wouldn't bother. That's not where we're at *(laughs)*.''

LUCKILY. BECAUSE in the context of ''Rattle And Hum'', the movie, that would have been a recipe for a self-regarding, insufferable bore. Far from being infatuated with the process, indeed, U2 give the impression of having got a necessary, if unpleasant, chore out of the way. Was it an intimidating experience, seeing your every wrinkle magnified to five or maybe ten times its natural size?

''Well, when we first met Phil Joanou, he promised faithfully that he'd make us all look like Montgomery Clift in his hey-day,'' Edge jokes. ''He turned out to be an absolute lying bastard (laughter), so we were all very shocked when we saw we looked like Bono, Larry, Adam and Edge, and we were very, very upset. What I'm really trying to say is that we could have gone like Hollywood and got all the real expensive lights and made ourselves look amazing, but this film was being shot to try and capture the way it really is. Warts and all.''

So what's the most embarrassing moment in the movie as far as the band are concerned?

''I would say the entire film,'' Edge says to the accompaniment of raucous laughter from Adam, ''from beginning to end. No, but I like the fact that he captured U2 in a way I was doubtful could be done, both live and in the studio. He's a great director, but not

ordered and civilised, but America is just this weird fucking jungle.''

And to discover what makes the jungle tick, it's necessary to swing from a few trees. You have to crawl before you can run before you can soar. That's what this epic voyage was about.

''The best American music is unrecorded and is to be found in obscure little bars around New Orleans,'' Edge reflects. ''Rock'n'roll, real rock'n'roll, ended when Elvis Presley left Sun Records, then it became a mass-media thing. But the real spirit of rock'n'roll is still occasionally found in little obscure places. And it's so hard to find, and so hard to keep that innocence or whatever it is that The Real Thing is about. And people like Dylan and Robbie Robertson have spent their whole lives trying to maintain that spark, that thing, which is so different to commercialism, so different to selling millions of records. And only is he a great director, he actually understands the band, so that combination — we just fell on our feet with him...

"Although it is frightening seeing yourself up there," Adam adds, "there's also a lovely feeling of distance. I don't actually *feel* like the person that's up there, but I feel like the person up *there* can go around the world and get through to people. So it sort of takes the pressure off you as an individual. It's quite liberating to have a representation of yourself that can stand up on its own."

Are they apprehensive about how the film might be received?

"I really couldn't give a shit," Edge says definitively. "We're not movie stars, we're a rock'n'roll band and it doesn't really bother me. I mean, I didn't even want to do it at the beginning. I felt it was just one headache we didn't need. Y'know, I've no doubt about what we do, what we're best at. As it turns out, I think it's a very good film but I didn't lose no sleep over the movie...

"I *was* concerned that the band would be portrayed accurately, that the film didn't paint a different picture to the one that was real. I think that hasn't happened. This movie hinges on music, and that's the most interesting thing about U2. There's no backstage scenes, there's no climbing into limousines, that's not what we're about. That would really be extremely uninteresting. It's also been done before. But what is interesting at the moment about U2 is where we're going musically and that's really what it is. That's the core of what this film says and is about."

"Besides," Adam laughs, "We can always go back to our day jobs."

W H I L E   T H E   film was intended to avoid the trap of glamourisation, it was made in the centre of the glamour illusion, Hollywood. It's a reflection of the kind of irony and contradiction which still fascinates U2 about America.

"It's a very, very strange place," Edge comments, "that's why I'm into it, 'cos it's so fucking weird. There's no heart to that city. I've been there 10 times, but it was only on this trip that I actually *found* Hollywood! I kept looking for it! We found the down-town area which was originally the centre of L.A. and, right now, it's like walking into "Blade Runner". It's a total no-go area after dark; the only way you go through there is in a car and quite fast!

"But during the day, it has this very interesting atmosphere. It's all, like, Mexicans, blacks, and it's a wonderful cocktail of influences — the things you see down there you just never see anywhere else. That's where we filmed a lot of the "Desire" video. We weren't trying to make any statement, we just thought: we're here, let's show L.A. as it is. With all the confusing angles to the place, it seemed to be the perfect visual

"What we do is much more emotional than political... We're not social workers. We're a fucking rock'n'roll band."

metaphor for the song "Desire". All the different colours, the lights, the whole thing."

"It's a very, very heavy place," Adam adds. "You have the people who live on the Hill, the stars. There's this *humongous* wealth — y'know every convertible is red and it's driven by a blonde-haired woman. And you have this street-life of massive homelessness. For a start, the mental patients they don't keep, you have this serious problem where if people are mentally sick and poor, there's no welfare, there's no nothing. So they live in these cheap hotels, they rent a room."

Edge: "In certain areas, it's like Beirut. There's probably 2 to 3 killings in L.A. every day, where the different districts of the ghetto areas are divided and controlled by the different gangs, the Crips and the Bloods, and so on."

Adam: "And poverty is rife, so they're running crack. They're making money — why wouldn't you? I think fear is running America at the moment, which leads to the whole arms issue. Everyone is carrying guns — you have ghettoes where the gangs have superior fire-power to the police. There's so much money coming in from drugs, and that's what they're all afraid of. There just doesn't seem to be any way they can close that door, because if you're poor in America you don't have anything."

With the result that those 'smart' enough to vote are going to put George Bush in the driving seat for the next four years, despite his appalling record on the Iran-Contra Arms Deal, among other thorny issues... "In a way, that's what makes America so interesting for a writer. You get an insight when a country is in descent, when things are falling apart."

That said, Edge is anxious that people shouldn't always expect the Big Statement from U2. Sure, all U2 have is "a red guitar, three chords and the truth." And yes "Rattle And Hum" does set about demolishing the myth of the No. 1 rock'n'roll band in the world by setting their achievements alongside the inspiration of the greats of rock'n'roll. But even that myth needs to be punctured before it gets out of hand. "We didn't sit down and say 'what big message are we going to convey in this?' We just write songs about what we're feeling at the time. Obviously we're trying to do something that's got a bit of bite and relevance but it's much less conscious than people think. It's much more emotional than political in that sense. We're not social workers. We're a fucking rock'n'roll band." (laughter)

The number one rock band in the world? "I find that hilarious," Adam responds, "it's a joke."

A MIGHTY LONG WAY DOWN

October 1988

Swapping notes: Bono and The Edge

I STILL HAVEN'T FOUND
WHAT I'M LOOKING FOR

So this is Christmas and what have we done... As U2 prepare to enter the final year of the decade, Bono devotes a long night at his home in Dublin to reflecting on his life, his music and U2's extraordinary career to date.
Interview: Liam Mackey

MEMO FROM The Eye Of The Storm: through the office walls comes the rattle and hum of typewriters and tape-machines as stout-hearted volunteers attempt to wrestle the contents of four hours' worth of cassette recording onto paper. Ah yes, I do believe we've been down this road before. I seem to recognise the territory. ''I'll always have plenty of time for Bono but rarely enough tape.'' I'm not much given to quoting myself (I leave that to others, har har), but that line which I wrote after interviewing U2 three years ago, applies just as forcefully on this mad Monday deadline afternoon, that follows another long, late-night conversation with yer man.

''An awkward sonuvabitch'', is how he, not unhappily, describes ''Rattle And Hum'' at one point, and so, at least in its preservation of *that* spirit, you might get away with describing the fruits of last night's labours as The Interview Of The Album (of the film of the book of the band of the controversy... of which more later). Then again you might not.

The world of journalism loves the concept of 'the definitive interview' — along with The Great Scoop it's a kind of Holy Grail of the profession. But you can forget about even getting close to the glittering prize as far as encounters with Bono are concerned, not least because here is a man who readily admits that *he* can scarcely define himself to any satisfactory degree. Which, of course, only serves to render even more glaring the supreme irony of his being perceived as rock's Man With The Answers.

Nope, what we have here is not a man whose personality can be so very easily gift-wrapped, tied and placed quietly under the tree — Joshua or otherwise — more a Jack forever popping out of whatever box people reckon they have him in. So no Definitive Statement, but between the public role and the private man, between the urge to get a lot off his chest and a guardedness that comes from knowing how print makes permanent and headlines distort, a lot of talk and thought and copious amounts of coffee, as 1988 unwinds and the first decade of U2 slips away.

Meanwhile, outside in the distance, a wild-cat did growl —but it's cool. It's only Niall, patiently asking, if there's any chance we might have this thing in print, by, say, the onset of Summertime. So, as the production staff plunge headlong deeper

Bono (above) as the decade draws to a close and (below) down all the days

into the maelstrom, let's go back to the midnight hour in a quiet room by the sea...

WE BEGIN on a sobering note with Bono describing how he came to write a song for, and then meet, the late Roy Orbison, who'd died just the day before the interview was originally scheduled.

"The song that stood out for me on the soundtrack of 'Blue Velvet' — which was a film I really liked — was Roy Orbison's 'In Dreams'. One night when I couldn't sleep in London, just before we played Wembley Arena, I stayed up listening to this tape. Y'know the way you can put a tape in and it just keeps going 'round and 'round and you come in and out of consciousness —well I always seemed to wake up on that song, 'In Dreams'. And I thought it was the most extraordinary song 'cos it breaks all the rules of pop music. And then there was that extraordinary baroque voice.

"So next day I woke up and I started on this song, 'She's A Mystery To Me'. I became a bore and talked about Roy Orbison all day. I played the song — or what I'd started of the song —to the others in the band and they liked that. Or maybe they liked the fact that it stopped me talking about Roy Orbison *(laughs)*. I was just going on and on about him. Anyway, after the concert in Wembley Arena I came back and I was sitting down in the dressing-room, working on this song and basically trying to order everybody into buying every Roy Orbison record ever made, when there was a knock on the door.

"It was our security man, John, and he says, 'Listen, I've got Roy Orbison outside — could he come in?' And everybody just looked at me and I said, 'Look, I didn't *know* he was at the show.' Nobody had told us he was coming. So there was much laughter and abuse...

"And he walked in and he just said *(quiet American accent)* 'I'm an instinctive kinda guy and I can't tell ya why I loved the show but I loved the show.' Then we got talking about songs and he asked for one, so I just took out the guitar and I played him 'She's A Mystery To Me'.

"Later when I was in Los Angeles I met him a few times and we started off a few things together. And his family opened up to me, were very good to me. I found him to be a very wise man, he had a lot to say. He seemed to be a man who was incredibly surprised at his own talent. I mean, he had the voice of an angel — and, well, now he is one."

LOOKING BACK on U2's '88, Bono pronounces himself "surprised and shocked" that "Rattle And Hum", an album he describes as "a wonderful mess of looking forward to the future,

bits from the past and bits from the present" should sell as well as it did.

"I don't understand how we sold *five million double* albums — I can't figure that out," he says. "I mean we do our best to shake off the not-really U2 fans and, we thought, if anything is going to shake 'em off, it's going to be this, 'cos we've essentially stripped the band of its sound."

The record certainly shook off some of their long-time critical support, as evidenced by an unprecedented amount of negative press, especially in America. "I always expected criticism," says Bono, "and in a way we were excited by the fact that people either loved or hated the album. We were getting reviews that said it was the greatest live LP in the history of pop music and reviews that said it was dog-shit. And I was thinking that it's been a long time since a record in rock'n'roll had that kind of impact — people just don't care enough about rock'n'roll usually to talk about it in such a heated way. So I must say we were flattered by the love-hate reaction to the LP but what I was disappointed in — in both the praise and the criticism — was the lack of insight into the LP, lyrically, in what it said about us, U2. There's so much in there, so many heavy things — it has a beginning, middle and end in its own ragged way. And that people didn't question the idea of why we did 'Helter Skelter' other than 'why are they doing a Beatles' song?' — that people didn't think further than that, I must say... amused me."

One of the central criticisms was that by invoking, in both image and song, such legendary figures as Billie Holliday, Presley, Lennon and Hendrix, U2 were engaged in a form of self-aggrandisement by association — a hi-jacking, for personal benefit, of the great rock'n'roll tradition.

"That was maddening because the intention was the exact opposite," Bono asserts. "I mean rock'n'roll *is* a great tradition, and we *are* part of it — and maybe you'll think this is funny —but we thought it was, kind of, the most *humble* thing to do. This was a record made by fans — we wanted to own up to being fans. And we thought rock'n'roll bands just don't do that — we all know they *are*, but they don't do it. The Rolling Stones did it on 'Exile On Main Street', sort of, and it was a kind of role model. But we wanted to go even further and have pictures, because there's people out there who probably don't even know who Billie Holliday is or who BB King is. We thought of it as: 'we have this thing, U2; now let's just put it aside almost and let's just get lost in this music.' "

So it was, at least in part, a tribute album?

"Yeah, but it wasn't meant to be a tribute to us *(laughs)*. It's very funny but things like that have happened to us before, so sometimes we can utterly misread a situation. I mean, I still think

"'Ratttle And Hum" was a record made by fans - we wanted to own up to being fans. Rock'n'Roll bands just don't do that."

Always someone looking at you

it was the right thing to do. We were in there as the apprentices — it was quite obvious. You only have to see the movie to see the look on my face of sheer embarrassment talking to BB King, sitting next to this great blues man.''

Again, Bono's introduction to the band's cover of ''Helter Skelter'' — ''This is the song Charles Manson stole from The Beatles; we're stealing it back'' — was seized upon as evidence of alleged delusions of grandeur.

''It was a totally off-the-cuff remark but it was meant in an irreverent kind of way,'' he responds. ''I don't want to seem to be defending myself — I don't see *why* I have to defend myself —but rock'n'roll has always had a little bit of irreverence. At the same time, I'm more reverent than anyone about music, about the spirit of it, about what's at the heart of rock'n'roll.

''But when you start off as a punk band in a garage, you do that everyday, you do wired cover versions of rock'n'roll songs and re-work them to suit yourself at that particular moment in time. And, y'know, we thought 'All Along The Watchtower' would really throw people but then when they saw the movie they'd understand it. The idea of learning how to play a song five minutes before you play it live is one thing — but five minutes before it appears on your album we thought was hilarious. That, for me, was the sort of thing a big band like us should do — let the air out of the balloon, not blow it up!''

In the overall context of U2's recorded work, Bono will allow that ''Rattle And Hum'' can be ''looked at the way people look at 'Under A Blood Red Sky' — but it's something we did *instead* of a live album.'' If that suggests a sense of modesty in his perception of the album's scope and ambition, it is not, however, to be confused with any lack of faith in its content. On the contrary.

''The reason it's a great rock'n'roll record is because it has great songs,'' he argues. ''There isn't a weak song on the LP. That's what makes a good or bad LP. The fact that it's an awkward son-of-a-bitch to listen to means that it can't be an album in the sense of 'album' with an American accent. But the songs on it... 'Desire', 'Angel Of Harlem', 'All I Want Is You'. There's no mention of 'All I Want Is You' in any of the reviews —it's better than 'With Or Without You'. We'll probably have to release it as a single before people realise that.''

In terms of quality, he could also have singled out the magnificent ''Hawkmoon 269'' but in a thumb-nail 'review' such as Bono's just delivered here it will inevitably be his assertion that the record is bereft of a single weak track which will be picked up and used as more fuel to fan the flames of critical discontent. Like, wouldn't he admit that the cover versions are off the wall?

''Yeah, they *are* off the wall,'' he cheerfully agrees. ''That's the way to *do* cover versions. The only reason we played 'All Along The Watchtower' in San Francisco was because the gig was in the financial district. It was, like, 'let's stop making big decisions — let's make some small ones'.''

The relevance of 'Watchtower' to the financial district had to do with the three lines from the Dylan song that had always stuck in Bono's mind: *''Business men they drink my wine/ plough-men dig my earth/but none of them along the line know what any of this is worth.''* The rest, he says, he picked up on the day.

''Literally,'' Bono asserts, ''by asking one of the local guys, somebody walking by, if he knew the words. We were collecting them on the spot.

''The sense of humour of this band is missed a lot,'' he elaborates. ''It's like some American papers reported that we had done a Save The Yuppie concert — the same band who did concerts for human rights and for the starving peoples of Africa were very concerned about the Crash. Honestly, it was reported without irony. It was like the time lightning hit the aeroplane when we were flying into America, and we were sitting opposite Sophia Loren and I said 'don't worry, it's only God taking your photograph' and she laughed. And then the story came out in a very *serious* way. It's just one of those things. Maybe people don't expect us to have a sense of humour so they don't look for a sense of humour in anything we do.''

U2's choice of ''Helter Skelter'' as the album's other cover-version, had an altogether different significance — as its placing at the top of side one suggests. The relevance of the song's portrayal of someone turned upside down and inside out in a world gone frantically haywire, was not lost on the band, according to Bono.

'' 'Helter Skelter' was exactly what we were going through on the Joshua Tree tour,'' he explains. ''It was one of the worst times in my musical life. First, a falling light cut me up and I had to be stitched up. My voice failed for the first week — the world press came to the opening of the tour and I couldn't sing. We were on the run the whole time and I busted my shoulder and was in a lot of pain. And I found that I was drinking a lot just to stop the pain.''

Going on stage drunk even?

''No, I never went onstage drunk. I would've drunk but I wasn't drunk onstage. It was madness. I don't want to overstate it but there was just times on that tour... there's this thing, y'know, we call it the heart of darkness. It was a series of four or five songs that began with 'Bullet The Blue Sky', then 'Running To Stand Still' into 'Exit' and 'Bad'. And we found ourselves in this heart of darkness, playing these songs every night, and not coming out of it, just feeling very black... we played some great concerts on that tour but there was a lot of madness.''

In the past Bono spoke of the ''War'' tour going somewhat off the rails — is it a case then that this 'madness' is an inevitable consequence of massive tours?

''I think it is and for different individuals at different times. We've agreed that we won't do one again, we'll just play when we want to play. That's the way we feel about it right now; we may change our mind. I don't want that to sound like rock'n'roll star cribbing, moaning about being on the road. There's a side of me that would go on the road and never come home but it's the mad side and it's the side of me that after one, two, three, four, five, six months, starts to lose sight of the other. Some days I don't know who I'm goin' to wake up as.

''There's a lot of laughter as well but there is a point when the laughter becomes hollow. There is a street-gang side to being in a band and there's a wild streak in U2 and there's a way in which a member or members can get a bit out of control on a tour and forget where they've come from and who they've left behind. You can live out any side to your character, and there *are* many sides to all of our characters...

''Outsiders can come and go from the tour, and they just see four guys in a band who go onstage and play — a lot of the time — great rock'n'roll concerts. That's all they see but you can start to live out the music a little too much sometimes, where the demons you're exorcising in the songs sort of follow you home. And they follow you home to what is the padded cell of a hotel room.

''Now this will sound like utter shite because people see a suite in the top of the hotel in Chicago and think it must be the most incredible place to be. But the more plush the surroundings, the poorer you feel in spirit sometimes.''

In documenting the dark side, Bono doesn't want to make it sound like he's lost sight of the light. ''The high of being onstage in front of 10,000 or 100,000 people,'' may, as he says, be followed by ''the low afterwards'' but the scales still weigh heavily on the positive side.

''I don't want to be the rock'n'roll star who's giving out about something he loves,'' he says. ''Because I *do* love this. I wouldn't do it if I didn't.''

FROM ''THE Joshua Tree'' through the tour of the album to the release of the new LP and film, an increasingly strong impression emerged of a band hugely — though not exclusively — preoccupied with The Big Country. With ''Rattle And Hum'' under his belt, can Bono now say that he's gotten America out of his system?

''I hoped living in LA for six months would get America out of my system, I hoped making 'Rattle And Hum' would get it out of my system. But now I've come home, I'm still living in America!'' he states. ''We all live in America in the sense that you turn on the television and it's America. As is a lot of the music we listen to. America slips under the door, it creeps all over you. It's something that we have to come to terms with. There are more Irish people in America than there are here... it's all mixed up, it's not as simple as America over there and Ireland over here. It's not like that. America's bigger than just the 700,000,000 people that live there. As Wim Wenders said, 'America's colonised our unconscious' — it's everywhere. So how on earth can I get America out of my system? I can't get it out of my television!''

As for Ireland, the decision of all four band members to continue living and working here is ample testament to their attachment to the old sod. However, as their collective star has soared ever higher in the rock firmament, their resultant celebrity

"There's a side of me that would go on the road and never come home but it's the mad side... "

In the hot-seat on Irish television

has made life a little more complicated at home.

"You're a journalist with an Irish perspective," says Bono, "and as Bill Graham so accurately pointed out in one of his articles about U2, here we have a problem of scale. People are talking about mega-this and mega-that, but in America, we don't sell half as many records as Bon Jovi or Def Leppard. We're only a dent in the side of the media in America but we're a gaping wound in this country. Even in the UK it's like 'Oh U2 have another album out.' I've got to be careful about how I answer these questions, because, while it's not really real in terms of the total world we live and work in, it *is* in terms of this country and we can't quite control that."

But the big fish in the small pool syndrome doesn't always work against you.

"If you make a mistake here, you could make a mess," Bono reflects. "I've been a bit out of hand once or twice, here or there, a bit drunk maybe at six o'clock in the morning or something, and you know, you make a mistake and you go to get into your car... Someone here is more likely to take you and put you in their car and drive you home, Irish people are like that. They don't really kiss and tell. You can make a mistake and they generally watch your back for you — I've had some experiences of that."

On the subject of the media he expresses annoyance at "the U2 stories being printed all the time which are completely untrue." For example , he cites a recent headline claiming the band were due to record the soundtrack for the sequel to "Chinatown", starring Jack Nicholson — a story, he says, that's totally without foundation. He was also irritated by the presentation in the *Irish Independent* of his contribution to a new book "Across The Frontier" edited by Richard Kearney. "They gave the impression that I was writing a book and that I had written this piece, when in fact it's from a conversation I had with Richard Kearney — somebody I respect for his book — that Neil Jordan and Paul Durcan were also a part of."

Without naming names, he also alludes, with evident anger, to more personal attacks on him which have been published recently.

"There have actually been lies about me," he says. "People saying things like I'm a liar. I'm not sure I really want to get into it but in the end the worst things people can say about you are not as bad as what you're really like *(laughs)*. But I'm becoming numb to it and I'm becoming numb because I'm so strung out on the songs and the music, at the moment. It's become so loud in my life that it's drowning out all the shite that has been following us around. And the bands that are sick and tired of being compared to U2, it's amusing again, because the same bands seem to talk about nothing but U2..."

It's back to that issue of scale, and at least until fairly recent times the phenomenon of U2 looming extra large in the Irish context, for want of any real competition. Bono agrees. "That's why I go to bed at night and I thank Holy Mary for the Hothouse Flowers and Sinead O'Connor and Enya and all these people, because we've been out on our own and sometimes we get a bit bored and lonely for the lack of company."

He pauses. "That was a joke by the way," he adds with a grin.

But at the end of the day, can criticism hurt?

"It can. The sort of criticism we got over Mother, for instance, from younger bands who wanted to put us in the cliched role of being Led Zeppelin and therefore casting themselves as The Clash and The Sex Pistols, without having a thimbleful of the talent that those two groups have. To be honest, I just got less interested in that whole thing. I realised that it was actually something I could do without. I'm at a time now where my philosophy is to simplify — not just musically trying to strip things down but in my own life trying to strip things down to get to the essence of what we want from U2. What is it about really? And in the end it's about records which are made up of four minutes, albums which are made up of some music and some statements about the way you see the world and what's going on in your life at this time. And trying to be — dare I say it? — artists.''

And, while writing songs and making music in the context of U2, is still Bono's prime vocation, away from the group he has got some personal artistic projects simmering. The background involves his attempts to be more rigorous in his style of lyric writing. "I thought it was important at one point to write in a beat sort of way, without editing myself as I went along," he observes. "It felt very Irish, very stream of consciousness. Allen Ginsberg approved of it too! It seemed to have all the ingredients that suited my lazy bastard approach to life itself. Y'know it seemed to suit me fine. But now I am a little bit more interested in storytelling and I've started to write some other stuff — like, now, I've got two stage plays and a book in progress.''

Though clearly excited by the challenge, beyond revealing that one of the plays, "The Million Dollar Hotel", is set in a flea-bag lodging house in downtown LA, he's reluctant to talk too much in public about the material in hand, not least because, as he puts it: "I might never finish the things. I just work on them when I feel like it — like earlier tonight, or when I'm on the road or when I'm not in the mood for writing songs. It's all very... *kaleidoscopish!*''

In relation to the real life inspiration for "The Million Dollar Hotel" and his first hand experience of the milieu while living in LA, Bono acknowledges the voyeuristic, if not exploitative, aspects which can be involved in the well-to-do artists' mining of lowlife for creative material. "I think artists are utterly selfish creatures and I don't approve of it at all," he says. "But I can't stop being attracted to that side of things. It's probably the violence in me that makes me interested in violence. The reason I'm attracted to the light of the Scriptures is because there's another side of me that is dark. The reason I'm interested in the men of peace is because I'm not like them and I would like to be. I'm *not* someone who in real life turns the other cheek... ''

''G O D   P A R T   II'', a song of irony and deliberate contradiction, is one of Bono's strongest lyrical statements to date, notable for a number of memorable lines including a savage denunciation of Albert Goldman, which was inspired, it

transpires, as much by his earlier book on Elvis Presley, as it was by his follow-up work on John Lennon, to whom the song is dedicated.

"Elvis changed everything," says Bono. "The America I know was born in 1956 when Elvis appeared on the Merv Griffith Show — because black 'n' white music collided in this guy's spastic dance. He had white skin with a black heart —and what I love about America is the fact that its melting pot of European and African culture keeps it from going straight. I think what's really significant about Elvis Presley and rock'n'roll culture was that everything changed in America after that. Racism was broken down as significantly as it was through the peace movement and MLK — not institutional racism but common racism. It was an extraordinary event: an *explosion* took place. Albert Goldman missed this completely and utterly and didn't see it as significant at all.''

So what made John Lennon stand apart in Bono's eyes?

"It's enough that he was an influence on my own musical life, never mind talking in terms of youth culture as a whole," he replies. "He had an incredible cut-throat honesty to his music that I always looked up to. He was saying this is what *I* think so here it is. Some people write about the country they live in — Lennon wrote about the mind and the body he lived in.

"I'm the sort of person who absolutely despises what Goldman did," Bono adds, "yet still reads the book. I had one advantage coming to it in that I never thought of Lennon as a hero really, more as an anti-hero. Also when the book came out Jimmy Iovine was reading it in the studio and he *knew* John Lennon so Jimmy could point out where the guy (Goldman) was completely wrong. The bit about Spector and his body guards tying up John in the house: Jimmy was there — he *untied* him but he wasn't in the book. It's laughable. I got an accurate picture of who John Lennon was through Jimmy Iovine. He saw him for the good, the bad and the ugly that he was. Personally I've got so much respect for him as a man and as an artist.''

Who, if anyone, qualifies as a hero for Bono these days?

"I don't have heroes like I used to have because I've met a lot of people who at 16 I would have called my heroes. But in a way, having met them, they appeared even more heroic to me because they were flawed. I suppose I suspect people who don't have flaws — it's a feeling that there must be something wrong somewhere. I don't negate one side of the person because you know there's another. Anyway, the people I'd look up to tend to be older. In music and in literature. Johnny Cash is a hero if you want to use that word. Willie Nelson, Bob Dylan, Lou Reed, Keith Richards. These are people who've survived rock'n'roll and came out the other side with interesting stories to tell to someone who's going in."

In those terms, Bono may still count himself an apprentice but there's no gainsaying the fact that he is himself an object of hero-worship to many. In "Love Rescue Me", the song he co-wrote with Bob Dylan, it's a theme that seems to be touched upon in the line *"They asked me to reveal the very thoughts they would conceal"* — a statement, one could suggest, that had equal relevance for Dylan and Bono. So whose was it?

"The line is mine I have to say," says Bono, "but it's not about people coming looking for salvation — it's more about people wanting to look into your soul. There's also the aspect of the performing monkey syndrome — like those Victorians that used to arrive at Bedlam and poke the demented creatures. *(Launches into hilarious toffee-nosed commentary).* 'There's Iggy Pop in there now, look at him, he's cutting himself. And there's that Johnny Cash — he's an alcoholic and he's on pills at the moment. Bob Dylan — he had a motor cycle accident. He was a spokesman for a generation and it was all a bit too much for him.' Poke poke poke. 'Now here's Bono, he's going to talk about God and Northern Ireland and sex — all at the same time. That's *his* trick.' *Whack* on the head!"

I N ''R A T T L E & Hum" the movie, the combination of music and emotion is at its most powerful in U2's performance of "Sunday Bloody Sunday", filmed in concert on the day of the Enniskillen bombing. Subsequent to the film's release, Bono has been heard to ponder, on more than one occasion, the possibility that the band won't play the song again. Why?

"Because it's almost like that song was made real on the day," he reflects. "It was made real for the moment, in a way that it's never going to be again. I think that that was the ultimate performance of the song and anything else would be less than that."

Had he ever hoped in originally writing the song, that it might contribute, in however small a way, to decreasing the likelihood of the kind of events it depicted, being repeated again and again.

"No, not really. I suppose in the back of your mind you hope you can help and turn things round in some way but that's not really your job as a rock'n'roller. Your job is to write a good song that expresses how you feel, how you see things. An experience I had, a very interesting experience which shows you how far and wide an audience can be in their understanding of U2, was when we played Belfast last year. It's got to be one of the greatest rock'n'roll houses in the world but we didn't quite know what they'd make of 'Sunday Bloody Sunday' after it had had a few years to sink in.

"As soon as we started into the song a tricolour shot up. Then a Union Jack shot up. Next thing, the Union Jack was pulled down and the Tricolour was pulled down by other people in the audience. Then some people in the front row started giving us the

Bono and Ali: "She is definitely the better half," he insists

'fuck off' sign. But as soon as the song ended and we went into another one, the same people went crazy and got straight into the next song. And I thought that was very interesting — that you could hate a song or something that U2 did but still love the band."

Has he experienced any particular reaction to the song's introduction in the movie, the 'fuck the revolution' speech?

"No, I think people understood where it came from, that there was a good reason. It was a reaction. It was taken not so much as a political statement but as an emotional one which a lot of people shared, including some supporters of the Provisionals, I would have thought. Everyone would have felt that way."

There have been press reports nonetheless that Bono has received death threats from the IRA because of his statement. Is there any truth in these?

"No. What I ask is: if you really hate me or hate U2 don't shoot me — that will only sell another 5 million records! Know what I mean? Like, I'm worth more dead than alive! If you really hate me don't make me a legend!"

Bono finds it disturbing, at the same time, that a story like that should have made it into print.

"Yeah. In fact, I was sitting on a plane opposite Robert Maxwell and I hit him with it between the eyes. I said 'Your paper printed some lies about me and our group. Lies that were harmful, that could have put an idea that wasn't there in somebody's head.' But then I get death threats all the time. Everybody receives death threats in a big rock'n'roll band. We've had them, we'll have them again."

Understandably, it's not a subject he likes to dwell on. Talking about the North, however, he's more expansive.

"With regard to the IRA, I know some people think 'he's got no right to talk, he doesn't live in Derry, he doesn't live in Belfast.' But I have the same right to talk about it as anybody in the pub. Even if I wasn't in a band, I'd be talking about it, and I have a right as an Irishman to have an opinion. And not even as an Irishman — I just have a right to have an opinion."

> **"I don't deny that some of the wishes of the IRA and their supporters are sincere, but they are, in my opinion, sincerely wrong."**

While placing on the record his opposition to the legislation banning Sinn Féin from the airwaves in Britain, he remains unshaken in his belief that the armed struggle is wrong.

"I think that the argument that the Provisional IRA puts forward, apart from the moral side of the issue, is just unintelligent — an unsound and old-fashioned idea that may have had relevance in the past but doesn't now," he says. "Revolution, where the overwhelming majority of the population are not behind it — and they are both a minority in the North and a minority in the South — won't work. Also, revolution to turn us into what? I don't think they *have* a political agenda in the real sense of the world. I don't see a real vision of the future that we could all buy into."

What about the withdrawal of British troops as an immediate item for negotiation?

"Yeah. I'd like to see that. In fact while I speak out about the IRA, I've also spoken out about the British presence in Northern Ireland on BBC Radio a few weeks ago. I said they don't want to be there and they shouldn't be there. It's obvious that Ireland is an island... The idea of borders is a bit dodgy anyway, not just between North and South but between anywhere.

"I think John Hume is the man with real vision. He realises that there is a bigger Europe that we are a part of, and we'll become closer, the North and the South will become closer, by both becoming part of a bigger Europe, a bigger world, with a bigger vision. It's so *small*, the vision of 'Ireland' and 'Eire Nua'. Who cares about Eire Nua? What about Europe Nua? The World?"

Can he understand or appreciate the motivation of someone like Bobby Sands?

"Yes I can, and I must say that you can't but be in awe of the strength of will that it took for Bobby Sands to go on that hunger strike but I just don't know — there are people striving to hold on *to* life. There are people in other countries who are dying because they have no food, not because they are refusing food. To me, *their* reality is something that we must not forget about.

"I don't deny that some of the wishes of the IRA and some of the people who support the Provisional IRA are sincere, but they are, in my opinion, sincerely wrong."

IT'S GETTING on for three in the morning now and the talk is of politics in general, specifically Bono's disillusionment with the options he sees available.

"The whole political picture right now is completely outmoded," he suggests. "The Right and the Left are ridiculous — they don't mean anything anymore. These are old ideologies. You can learn from Marx, you can learn from Lenin — but my worry is: why are there no new Marxes or Lenins? Why is there such a void in political thinking at the moment? Why are we using solutions to problems of an industrial revolution when we're going through our own revolutions — technological, ideological, *everything-ological*. It's different now and different problems need different solutions."

Are there any people on the political landscape that he looks to with a degree of hope?

"I don't know. I don't see anyone with vision anymore. Nobody has big vision. I'd belong to a world party if there was

U3

one, I would. On a purely local level, which you have to get down to eventually, I find my sympathies more and more, issue by issue, with people like The Workers Party — Proinsias De Rossa I really respect. Tony Gregory I also respect. But it's issue by issue with me. There is this black hole, this void right now, as the world awkwardly changes gear from the twentieth century to the twenty-first and I think, in general, this will be looked back on as a really empty-headed period in political life.''

Would Bono describe himself as a pacifist? ''I would love to be,'' he replies. In that context how would he view, for example, the prospect of all-out armed revolution in South Africa, a subject he refers to in ''Silver And Gold''.

''I can really understand the overwhelming majority deciding to take up arms against the system of apartheid,'' he answers. ''I could really understand and relate to it — but I hope they don't have to do that. It would be better if it didn't have to happen that way. But I mean, *there's* another contradiction, another ugly contradiction of Ronald Reagan's America — that they would support the Contras to undermine a state like Nicaragua which they see as illegal and yet they make no effort to undermine the Apartheid system which they also say is illegal.''

He pulls himself up short. ''When it comes to discussing politics,'' he reflects, ''I just want to be the man at the bar talking, that's all. No more or less educated about anything than anyone else.''

Except of course that once the lead singer of U2 expresses (or is asked to express) an opinion on anything, there's a fairly widespread perception of Bono getting up on his soapbox again.

''Yeah sure, but *everybody's* on their soapbox,'' he responds. ''You know, you hear people saying that religion and politics are things you shouldn't talk about but they are two of the few things actually worth talking about. And everybody else in Ireland talks about them.''

WHEN THEY aren't talking about money, perhaps. In ''God Part II'', Bono writes the following lines: *''I don't believe in excess/success is to give/I don't believe in riches/But you should see where I live.''* Has he personally learned to resolve that paradox?

''I have. OK, the contradiction is, essentially, writing songs that criticise the system and, at the same time, benefiting from the system. But I don't think that's bad. You *ought* to bite the hand that feeds you *(laughs)*. Bite it. Why not?''

To put it more bluntly — does he feel guilty about his wealth?

''Well, we have two ways of dealing with our wealth. We have what U2 does as a group — decisions that are made collectively about income — and we have our own personal responsibilities. Both we keep secret and while that doesn't absolve us from all the guilt of having a lot of money in a society that doesn't have much, at least it makes us feel we're doing something worthwhile with

Bono: the man at the bar talking

that money. There are still contradictions to be tackled but if I have to choose what I'm going to tackle in a day, I mustn't put it before being in a band making music. You know it's almost harder to give away money than to earn it because of the responsibilities involved.''

Is he philanthropic by nature?

''Giving it away? I think to answer yes would be vain and if I said no? *(laughs)*. You tell me!''

It's an invidious position in a way. Secrecy on financial matters is understandable, yet it can mean the band is left open to a certain kind of sustained, and generally, ill-informed criticism.

''I couldn't care less,'' he replies. ''But I'll tell you what, U2, for all the flak we get on this level from the middle class, we still have a huge working class audience. I would get more flak in a pub in Foxrock than I would in the Ballymun House. There, I think people feel 'well, it's his business'. And they know we pay taxes and they know we make a lot of money for the country anyway. I mean, I don't mind paying taxes though I try to pay as little as I can obviously — I prefer to equally distribute my own wealth *(laughs)*.''

The acquisition of wealth for its own sake, is not something that motivates him.

''I think I've said before that I always felt rich. When we were growing up, the Lypton Village gang, some of us had money, some of us didn't. I didn't notice. I was being supported by my mates, by Ali, by everything. But I'm not stupid. I know how to make money, and probably have some sense in that area, but I'm not interested in it for its own sake and never have been. You know, my old man laughs at me — he finds it hysterically funny 'cos I was never interested in money. He thinks this is evidence of

God's sense of humour because I'm just not that way. I'm probably greedy in other ways — possessive about people maybe."

"I LOOK through the songs," says Bono, "and I see all these repeated images. There's a whole vocabulary there which is virtually my own; okay, I may have shared a river with a few people *(laughs)*. But there are a lot of images relating to borders, death, heroin addiction — I can't really explain these, they just come out of my subconscious memories and say something about me or the way I see things."

From "Bad", through "Running To Stand Still" to "Desire" and "Hawkmoon", it's the image of the needle that recurs. Why the fascination?

"All I can say is that I'm probably an addictive kind of person myself. Also I have some sympathy as I had some friends who were addicts — even in Cedarwood, which is a fine and okay neighbourhood, there was a lot of heroin at one time. Heroin is the drug that fascinates me because under the influence of it, it seems people think that that's how they *really* are, and when they come out of it, that isn't really them. It seems very like what fame and stardom does to some people — sometimes they think they really are the image they project, and eventually they can't live without this image of themselves. Also there is the fascination of death and flirting with death that's also part of heroin use."

Was he in any way traumatised by seeing the effects of heroin on friends?

"I'll tell you — and this will sound bad — but I felt left out rather than traumatised. I felt like I almost wanted to be a part of it, so I could understand better. It's like if you see things tearing at people, you want to try and understand the way that they feel. And in the case of drugs, you're very much on the outside if you're not doing them — it's very hard to get on the inside."

With heroin use happening virtually under his nose at one stage, what stopped him going down the same road?

"In the end I got something better. There are very few things, I would imagine, that can rival the high of heroin for people looking for a way out of a low life. And it was my faith that brought me higher. It *is* a higher love." But was he ever seriously tempted to try heroin?

"I don't really want to talk about this. If I talk about drugs I'm going to have the Customs looking up my bum every time I come into the country. It's a bit of a minefield really doing an interview with U2. There are all these things I want to talk about ... sometimes I'd love to be in REM and talk about Athens or — who else would I like to be — I'd like to be somebody who talks about the Velvet Underground and their influence on us."

The hedonism for so long synonymous with rock'n'roll, the old 'nothing succeeds like excess' schtick that predominated for two decades and more, was something U2 conspicuously rebelled against when they emerged in the late seventies.

"Yeah, these were cliches — and they were daft and outmoded. I think that when people look back on U2 they'll realise that we pointed out the contradictions; that the leather jacket does not equal rebellion, that smashing a hotel room is something the system wants, even encourages — the record company loves to pay the bill, it's the cheapest press they can get and the hotel likes it because they get a new room. Again, smashing a guitar is only an endorsement of its in-built obsolescence like people building cars that won't work in a few years. Destroying your own guitar just means you'll have to buy another one. There's nothing rebellious about that — that's part of the establishment.

"Punk was a middle-class movement that conscripted the working class, basically, to give it credibility. It was about anarchy as a coffee-table concept. Mind you, I'm fascinated by anarchists. In terms of belief they're the only ones, I feel, because I think that the Judaeo/Christian belief in love as the higher law, the spirit leading you and no-one knowing where it goes to — I think that's very close to anarchy. Religion has suppressed this aspect of Christ's teaching about living by the spirit, which is, essentially, 'hands-off motherfuckers — this is my life and it's between me and God and no-one else'.

"But, anyway, where were we? Rebellion. I'm trying to point out that, say in the 50's when sex had been hidden away and not owned up to, expression like you had in rock'n'roll then was genuinely rebellious and shocking. But not any more. Now, Coca-Cola sells the same sex that rock'n'roll sells. It's the same girl in the ad as on the rock video on TV — the same girl, the same version of 'tits'.

"And, by the way, I think that The Pogues have pointed out another redundant concept. I think that the most radical thing about The Pogues is that you'll find a sixty-year old man in a pub singing one of their songs and fully understanding what it is all about, maybe more than his son does. The generation gap doesn't exist anymore. I know old men who are more interesting than their children or their children's children and I know people of twenty-five who are dead and they're just postponing their funeral 'till they're seventy or whatever."

SOME MIGHT consider it ironic that ten years on, Bono and U2 would find themselves working with Keith Richards, a man who even by the outset of U2's career, had long since come to represent the definitive example of the so-called elegantly wasted

> "The Edge and myself left the band for a while, certainly in our heads. But nobody else would have us!"

rock star, a role-model embodying precisely those qualities U2 stood four-square against.

"But if Keith was twenty years old in the 80's I don't think he would have got into junk, he wouldn't have been into heroin as rebellion," Bono counters. "The 60's were a different time and in terms of rock'n'roll it was the *first* time. People were dizzy with it and maybe it seemed the right thing to do at the time or whatever. But it is quite obvious it was the wrong thing to do because a lot of people died. Now we know that, but then they didn't. That was the generation that thought it could live forever; they thought they had their immortal number plates on their car."

At the same time Bono concedes to a loosening-up, over the years, in the band's dealings with the world of rock'n'roll.

"Yeah, we were a bit uptight at one stage, though you must remember that with Lypton Village and so on, we weren't coming from an at all pious or monk-like existence. But at the time when we first started exploring the teachings of Christ and studying the Scriptures, we got involved in something that on one level was opening our minds to a wider reality but which on another just closed us off to certain experiences. But, you know, you go through things."

Was there a point when it seemed like there was a clear-cut choice between rock'n'roll and some members' religious convictions?

"There was that point. Yeah. The Edge and myself left the band for a while, certainly in our heads. But nobody else would have us *(laughs)*."

In Bono's conception, God is not a puritanical force.

"Oh no, God is much bigger than that. Religion is much bigger than any one point of view. It's much bigger than my point of view or the Catholic Church's point of view or the Protestant Church's. But you can explore things and I'm very curious — that's probably my strongest character trait actually. I will go wherever I have to go to see something through. And it sometimes gets me into lots of trouble. I've experienced a lot in the life that I've had and I've met a lot of interesting people whether in Ballymun or in a village in El Salvador or with a nurse in Ethiopia or with a bum in L.A. or with a star in Hollywood or with a Prime Minister of a country. Whatever. I'll listen to anyone.

"It's funny, but I think there is a real lack of understanding about what we are, the band members and myself. We're all either seen as saint or sinner, when we're all of us — not just the band — a mixture of both. A lot of people seem to me to write about caricatures of U2. Nobody shades in the fact that I'm just curious. You know, why did Bono go up to Garret Fitzgerald? Why would he? Curiosity. The sort of thing that any writer has. It's what he was born with. I think it's quite amazing that people don't understand that."

Is Bono's faith as much of an anchor in his life now as when he first embraced it?

"It's more than that. It's the paradox that God is for the Godless. People who can swim don't need a life-guard. It's just that in the madness of my own life I find sanity in studying the Scriptures when I can and if I can. I'm not a big Church-goer and I don't have any formal religion."

The cliche, of course, is that the world of rock'n'roll is a Godless world.

"Yeah, that's why all great rock'n'roll music comes up against God I suppose. That's why Prince, that's why Bob Dylan, that's why Marvin Gaye, that's why Elvis, that's why Jerry Lee Lewis, that's why Patti Smith, that's why B.B. King, that's why Van Morrison, that's why U2, probably that's why Pete Townshend — in some ways this is what probably separates pop music from rock'n'roll. I mean rock'n'roll is about sex and pop music is supposed to be about sex too isn't it? So what's the difference? Is it that rock'n'roll is a bit bigger than that? It seems to explore more. I used to think we were the odd ones out. Now I realise that our generation *is* the blank generation. And we're not the freaks. We're totally in line with all these artists and maybe this explains the reason why we go back to them."

Bono's avowed belief in an all-loving God remains unshaken by the immense problems facing humanity.

"I can't understand how people could blame starvation and famine on God. That's to suggest we live in God's world but I don't think that *this* is the world God created. This is the world *we* created and sickness is a part of it. I believe that God inspires the minds of men *towards* medicine and towards advances that can inoculate a whole world. You know, there's enough food in the world to feed everybody — don't blame God for the fact that we don't share it out. That's something that I got over very early on — the idea of how *could* he.

"At the same time I don't expect this pie in the sky when you die stuff. My favourite line of prayer is 'Thy Kingdom come on earth as it is in Heaven'. I want it all and I want it now. Heaven on earth now — let's have a bit of that. But religions won't buy into that."

Because they're primarily interested in power?

"Well, to me faith in Jesus Christ that is not aligned with social justice, that is not aligned with the poor — it's nothing. How can you read the Gospel of Luke the physician and call yourself a Christian and have health cuts? How can you not work towards the ends of social justice?

"One thing I think people forget is how radical Christ was. People were put to death for the idea that all men were created equal, which meant essentially that Jewish peasants were equal to Roman emperors. That was radical. And to me, there's nothing

more radical or revolutionary than love — the love two people have for each other for instance. Because it's so hard to find. My version of love is not soft, it's hard. You know, the Christ I read about in the Gospels is steel not straw."

Bono acknowledges that, though not at all enamoured of organised religion — which he considers "almost entirely a betrayal" of the teachings of Christ — there are certain ceremonial and symbolic aspects which he finds attractive.

"There are some interesting symbols going on like that of baptism, immersion in water," he observes. "I find generally that I'm attracted to images that have a double meaning like fire which can be destructive or a sign of life or the desert which symbolises a lack of living things yet where things can become clear and there's no obstruction. But I think you should take what you want and leave the rest. Everyone is trying to find their own way in the world and in terms of the way you live your life and religion and all that, it's between you and God. It's nobody else's business. And can we change the subject now please? *(laughs)*."

One last observation: for a lot of people, religious faith seems to be not so much a source of inspiration as a simple refuge from the storm, something to fall back on at times of crisis.

"My vision of love is not soft, it's hard. The Christ I read about in the Gospels is steel not straw."

"Well I've used God as a drug sometimes, when I was troubled, and when I'm out of trouble I've walked away from him. But to me it's been more of a source of pain because it's affected the way I see the world and, essentially, it's been the matchsticks that keep my eyes open and stop me from shutting out the things I see around me."

Were it not for his faith, would he, in rock'n'roll terms, have burned out a long time ago?

"It's probable that a person with my kind of personality would have. But, you know, I can't say for sure. I'm nearly burnt out as it is and I *have* faith."

THE NIGHT grows old and, by now, Bono has a guitar on his lap, quietly plucking the strings as the conversation moves towards a conclusion. At this late hour, talking about anchors in his life, it seems natural, if not a little intrusive, to enquire about his long-time relationship with Alison. "Well I just love women," he grins. "I love women, they're definitely the stronger sex. Some of my best friends are women. Some of my best friends dress up as women too *(laughs)*."

Why does he see women as stronger?

"In their discipline, in terms of the level of pain they can take before they cry out. That they can go through the pain of childbirth at all is remarkable to me. I just have a real respect for women and I suppose the woman I respect most of all happens to be my wife. And she is definitely the better half. She just is. She is smarter, more secure, much more disciplined, has things in much better perspective… you know, the list goes on.''

Sounds like Bono's pretty much of a write-off then!

''*(Laughs)* I dunno! When I say smarter that does not mean that I'm dumb. Not as smart, in this case, could still be *very* smart *(laughs)*.''

It's the most cliched of showbiz questions, but has Bono's success, and the life-style it entails, placed a strain on the marriage?

''If it had I wouldn't tell you,'' he replies evenly. ''I wouldn't.''

Does it piss him off that that kind of interest exists, that the press will want to take photos of Ali and so on?

''No, but it might piss Ali off,'' he responds. ''And this is one person who wishes to make it on her own, who was never *my* girlfriend and she's not *my* wife…''

As in chattel, possession…?

''Yes. Thank you, Liam.''

Is he at all interested in the idea of having a child?

''I probably have a hundred of them — oops, did I say that!!?'' he laughs. ''But yeah, I probably need a child, somebody else to look after me. Ali's getting fed up with the job…''

Some people speak of a very strong paternal instinct but Bono doesn't reckon he has it. Or at least not yet. ''Some people say I'm gonna get it but I don't know. I really like The Edge's kids and my brother's family have helped me to figure it out a little bit. I think I've decided I like children who like me!''

There's an enormous responsibility involved.

''Yeah, I'm big on that. There is a side of rock'n'roll which can give you a way out of facing up to responsibilities and even growing up — just becoming a *man*. I suppose, indirectly, I have a lot of responsibilities to a lot of people whose lives depend on U2 — so one more maybe wouldn't make that much difference! But I hope that if I do have a child, the child will be a lot more at ease than I was with his world or her world.''

We're nearly there. It seems the right moment to ask The Big Question. We'd talked for a bit about ''I Still Haven't Found What I'm Looking For'', Bono observing that the reason the song struck such a deep, popular chord was because it concerned ''the truth of most people's experiences''. But can he define in any concrete way what it is he's looking for?

''Oh that was Edge's phrase,'' he replies. ''Edge said it and I wrote the song around it. One thing I know and I must say this to you…Coca Cola is *not* it *(laughs)*.''

THE MASTER tapes of ''Rattle And Hum'' may still be warm to the touch but already, Bono reveals, U2 are doing the groundwork for their first album of the nineties. ''If people didn't like 'Rattle And Hum', they won't like what's coming,'' he asserts, ''I don't mean that in musical terms — I mean that we're going to continue to put out records in that kind of way.

''I think a lot of people who don't like the record, and a lot of people who don't like U2, actually haven't listened to U2. It tends to be that they hear a record on the radio or someplace else. But we've started to make records now for ourselves and for our own audience who *do* listen very carefully to our records and who do spot all the subtleties. So that's really it.

''Basically, we're the Grateful Dead of the 90's!''.

I STILL HAVEN'T FOUND
December 1988

While the entity that is U2

continues to be the dominant

focus in the creative lives of

its four members, away from

WITH AND WITHOUT U2

the band, Bono, The Edge,

Adam and Larry have all

indulged in extra-curricular

activities, bringing them – and

their music – into contact

with such legends as Bob

Dylan, Robbie Robertson,

Keith Richards, and Roy

Orbison, By Dermot Stokes

THE PHOENIX Bar in Cork on a hot sweaty Thursday night, and Robbie Robertson's "Testimony" pounds out of the speakers, all beef and brass and gospel funk, and suddenly you remember, that's Larry Mullen on the drums, Adam Clayton on bass, The Edge chopping stevecropperly on guitar, and Bono's voice gospelwailing, all of them weaving in and out of the rhythms and the brass lines as though to the manner born. The whole bar chugs to the mighty pulse. This wheel's on fire. Turned full circle...

Cut back to the summer of 1981, U2 having just returned from one of their early tours of the States. Yours truly was upstairs in Bewleys, nursing a black coffee and reassembling some fragments of the previous night when Bono entered the room, on his way to meet some new American friends who'd made the pilgrimage.

We wound up talking for an hour, about America, about American music and about the contrast between the young bands of the era who had largely come to music anew, learning their instruments on the run, as they attempted to assemble an idiom that reflected their own experience, and their older counterparts whose music encompassed a range of traditions, but had lost the

freshness and fire that was so evident in a band like U2. We also talked of God and the vocal affirmation most manifest in gospel music.

Typically, Bono wanted it all. To be himself in U2, learning as he and they went, but also to understand the roots, to absorb them into his own canon. He hadn't listened to much roots material at the time, so I promised to put a tape together of some of music's finer moments.

In the way of these things it was some time before the tape was ready, and I delivered it during the recording of "War". "I'm going in there in an hour to record a very heavy song, and I don't know what I'm going to do on it yet," said Bono as we settled down to listen to the tape. The song in question was "Sunday Bloody Sunday".

The stuff on the tape was culled from a whole bunch of sources, and included tracks like "Trouble In My Way", a stunning gospel performance by the Swan Silvertones, "Dark Was The Night, Cold Was The Ground" by Blind Willie Johnson ("Slide Guitar! Wait till the Edge hears this!"), "Jesus On The Mainline" from Ry Cooder's live "Showtime" album, stuff by

Muddy Waters, Louis Jordan, bits of country, soul and folk...

Later that day "Sunday Bloody Sunday" was recorded and the "War" album was well and truly on its way. The big wheel kept on turning. The band hit the road again on the "War" tour that eventually wound up at Red Rock, the video of which — by capturing their power for mass consumption in passionate close-up — elevated them to the front rank of live acts. Even then, the desire to broaden their musical canvas was in evidence, in the rather odd inclusion of a chunk of the Steven Sondheim MOR classic "Send In The Clowns" during "Electric Co", a musical quirk which is captured live on "Under A Blood Red Sky".

It was to be a chastening initial foray into the world of cover versions — with the release of the video, and the six-track live album in the United States, the band were sued for royalties by Sondheim's publishing company, who eventually won the case.

A costly experience, it would not, however, deter the band from pursuing the policy of digging deeper into the music's past.

AFTER "UNDER A Blood Red Sky", U2 began a rethink. For their next album, "The Unforgettable Fire", they brought in Brian Eno and Daniel Lanois to handle production and engineering duties. It is usually assumed of the former that he represented a Europeward move, given the normal association between the name Eno and European-styled avant-garde music. Not so simple. Eno is a musicologist by disposition, with a wide ranging interest in all areas of ethnic as well as contemporary music.

"You really ought to meet Eno", was Bono's introductory remark when we met at Slane during the Bob Dylan concert there, "he's got the most amazing gospel collection." In fact the association with Eno and Lanois was part of a wider change of bearings which U2 were going through and which involved at least the temporary abandonment of formal recording studio facilities; for "The Unforgettable Fire" the band had taken over large sections of Slane Castle, into which a mobile studio was wheeled, thus beginning their shift to the "live" approach to recording which has subsequently become a trademark.

The band's temporary residence at Slane meant that the venue was like a second home to the singer at the time of Dylan's visit and he became involved in the thick of the action a couple of times during the day. Initially he went backstage to interview Dylan for *Hot Press:* both had been intrigued by the idea when it was mooted first. In the event, the cub reporter actually confronted two of the cagiest and most practised media gameplayers in music, Dylan being accompanied by an unexpected associate in Van Morrison.

That pair do not always like to give much away, and the

"Dylan asked me if I knew 'Blowin' In The Wind' and I said 'sure.' But onstage I realised that while I knew the song I didn't know the words... "

published results give a fair impression of the sometimes awkward and often humorous encounter that ensued, with Bono winging it, filling the gaps with freewheeling associations, and in the end almost out-talking the interviewees.

But Dylan seems to have been engaged. On his way back to the stage for an encore he passed Bono, who later recalled the occasion: "He asked me if I knew 'Blowin' In The Wind' and I said, 'Sure. Everybody knows it.' But on stage, when he threw a verse at me to sing, I realised that, while I know the song, I don't know the words... "

So he made them up. To unsympathetic ears it might have been a travesty but to the rest of us that verse lasted forever, with all the spinetingling sense of possible doom that accompanies a highwire act, as Bono wrestled with the song's meaning and let his feelings flow in a torrent of words and emotion. It was an occasion when he seemed exposed and vulnerable — but one on which his ability to give something extra, even in the most difficult of circumstances, was also established beyond dispute.

In some ways that unplanned live collaboration saw Bono cross the great divide in musical terms. If punk, and the inheritance of its do-it-yourself philosophy to which U2 had been privy, involved a rejection of established rock heroes and the legacy of the sixties and seventies, then Bono was re-writing these rules in stepping on stage at Slane and trading vocal licks with Dylan — a man who was old enough to be his father. With the one gesture he was also staking a claim to credibility with a new audience, those for whom tribal allegiances were a matter of indifference but whose fundamental musical commitment was to great songs, and great rock'n'roll, from writers and performers of any age and any generation.

Almost certainly none of this would have been considered by Bono or anyone else in the U2 camp at the time. Indeed there seems to be little doubt but that the experience will have confirmed for the singer just how much he still had to learn about the great tradition of singing and writing and musicianship of which he wanted to be part. But the important point was that U2 did now want to *be* part of that great tradition.

THAT PROPOSITION would be confirmed with the much-anticipated release in October of 1984 of the band's follow-up to "Under A Blood Red Sky", the magnificently atmospheric Eno-Lanois produced magnum opus, "The Unforgettable Fire". For the most part a carefully crafted labour of love, it was also the album which saw Bono emerge as a songwriter of real subtlety and substance. And in "Pride" and "MLK" it contained the first U2 *songs* which could aspire to classic status, ones which might outlive the band and their time, to become part of The Big Picture, and be covered by other singers and bands for years to come.

Nurtured into life over a lengthy gestation period, "The Unforgettable Fire" marked the point at which U2 as a unit opened out to broader landscapes in earnest — but part of that broadening included an involvement in spare-time activities, with other musicians and in other contexts, as the members of the band separately explored the new parameters they had begun to shape for themselves.

In some ways U2 were reflecting the growing involvement of rock musicians in general in wider social issues. Indeed the band were in the vanguard of this upsurge of commitment, "Pride (In The Name Of Love)" and "MLK" in particular signalling a willingness to challenge and confront audiences with statements of an overt political nature. But these aspirations to changing hearts and moving minds were given a more practical dimension entirely by fellow Irishman Bob Geldof who galvanised the goodwill of the pop industry for the Band Aid single "Do They Know It's Christmas?" in December 1984, in which Bono participated as one of the featured vocalists, and the proceeds of which went to famine relief in Ethiopia.

The following summer saw the concept extended with the "Live Aid" concerts run simultaneously on both sides of the Atlantic and transmitted by satellite to a global audience of hundreds of millions.

U2 were among the bands who grabbed the moment, turning in a show-stealing performance which many see as having irresistibly accelerated their transition to megaband status. Typically, however, they did not let their involvement with Ethiopia rest there. Bono and his wife Ali travelled to the famine and war-stricken country in 1986 to do a stint as Famine Relief Workers, a voyage which resulted in an exhibition of photographs and a book, published in co-operation with the Irish Famine Relief Agency, Concern, to whom all proceeds were donated.

Another excursion into extra-curricular political pop came with the "Sun City" album, brainchild of former E-Street Band mainstay Little Steven (aka Miami Steve), late in 1985. Bono's contribution here was self-penned, a simple driving blues, "Silver And Gold"; with Keith Richards in support playing slide guitar, its pared-back country blues feel powerfully underscores the song's anger and emotion.

"Silver And Gold" was a marked departure from all that U2 had released previously, although subsequent versions have, with the other members of the band on board, linked it more explicitly with the mainstream of their *ouvre*. But at the time, there it was, Bono and his song, almost alone... and still most effective.

It was another statement of growing maturity, with U2 defining their place individually and collectively, at the forefront of global rock. In Bono's case it was further confirmation that he had, in Robbie Robertson's phrase, *caught the fever.* Music had become a way of life.

Few other musicians of U2's era would have been seen in the company of the likes of Keith Richards; indeed in the band's own early days, U2, in common with most other post-punk performers, might themselves have been seen as antagonistic to all that those older generation musicians stood for.

Bruce Springsteen, like the streetwise Little Steven, acted as bridge between the generations. The Jersey Devil was among their strongest supporters from their early days. He and Bono found common ground in talking of songs and U2 repaid the

The Edge with Annie Lennox of Eurythmics who supported U2 at the Phoenix Park festival in Dublin in 1983

compliment with a ragged, but utterly engaging version of Bruce's "My Hometown" at their 1985 homecoming in Croke Park, Dublin.

The narrow worldview of rock music as the exclusive possession of the young was now officially consigned to the dustbin of the 70's...

I T   W A S   around the same time that Bono recorded his contribution to Clannad's "Macalla" album, released in 1985. The track was "In A Lifetime", which during 1989 enjoyed a second lease of life in the UK and Irish singles charts. At the time Ciaran O'Braonáin of Clannad expressed amazement at Bono's brilliantly empathetic reading of the song: it wasn't so much the quality of the vocal performance itself, which is exceptional by any standards, as the sureness of the U2 singer's instincts, which enabled him to put it down almost instantly.

"He was in the next studio, and we asked if he'd like to try a vocal, and he said sure," Ciaran recalled, "and he just walked in, listened through it, got the hang of it, and did it. Just like that."

The song's renewed success affords us an opportunity to recognise afresh the still-young Bono's vocal assurance, his combination of passion and technique on what is, in fact, a comparatively complex song.

Meanwhile The Edge was also branching out again, this time for the soundtrack to the film "Captive", released in 1986. Three years earlier he'd collaborated with Jah Wobble and Holger Czukay on the mini-album "Snake Charmer", but "Captive" was a much more substantial undertaking on his part.

The album of the movie is most widely remembered for the presence of a young Sinead O'Connor on the song "Heroine" —an underrated performance in hindsight — which was released as a single in the months before "The Lion And The Cobra". The track also featured Larry Mullen on drums. The rest of "Captive" is by and large, a highly-effective piece of soundtrack sound sculpting; outside the context of the film it works best as mood music, confirming The Edge's fascination with the evocative power of orchestration.

Placing it in the context of U2's work, it is an exploration in the European mode, of textures and patterns. And yet, there is a clear link to the band's development, from "The Unforgettable Fire" onwards. If "Silver And Gold" can be seen as an advance on the western front, then "Captive" is an exploration to the east. And, as the axis of U2's sound moved ever westward, it may also have been important in convincing The Edge that there were other avenues via which he could ultimately —where time and tide might allow — explore this aspect of his muse.

Bono and The Edge were joined in the extra-curricular

activities by Larry Mullen Jnr., who not only played on the "Captive" soundtrack, but also contributed handsomely to Paul Brady's album "Back To The Centre", on the track "Airwaves".

The sound that U2 had begun to explore in "The Unforgettable Fire" was altogether more spacious than the U2 of old, and both Larry and Adam found themselves with a great deal more room to manoeuver. This freedom also carries responsibilities: in this case they had to be able to control the space and time of the performance, and integrate their contribution into the overall sound.

That ability was effectively brought to bear on "Airwaves" in a performance that emphasises Larry's maturity, not just as a drummer and marshal of time, but also as (that most difficult of roles) — an accompanist. The cut may not have had Steve Gadd quaking in his boots but it was a mighty long way from the Artane Boys Band and the Drifting Cowboys — a country band Larry toured briefly with in the 70's — nonetheless...

"There were cars floating down the street," Robbie Robertson recalled. "It was really frightening. Thank God, U2 were up for some spontaneous combustion!"

T H E R E   W E R E   other landmarks along the way. One occurred when the new looser U2 surfaced on RTE's *TV Ga Ga* early in 1986, Bono resplendent in a buckskin jacket, boots and a beard, his newly long hair tied up for the first time in an outlaw-style bandana.

The ramshackle image aptly reflected the character of the music unveiled on a night that was destined to challenge every assumption about the nature of the beast U2. Renowned for the tightness, precision and organisation of their sound, here they opted for a sprawling raucous noise, with Bono blowing an ornery harmonica in a Dylanesque folk rocky version of the then unreleased "I Trip Through Your Wires". A rockabilly-based original with the working title of "Womanfish" was also on the agenda before the band launched into Bob Dylan's "Knockin' On Heaven's Door" by way of finale, with the audience gradually taking over the singing and playing.

That gig was undertaken on the explicit agreement with RTE that it was to be a once-off performance, never to be re-screened. Inevitably, however, bootleg video tapes of the occasion — complete with an interview with Bono and Larry — have since surfaced, capturing a performance for posterity, the full significance of which could hardly have been lost on those involved. Following the huge Stadium Rock success of The Unforgettable Fire Tour, *TV Ga Ga* saw U2 reincarnate as garage band, rough and raw and untutored. But this time round, rather than aiming to soar into the stratosphere, the collective had their feet planted firmly on *terra firma*. They were putting down roots, relearning their trade, only this time as journeymen musicians of the kind that are in the music game for good.

U2 with Eno in Slane Castle during ''The Unforgettable Fire'' sessions

U2 meet The Coconuts during the recording of ''War''

Larry, solo

The same spirit informed the band's appearance at the "Self-Aid" gig at the RDS in Dublin in May of 1986. The set opened with a storming "C'Mon Everybody" and featured "Pride", a balladic "Sunday Bloody Sunday", "Bad" in its most tortured performance ever, as well as a violent and menacing version of "Maggie's Farm", which is to be found on "Self-Aid", the album of the concert, which was released by MCA. Ragged, angry, spontaneous, anarchic — "Maggie's Farm" is all these things and more, with its mocking references to "Old MacDonald's Farm" and its furious surges and declamations on Chernobyl and Sellafield, underscored by the rumbling rhythm section and The Edge's searing slide guitar.

It is a performance of power, intensity and passion that's well worth hunting down in its recorded form.

U2 have seldom been so naked.

"THE UNFORGETTABLE Fire", according to the credits was "produced/engineered by Eno/Lanois." Its successor marked a subtle shift: it was "produced by Daniel Lanois and Brian Eno."

The implied elevation of Lanois in the overall scheme of things was significant. Lanois leans towards a more rough and ready style, and was instrumental in the band's rejection of the clinical studio environment from "The Unforgettable Fire", through "The Joshua Tree", and on to "Rattle And Hum". He was also co-producer of the solo album by his fellow Canadian, former Band guitarist Robbie Robertson, in which U2 became involved...

Robertson arrived in Dublin at the end of August 1986, in the middle of Hurricane Charlie. "There were cars floating down the streets," he recalled in a *Hot Press* interview with Declan Lynch, "... it was really frightening. Thank God these guys (U2) were up for some spontaneous combustion!"

Robertson admitted that he wasn't prepared for the exercise because he had been too busy writing the score for the film "The Color Of Money". "I had one little clue, inspired by a song I heard by Mahalia Jackson when I was a kid, called 'Didn't It Rain, Children'. I put it on a tape with Daniel Lanois — just a tom-tom and a guitar playing this groove, and it had something.

"I also had a tape of a thing that Gil Evans wrote for 'The Color Of Money'. So I put that down on tape, and thought there was something about it I liked. It's got this kind of bizarre, trance-like throb.

"Then I had a few scraps of paper with stuff written on them, and when I got there, their enthusiasm was just so fantastic. They were so great at rising to the occasion. Saying 'let's jump all over it' and 'let's hit it every way until we get it'."

The two tracks recorded with Robertson worked well in the context of the album, yet maintained the integrity of U2's sound, a tribute to Lanois' production mastery. Of the two tracks, "Testimony" is the more successful, working the brass riff originally composed for "The Color Of Money" into a dense, powerful, blockbuster of a soul stomper.

The other side yields up "Sweet Fire Of Love" where, it's fair to say, the former Band leader meets U2, and youth too, half way. While this is not as interesting a track, it features Bono more prominently in an effective vocal part which shifts smoothly between harmony and counterpoint.

Robbie Robertson's eponymous album was not finally released until the latter half of 1987. The same year saw the release of U2's fifth studio album, "The Joshua Tree", which signalled an emphatic shift towards an exploration of the enigma of America.

Before they hit the road, however, they repaid a debt to their own roots — this time through an American-style folk ballad. When RTE's *The Late Late Show* presented a 25th anniversary tribute to folk scene veterans, The Dubliners, U2 played an impassioned version of "Springhill Mining Disaster", learned from the singing of one of Bono's spiritual forebears, the late Luke Kelly, a founder member — insofar as such an animal existed! — of The Dubliners, who had died not so long previously of a brain haemorrhage.

Kelly was a great and garrulous artist, never short of an opinion and never wanting for a song or poem. He was full of curiosity and hungry for new challenges, like appearing in theatre and playing with rock bands. He was politically committed too, and notably generous, both with money, being a patron of the arts, and with praise, for those whose efforts were made with sincerity and what that era unblushingly called soul.

The video of that *Late Late Show* is available on general release, and repeated viewings reveal an authority and assurance to U2's performance, and an empathy with the genre that make marked contrast with Bono's youthful exuberance, onstage with Bob Dylan at Slane a few short years before.

Against a stark, sparse backdrop, Bono recounts the song's story of greed and exploitation with passion and commitment. Unburdened of the trappings of rock'n'roll, the voice can come into its own, a wonderfully powerful instrument delivering a simple folk song with devastating power.

Quite clearly, U2 were beginning to take command of the roots they'd been digging through...

IN SOME ways, all of these extra-curricular activities found their logical culmination in "Rattle And Hum", the album on which U2 officially explored the musical continent of America. Throughout the tour which became the album and the film, they'd endeavoured to connect with the great tradition, not just by seeing and listening, but also by *doing*.

Unwinding after gigs in bars and hotels they were prone to adopting the guise of The Dalton Brothers, a kick-ass country combo. But it wasn't all played strictly for high jinks. Reflecting their increasing fascination with the sources of the music's primal power, they journeyed to Memphis to record in Sun Studios with Cowboy Jack Clement and Dave Ferguson, in the room where all the great hillbilly cats turned the rootstocks of blues and bluegrass and country into the heat of rock'n'roll. Not just for tourist nostalgia either: now they would know how those guys *got* that sound. And in a similar vein they recorded "God Part II" with Jimmy Iovine, who had himself worked with John Lennon on his solo album.

They also played a host of cover versions drawn from different sources and eras: "Stand By Me", "C'mon Everybody", the furious upstanding version of The Beatles' "Helter Skelter" which features on the album and a decidedly ropey unrehearsed once-off of Dylan's "All Along The Watchtower". Add in the joyous version of the old Love Affair hit "Everlasting Love" and the classic "Unchained Melody" (both recorded in Dublin's STS Studios and found on the flip side of "All I Want Is You") and you begin to get a full picture of the magpie instincts which have begun to prevail in U2, where any and every aspect of popular music's rich heritage is seen as a potential source of inspiration.

For "Rattle And Hum" also found U2 exploring forms: there is the homage to Billie Holiday on "Angel Of Harlem"; an Irish transportation ballad — The Edge's plaintive "Van Diemen's Land"; and, most triumphantly, an exhilarating gospel version of "I Still Haven't Found What I'm Looking For."

Part of the excitement of these explorations was finding it happening right beside you: "Rattle And Hum" records Bono's palpable joy at the impact of the New Voices Of Freedom on this latter track, but he also refers to "hearing the horns breathe", to that urgent and immediate and utterly *live* approach to recording which the band have come around to.

And then there are the collaborations: with Bob Dylan on the lonesome campfire ballad "Love Rescue Me", and with the king of the blues, BB King, on the rich, swaggering "When Love Comes To Town". On the basis of performances like these, by "Rattle And Hum" U2 have attained that plateau where they can reach out and successfully embrace other forms of music and ideas — often without guile or artifice or apparent sense of purpose, but always with intense curiosity and commitment. IF ''TESTIMONY'' saw U2 riding the crest of a pounding, raunchy soul rhythm, another collaboration reveals a different kind of authority. Perhaps the pinnacle of U2's recent explorations

is the beautiful love song "She's A Mystery To Me", written by Bono and The Edge for the late Roy Orbison, and produced for Orbison's "Mystery Girl" album by Bono.

It ties in with Bono's work with T-Bone Burnett — they co-wrote "Having A Wonderful Time, Wish You Were Her" for the long fellow's album, "Beyond The Trapdoor", and "Purple Heart" for his last LP "Talking Animals", on which Bono also gets a vocal credit — in that an aspect of the U2 singer's ambition in relation to songwriting has been to escape from the specifics of band composition. He wants to write songs that transcend time and place — classic songs. He talks of writing for Nina Simone and Willie Nelson. He says he'd love to write a song for Frank Sinatra. The Orbison opus whets the appetite for what's to come...

> **"Uncluttered, literate, intense and classic, 'She's A Mystery To Me' is the perfect torch song for the greatest torch singer in rock'n'roll."**

Uncluttered, literate, intense and, yes, classic, "She's A Mystery To Me" is a wonderful thing -– a perfect torch song for the greatest torch singer that rock'n'roll has ever produced. Its classic lines offer the ultimate statement regarding the efficacy of U2's extra curricular explorations and collaborations. From here on, anything is possible...

And still the big wheel keeps on turnin'. Summer 1989 found Adam joining country chanteuse Maria McKee onstage in Dublin. Bono meanwhile was to be found alongside Bob Dylan again, this time at the RDS (performing "Maggie's Farm" which the U2 singer transmuted to "Charlie's Farm", in deference to the uneasy political times in Ireland in Summer 1989), and onstage at Dublin's Abbey Theatre, reciting poetry by W.B. Yeats against his own atmospheric musical backing.

But the traffic hasn't all been one way. Joan Baez' latest album featured a folksy version of "MLK". Colm C.T. Wilkinson has recently been performing "I Still Haven't Found What I'm Looking For" in his stage show. On a lighter note, there was the recent single "A Bit Of... " by London rappers Kiss AML which sampled the bass and keyboards riff from "New Year's Day" with decidedly infectious results. And then there's The Joshua Trio, currently making a career out of covering and parodying U2...

It's ironic. The group that were once, by their own admission, the "world's worst covers band", now inspire a thousand cover versions by garage combos across the globe —while the fab four themselves, collectively and individually, continue to expand the limits of their own musical ambitions by collaborating and conspiring with the greats of rock'n'roll past and present and by covering whatever — or whoever — takes their fancy.

Against that compelling backdrop, it's worth pausing to reflect that the second decade of U2 is only just dawning.

WITH OR WITHOUT U2   August 1989

THE VERDICT

When Adam Clayton was arrested in Dublin in August of 1989 and charged with possession of 19 grammes of cannabis with intent to supply, it placed U2's immediate future as a live band in jeopardy. Trial report: Liam Fay.

YOU COULD be forgiven for thinking that most of the national newspapers had sent along their fashion correspondents to cover the trial of Adam Clayton, on drugs-related charges.

"Clayton in an expensive but crumpled check suit sat flanked by Mullen in a crombie overcoat pulled over a denim jacket and McGuinness in his customary immaculate double-breasted business pin-stripe," said the *Irish Independent.*

"Mr. Clayton was wearing a Prince Of Wales check suit with a black shirt and silver chains around his neck," said the *Evening Press.*

"Clayton was soberly dressed in a light black and white check suit and a dark shirt," said the *Evening Herald.*

None of the papers, as you can see, made any reference to what kind of shoes the defendant and his two friends were wearing. Well, I can now rectify this glaring omission by exclusively revealing that Larry Mullen Jnr. wore a pair of runners, Paul McGuinness had a pair of stylishly-cut, leather slip-ons and Adam himself sported grey loafers, with black socks that stretched upwards, three and a half inches above his ankle. I gleaned this invaluable piece of intelligence when I grabbed his foot so that our photographer could get a shot up the leg of his trousers. The public has a right to know, after all.

Make no mistake, this whole incident has been a field-day — or a field-month, rather — for the Irish media. Adam Clayton did the press an extraordinary favour by getting arrested on Sunday, August 6th, the day before a Bank Holiday Monday, thus allowing them to fill what would normally have been a drab front page with pictures of the country's most famous bass player outside a courthouse, alongside headlines like "U2 MAN ON DRUGS CHARGES"! Then he unwittingly did the media a second favour, having his trial set for Friday September 1st, the official end of school summer holidays. This was the perfect story with which to finish off the year's silly season.

JUST BEFORE 10.30 am, a huge black Mercedes reversed into the yard outside Dundrum courthouse and Adam, Larry and Paul McGuinness were bundled in through the waiting phalanxes

Press photographers vie with each other for pix for that evening's editions   Pic: Michael J. Quinn

of reporters, gardaí and about fifty young fans. They were barely in the door when Justice Desmond Windle appeared at his bench and started the proceedings. The Judge, who was dressed in a knee-length, bright red mini-skirt, a skimpy blouse and pearl necklace (well, that's a lie actually but I just thought I'd have a go at this sartorial reporting, seeing as everyone else is doing it), seemed genuinely distressed by the number of people in his courtroom and reminded us all that we were in the presence of 'the law' and that we should mind our manners.

In a previous incarnation, I spent a great deal of time in District Courts and remembered them as breathtakingly boring places presided over by ancient men suffering from physical and mental rigor mortis in varying degrees of advanced-ness. The cases too always seemed faintly ludicrous (once, I distinctly heard a judge say that a young man had been charged "with cycling in a built-up area without a bicycle"!). However, there was something about the gravity of the cases on this particular morning which concentrated the mind, in sharp contrast to the giddy media circus outside.

Detective Moody said he discovered a resinous substance, which later proved to be 19 grammes of cannabis.

The first young man before the dock was charged with using an imitation gun in a series of assaults and over the next hour or so we heard of many other cases of muggings, car thefts and burglaries. While all this was going on, however, most of the reporters had their eyes fixed on the U2 rhythm section and their manager. McGuinness was impassive throughout, Mullen nervously tapped out a paradiddle on the seat in front of him and Clayton adopted that grimace of intense concentration that he uses when he's playing something like the bass break in "Gloria". The only person who had managed to squeeze in beside the three of them was an eight or nine year-old hard-chaw with a tight haircut and a Guns N' Roses jacket. This kid was well aware that he had one of the most sought-after positions in the courtroom and he wasn't afraid to flaunt the fact. He made faces at the row of reporters, gave the finger to his mates who were peering in through the courtroom door and amused everyone by mimicking McGuinness' crossed-arms and stern-looking face.

At one point, an elderly couple who were in court to testify on behalf of their son approached Larry and, mistaking him for Adam, wished him the best of luck. Larry didn't correct their mistake and told them he was sure everything was going to be fine.

Just after 11.45 the Clayton case was called and Adam walked to the centre of the court, his hands clasped in front of him. It was immediately established that the intent to supply charge was being dropped by the State, and Clayton pleaded guilty to the charge of possession. Then Detective Garda Michael Moody recounted how, on August 6th, he and another Garda had gone to the car park of the Blue Light pub in Glencullen, as a result of a call from Garda communications. There he observed a number of people standing around a black Aston Martin car with one man, who he identified as Clayton, sitting in the boot. Carrying out a search under the Misuse Of Drugs Act, Garda Moody said that he looked in the boot and discovered a resinous substance which later proved to be 19 grammes of cannabis. Justice Windle enquired as to how many 'cigarettes' you could make from 19 grammes . "About 150," replied Garda Moody. Windle then chuckled and said, "Oh, people are allowed bring 200 cigarettes through customs from duty free — but not cannabis." Larry Mullen thought that was rather funny. Paul McGuinness didn't.

Garda Moody then further recounted how he had brought Clayton to Dundrum station and then searched him, discovering a black Swiss army-type knife containing traces of cannabis. (While testifying, Garda Moody was dressed in a light blue shirt, navy tie and, er, sharply creased slacks).

Defence solicitor Garret Sheehan had no questions to put to Garda Moody. He did, however, inform the court that his client, Mr. Clayton, was 29, single and a musician by occupation. "He is a talented and successful musician," added Mr. Sheehan. "He has brought honour to the country and not inconsiderable employment." Mr. Sheehan then pleaded for leniency for his client and emphasised that a conviction on a drugs charge would cause major visa problems for Clayton, who frequently had to travel abroad with his band. Justice Windle made it clear that he understood the objective of the defence case and then ordered a 30 minute recess so that Mr. Sheehan could confer with Prosecuting Barrister, Maurice Hearne, about a suitable penalty. Garret Sheehan, by the way, was dressed in... Oh, never mind.

AS SOON as the Clayton case was called again, it quickly became apparent that this was Justice Windle's gig and *no-one* was going to upstage him. He played a blinder, every inch the impartial District Justice — unimpressed by rock stardom and *determined* to dispense the rigours of the law without fear or favour.

Windle made it clear that he wasn't exactly an expert on rock'n'roll. Indeed, if he'd said that he ranked the musical profession somewhere between rat-catching and the mugging of old ladies, no one would have argued. "I don't know anything about these singing groups," he announced, with perhaps a hint of disdain, "but I understand that they have some influence on children, youths and — how long do they listen to this stuff? —until they're about thirty, I suppose."

He made no pretence to having been aware of Mr. Clayton's band. No, not only does he not 'like' U2's music, he doesn't even know who they are! Could that have been a chink of inconsistency in his attitude, then, when he began lecturing Clayton on the 'dreadful example' he had shown to those fans who regard him as a 'hero'?

The Prosecuting Barrister next informed the court that, following his consultation with the defence solicitor, they had decided that the Probation Act could apply in this case, if the Justice saw fit to do so. Mr. Sheehan added that his client was willing to make a "substantial contribution". "A *very* substantial contribution?", asked District Justice Windle. "Yes," replied Mr. Sheehan.

The Judge's summing up was brief. He accepted that Mr. Clayton was a man of good character, that he had been given the cannabis as a present and that he "bitterly regretted this incident". He was, however, 'distressed' to hear that the defendant had a previous conviction under the Road Traffic Act. He also conceded that, in terms of drug offences, possession of 19 grammes of cannabis was "on a very low scale of importance" —but he went to great pains to remind us that all illegal substances caused a stench in the civic nostril. He then made his judgement...

Justice Windle may not be able to tell the difference between Bono Vox and a corpus delecti but he certainly seemed to know who he was dealing with when it came to deciding on an appropriate fine. "Would the defendant be prepared to pay £25,000 to The Women's Aid Refuge Centre?" he asked. Mr. Sheehan turned to Paul McGuinness. The U2 manager's eyebrows had shot up his forehead in a look of incredulity but he quickly retrieved them and nodded his assent. The Judge, however, was taking no chances, asking that the money be paid straight away.

The District Justice then said that, under the Probation Of Offenders Act, he would dismiss the charge without conviction, having regard to the character of the accused, the nature of the offence and the prospect of rehabilitation.

So that was it. In less time than it takes to roll a joint, it was all over. McGuinness, Mullen and Clayton were hustled through the assembled throng and into their waiting Mercedes. "Where's Bo—no," and "Gis an autograph," a couple of kids shouted, as a mob of photographers literally kicked and gouged one another in a bid to get a snap of three men sitting in a car.

Back at the U2 office, they'd been waiting anxiously by the radio all morning for news from the courthouse. Now that it was all over, there was, simply, a sense of relief, that the worst possible outcome had been avoided. When the Probation Act is applied, there is no conviction. Adam's record would remain clear of drug offences, thus making the task of getting visas for Australia, Japan and the US that much more straightforward. A major trauma, which might ultimately have placed a question over the band's ability to survive as the finely-integrated unit we know, of over 10 years standing, had been avoided.

They were not alone in feeling relieved. Indeed the general consensus seems to be that — the £25,000 loss to Adam or the band notwithstanding — in a sense, it turned out well for everyone in the end. The State got its satisfaction, a deserving charity got its money and Adam Clayton didn't get a conviction.

However, there was another sound to be heard in that Dundrum courtroom apart from the sighs of satisfaction at a job well done, and that was the baying of an ass-like piece of legislation, which makes the possession of cannabis a crime. When is that stupid, irrelevant and time-wasting statute going to be amended? We'll be waiting...

As the U2 Mercedes drove off into the Dundrum sunset, an old man who had been hanging around all morning and had clapped Adam on the back as he left the court sighed deeply and said, "Ah well, sure he's a great singer. A great singer."

September 1989

Adam follows Paul McGuinness out of the courthouse. Pic: Michael J. Quinn

 *Hot Press* has been acclaimed by musicians, fans and the music industry for its incisive, informed, accurate and comprehensive coverage of contemporary rock'n'roll. However, *Hot Press* is not just about insightful critical writing and in-depth interviews. A number of important musicians have themselves written articles for *Hot Press*, including Adam and Bono of U2, Elvis Costello, Bob Geldof, the late Philip Lynott of Thin Lizzy, Philip Chevron of The Pogues, Hugh Cornwell of The Stranglers and Feargal Sharkey (formerly of The Undertones).

Published fortnightly in Dublin, U2's hometown, *Hot Press* subscribers correspond with both *Hot Press* and each other in a global network of genuine music enthusiasts.

If you would like to become a *Hot Press* subscriber, write to *Hot Press*, 6 Wicklow St., Dublin 2, Ireland.

UK Trade Orders from Music Sales Ltd,
8 – 9 Frith St., London W1 U.K.

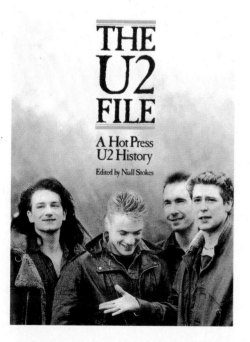

ALSO AVAILABLE FROM *HOT PRESS*

A blow by blow account from the vaults of *Hot Press*, "The U2 File" traces in words and pictures the evolution of U2, from their humble beginnings as a school band, through to their appearances in the gigantic stadia of the world. Featuring a series of revealing interviews with Bono, Larry, Adam and The Edge, reviews of all the albums up to "Unforgettable Fire", major concert coverage, exclusive archive material and hundreds of photographs in colour and black and white, "The U2 File" presents an intimate, critical and entertaining portrait of the greatest Irish rock band of all time.

• Available from *Hot Press*, 6 Wicklow St., Dublin 2, Ireland. Price £7.99 (Ireland & the UK); £9.50 (surface mail Europe & the rest of the world); £13.50 (air mail Europe & the rest of the world).

AND NOW FOR SOMETHING COMPLETELY DIFFERENT...

In the following pages, hear about Bono's top secret solo album; meet The Joshua Trio, the band whose mission is to bring U2's music to a wider audience; thrill to an appreciation of The Fab Four in their native tongue; and, last but not least, discover The Greatest U2 Fan Letter Ever Written! And, remember, don't believe everything you read...

THE TOP SECRET ALBUM

Industry insiders have dubbed it The Thing That Dare Not Speak Its Name. Even the members of U2 are unaware of its existence. It's Bono's unbelievable solo debut. Review: Mail Lackey

B O N O : ' ' B O Y O ' '
(Motherfucker Records)

For months now, industry insiders have been referring to it as "the best-kept secret in the West".

All calls to Principle Management offices about the project have been met with a wall of silence and, as for U2 themselves, if the topic was even so much as hinted at in interviews, they would quickly change the subject to something less contentious. The author knows this from first-hand experience. "Relax, take it easy," Bono admonished, when I raised the grim spectre of The Thing That Dare Not Speak Its Name. "Let's just cool down here a minute," he continued, "let's bat the breeze awhile, kick around a few less *weighty* themes for a change."

"Such as?", I enquired, feigning nonchalance. "Oh, I dunno... how's about the military-industrial complex and its profound implications *vis-a-vis* the crushing financial debts of emerging Third World Nations?", he said pleasantly. Readers can be assured that your tenacious reporter wasn't so easily put off.

"Righty-o then," I parried, "whatever you say, Bo." (You learn fast that it pays to be subtle in this business — especially, when, as I thought at the time, one is talking to one's actual employer. I have since, of course, learned that this is not the case — it's Adam who owns *Hot Press*; Bono merely owns the building. And as for Larry and The Edge, all they have is the minor, peripheral involvement of a joint 51% share-holding in The International Bar. But I digress and I sense my readers are becoming impatient).

So what is this hidden thing of which we speak? Well, at long last, all can be revealed. *Hot Press* has gotten its paws on the master-tape of the record U2 don't want the world to hear: it's called "Boyo", and it's Bono's extraordinary, ground-breaking debut solo album.

Extraordinary, because this was the record that resulted from his so-called long-lost weekend, a six-month period between the release of "The Unforgettable Fire" and "The Joshua Tree", during which the charismatic, lion-maned U2 vocalist totally lost the run of himself in the dark, infested underbelly of New York city, in the company of some of rock'n'roll's most notorious hell-raisers and hooligans. The album's sub-title offers more clues: "Tales Of Shame & Degradation In The 80's", it reads, adding, ominously, "Vol 1". The few intimates who have been aware of its existence from the start call it by a different name: "Debasement Tapes".

On even a cursory hearing it's not hard to work out why. Recorded 'live' onto a portastudio in the back room of Dirty Dick's, a biker hang-out in the Bronx, "Boyo" brings the stocky, ear-ringed U2 front-man together with such quintessential outlaw figures as Johnny Thunders, Lemmy, Ted Nugent, P.J. Proby and Ozzie Kilkenny...sorry, Ozzie Osbourne. Lightening the belligerent mood somewhat, drums and percussion are supplied by all the members of nice boy collective Guns N' Roses.

The result is an album that throws a rather different light on some familiar U2 classics and unveils a bunch of never-before-heard originals to boot.

The opening salvo, the tenacious "(In The Name Of Jaysus) Get Out To Be Fucked", sets the tone. Backed by a furious guitar barrage, underpinned by the last word in thunder-drumming, 'Fucked' allows the garrulous, stubble-chinned U2 lyricist vent his spleen on all those who've numbered him as rock's sole salvation. The opening verse carries the authentic ring of truth. *"They liken me to Buddha/They liken me to Ghandi/They liken me to God above/When all I like is brandy"*, wails the shamanistic, pony-tailed U2 prime-mover, before being joined by his motley back-up crew on the raging terrace-style chorus: *"Get out to be fucked/Get out to be fucked/In the name of Jaysus get out to be fucked."* Stirring stuff indeed.

Next up is "Angels Of Harley" a tribute to the New York chapter of the world's scurviest motorcycle gang. Full of striking juxtapositions of image (check *"throttle and scum"*), the song ends on a real *audio-verite* note as, with the tapes still rolling, a bunch of disgruntled bikers are heard entering the room and demanding 18 cases of beer for favours unspecified, before commencing to trash the place with tyre-irons. The resulting cacophony of feedback, human shrieks and shattering glass amounts to the single most corrosive slice of vinylised 'rockumentary', since Iggy nailed down his own coffin lid on "Metallic KO" way back when. Uplifting stuff — and then some.

Inevitably, the drugs issue raises its controversial head on "Boyo", in the form of a bunch of radically re-worked U2 classics including "(Out Of My) Joshua Tree", "I Still Haven't Found My Stash Which I'm Sure I Put In My Guitar Case Last Night" and, a genuine *tour de force*, "With Or Without Glue". *"I can't live with or without glue"*, snarls the iconoclastic, Dublin-born U2 mainspring, articulating the ultimate, grisly paradox of solvent abuse. Sticky stuff — to be sure.

But it's not all rough and tough — "Boyo" has its lighter moments too, specifically the ingenious "Pullet The Blue Sky", a

"They liken me to Buddha/They liken me to Gandhi/They liken me to God above/When all I like is brandy."

song about the first chicken in space. Then there's "God (Continued On Page 94)" in which the behatted, Grammy Award-winning U2 focal-point reels off a kind of reverse credo. Key lines: *"I don't believe in Dunphy, his type like a curse/he wasn't much of a footballer/but Giles was even worse."* Adding a topical Christmas appeal here the fast-talking, beer-drinking U2 lynchpin also reveals that he doesn't believe in Santa Claus. Unbelievable stuff. Totally.

For the finale, however, the restless, leather-clad U2 pivot returns to band tradition, closing proceedings with a hymn-like, serene ballad. In what is surely his most compellingly literate statement to date, the amply-proportioned, well-hung U2 major-domo, poses the metaphysical-cum-existentialist question of the decade; *"How long/how long/how long/how long/how lo-o-o-ong/how l-o-o-o-o-ng/how l-o-o-o-o-o-ng/how l-o-o-o-o-o-o-n-g/Is a piece of string?"* Inquisitive stuff entirely.

And there you have it. Or rather, you don't. Because there's only one copy in existence and it's our's. But it *could* be yours. Yes, to earn your chance of winning this fantastic copy of "Boyo" (individually numbered by Jackie Hayden to ensure authenticity), send £40,000 — no let's make it £50,000; a bit of profit wouldn't go amiss — to The Hot Press Libel Action Fund, c/o 6, Wicklow Street, Dublin 2, Ireland. And complete the following slogan in not less than 10 words: "Our names are Wendy and Marlene. We live in Melbourne and we think it's high-time that U2 played Australia because..."

Competitive stuff.

• **Mail Lackey**

The Boyo Himself

THE BAND

THE MAN who is called Paul Wonderful sweeps his raven-black hair from his eyes and laughs delightedly. He is thinking back to the days when the crumbling, monstrous beauty of The Joshua Trio was born. There is still some raven-black hair stuck in the corners of his mouth, however, and he coughs violently before being able to continue.

"It's funny, but when we started we could hardly even play our instruments," he tells me, smiling softly. "We still can't, really...", he adds in that humble yet honest way that has earned him the title of Lead Singer Of The Joshua Trio. Looking at him, it's easy to see why he has won the undying worship of more than twelve people. He has the look of a fallen angel, and not just because of the bruises along his arm which certainly point to a fall or stumble of some kind. Paul Wonderful has known pain.

We're sitting at Stonehenge, supping on Guinness and watching the blood red skyline. Paul asks if I would like to begin the interview. I reply in the affirmative, but wonder where the other members of the band, Kieran (bass, whistling) and Arthur (drums, poetry) are. As if by magic, they appear behind Paul, emerging from a white cloud of fog that I hadn't noticed till now.

"Hello Arthur. Hello Kieran," says Paul without turning around.

"Hello Paul," says Arthur.

"Hello Paul, my brother," says Kieran — for Paul is indeed his brother.

I place my tape recorder on the table and switch it on.

"There will be no need for that," says Paul, and hands the machine back to me. We begin.

When The Joshua Trio formed, they had but one goal, and that was to bring U2 to a wider audience. They've certainly done that, with sell-out nights at Dublin's Baggot Inn (upstairs, Tuesdays) leaving people exhausted, elated and, most importantly, hungry for *that* sound.

"We want to wean people onto U2. We want to bring U2 to the old, the sick, the infirm, the handicapped, and members of Cactus World News," Arthur tells me. "We are to Jesus Chr— we are to U2 as John The Baptist was to Jesus Christ. We are but the vessel for their words."

Do you not worry that you might overshadow them in some way?

"It's a constant danger," Arthur agrees, nodding. "A constant danger, and we often have to pull back, whenever we feel we are reaching that point."

"I was practising a few, um... whatjacallem... *chords* a few weeks ago at rehearsal," begins Paul, his voice low, almost inaudible, "... when Kieran walked in and said 'Hey, that really sounds like The Edge.' I just... I just couldn't... I threw down the guitar and went to my car and drove deep into the country, as fast

The Joshua Trio: (l-r) Kieran, Paul and Arty

and as far as I could. I honestly thought that would be the end of the band."

"We live in fear of going that far," says Arthur. "We could even become a case of the baby spiders eating their mother."

A cold wind seems to pass us, and I shiver. Frightened by the turn the conversation is taking, I decide to try and cheer everyone up by asking Kieran a question.

You don't talk very much, Kieran.

"No," says Kieran, quickly adding, "I don't talk very much."

You're very quiet.

"Yes," he says, before continuing, "I don't talk very much."

We laugh uproariously. Kieran, once again proving himself the joker of the band, smiles softly. Suddenly, a white dove flys towards us, circles three times over Paul's head and shoots off.

"That's been happening a lot lately," says Paul, watching as the bird becomes a dot in the clear-blue sky. "I wish they'd just fuck off," he continues, and begins to look for a hand sized rock.

Cheered up immensely by what's just taken place, I ask about the new film "The Last Temptation Of Chris de Burgh", which is in its pre-production stage at the moment.

"It's all set to roll," says Paul. "We have the cast mostly worked out and all we need now is some money. Chris is hopefully going to play himself. In fact, he was supposed to call earlier on today but he didn't. By the time this interview is out we'll probably have him. His is certainly the most demanding role in the film."

How so?

"He's filmed throughout from the viewpoint of a sniper on a nearby building."

Why is that?

"Well, all we can really tell you is that it introduces a note of tension into the film, but we can't exactly say why it's there because that would be giving too much away. All you really need to know is that Chris spends the entire film in the cross hairs of a gunsight."

"But the question is," says Arthur, "is it *really* a gunsight? Or is it something far more ominous?"

"No, it's really a gunsight," says Paul, giving Arthur a strange look.

Arthur: "The film also includes a car chase that acts as a metaphor for the Irish Music Industry. In the first car there's Chris, then there's us in a Ford Escort and behind us both, Mother Teresa of Calcutta in a Volvo, but she has to do with a subplot that really has nothing to do with the Irish Music Industry."

Are you hoping to equal the success of "Rattle And Hum"?

"Oh, we couldn't," says Arthur. "We just couldn't. 'Rattle And Hum' has to be the greatest film ever made. So far, I've seen it the most times — probably seven or eight times more than Paul or Kieran — and each time I spot something new."

"Yes," agrees Paul. "Like the kangaroo that crosses the stage in 'Bullet The Blue Sky'. That bit gives me the chills."

"Or that plague of mice that happens just after they leave Toronto," says Kieran.

Arthur has fallen quiet, and I am once again reminded that it is he who holds the dark secret of The Joshua Trio, something in his past that digs its taloned claws into his heart every day of his life. Something that gnaws away even at his very soul. I ask him to tell us as much as he can about it.

"I'm not telling you," he replies. "It's a dark secret."

I ask Paul if I would be right in saying that he looks to Bono as a help in hard times.

"Oh, absolutely," he tells me. "Without a doubt. I feel the deepest empathy with Bono because I play the guitar and so does he. Also, I have long black hair that I sometimes tie in a ponytail. And, like him, I was raised in a shack and beaten regularly.

"But he's also much more to me," he continues. "I look at Bono like a well. When I'm thirsty for love, for comfort, for inspiration, I turn to him."

"One pint please," jests Arthur. "Fill 'er up."

"Yes," concludes Paul. "He is our petrol, our Complan when we're not really ready for a big meal."

Even in an interview, Paul cannot help being lyrical and he becomes slightly embarrassed at the poetry of his own words. We all smile and contemplate the lowly mustard seed that longs to grow into a beautiful swan.

I ask if they think that music can change the world.

"If it can't," says Paul grimly, "then why do it? Of course it can change the world. U2 changed *my* world. I started going out

for long walks and I began to cure the sick after hearing them."

I tell them that I agree, and that after the last Banshees album review I had written, six Chilean political prisoners were released.

"There ye go," says Arthur. "People think that music and politics can't mix, but I think that's a load of rubbish. Look at Supertramp. They're not political at all."

"It's not that we don't like Supertramp's music, though," says Paul. "It's just that we think their records are atrocious."

What's the worst example of man's inhumanity to man?

"People who don't like U2 actually saying so."

I figure it's time for me to move on to something profound. Where did the name The Joshua Trio come from, Paul?

"It comes from the name of a U2 album," replies Paul.

Of course! Why didn't I think of it? But how did the band get together in the first place?

Arthur: "Paul used to heal people at the wall outside Windmill Lane, and soon he and Kieran were holding daily workshops for guitarists who wanted to be invited up on stage by U2 to play some songs. I thought they were great, and asked if we could get together and jam."

It was the beginning of something momentous. Deciding to perform jazzy, Sinatra-type versions of U2's greatest hits, the band took to the road and never looked back. The result is a residency at Dublin's Baggot Inn, possibly Ireland's most prestigious venue.

"We were a little worried about playing The Baggot," Paul tells me. "I mean Tracy Chapman had played there only a few months earlier, and subsequently went on to have a big-selling single and album. We're not sure if we're really ready for that yet, seeing as we can't really play our instruments or anything."

I beg to differ. The band's talent is obviously only exceeded by their modesty, and the truth is that their music is as darkly mysterious and melodic as you could wish for. They are not the next U2, of course, neither do they want to be, but they could take over for a few gigs if the band caught the flu or something.

"Let me put it this way," says Paul, as we begin our long walk back to the city. "I would rather listen to a U2 record than do just about anything else in the world, whether it's going to the toilet or sleeping — but I also think that fanaticism of any sort is basically wrong."

A man, and a band, of contradictions, ready to take on the world. Ladies and Gentlemen, The Joshua Trio.

• **Graham Linehan**

THE FAN LETTER!

In view of the recent controversy about U2 selling out, may I relate my experiences with the band on their current American tour. After a brilliant two and a half hour gig at the LA Colosseum, myself and some friends waited for U2 in the car park outside. After about 50 minutes, all four band members arrived outside and started talking to us. Then they invited us back to their hotel room, and we had a long chat and some drinks. Then we had a delicious four-course meal and went for a swim in the hotel's luxury swimming pool. Then Bono noticed that I had a slight cough and he offered to pay for a heart and lung transplant operation. A friend of mine also happened to mention that her mother had an incurable illness, so Larry and Adam stayed up all night working an antidote. Luckily the antidote worked, and my friend's mother is now a big U2 fan! ("Sunday Bloody Sunday" is her favourite song!). The Edge was also really nice, and gave me a guitar which Keith Richards had given to him. Then Bono gave us £10,000 each. Not to be outdone, The Edge promised to buy every one of us a luxury home in the Caribbean!

Surely no other band in the world cares as much about their fans as U2 do. U2, you're the greatest!

Sharon Dulux , Wide Awake In Mulhuddart

THE APPRECIATION

For this week's column, I would like to depart a little from the norm and conduct affairs through the medium of Irish.

I have always had a great affection for our native tongue, although, as you will observe, I never fully mastered all the subtleties of the idiom. However, I'm sure you'll bear with me, as the topic is a familiar and simple one — U2. From time to time, like Liam O'Murchú on *Trom Agus Éadroim*, I will insert an English phrase to jolly you up, and expedite the process of comprehension.

Indeed I hope that by showing that rock'n'roll can be interpreted *as Gaeilge*, a few young bands will set their minds to penning a few numbers in the ancient language of Ireland. What they produce in English is no great shakes, so they have nothing to lose, and the Yanks would think they were deep and mysterious. They could start off with a few standard covers like "Go, Johnny, Go" ("Imigh, A Sheánín, Imigh") or "Jailhouse Rock" ("Clock Sa Phriosún"), progressing on to their own numbers.

So then, wish me luck as I describe the wonders of U2. *(Good luck, you great pillock! — Ed)*.

Tá ceathrar seinmeoirí ins an banna ceoil U2 — sé siad Bono, Adam, Labhras agus An t-Edge.

Nuair a seinm siad i bPáirc an Crócaigh, no na Madison Square Gardens, bíonn rí rá agus ruaille buaille, bíonn na cailíní agus na leadíní ag deoch Bulmers Cider until it comes out their arses.

Rinne siad a lán ceirníní mór agus ceirníní beag, cosúil le "Buachaill", "Deireadh Fomhair", "An Tine Gan Dearmad", "Cogadh", "Faoi Spéir Fola Dhearg" agus "An Crann Joshua".

Nuair a cloiseann na páistí na ceirníní úd, deireann siad "A Bhono, A Bhono, be mhaith lion do thóin a phógadh." Agus "A Labhráis, A Labhráis, is tú an buachaill is áille ar fud an domhain. Agus "A t-Adam, A t-Adam, cen chaoi do you do it." Agus "An t-Edge, An t-Edge, shake that funky thang. Yo!"

Tá U2 an-mhór sna Stáit Aontaoithe, san Astráil, sa Bhreatain, san Fhráinc, san Íodáil, agus beagnach gach áit except Albania.

Ní gá Bono aon rud a dhéanamh ach a willy a thaispeáint, agus titeann ne páistí ar an urlar, ag screacháil "buíochas le Dia do U2".

Ba é mise, Seam Mac an tSnort, who discovered U2. Mé féin agus Liam Graham.

Duirt mé don t-Edge, "cuir hata ar do cheann, agus faigh giotar leis an funny shape. Tá mé cáirdiúil le bainisteoir iontach. Pól Mac an Guinis is ainm de. Tá sé an-mhaith ag déanamh airgead, agus tá guth an-dheas aige, so they won't think ye're complete bogmen sa Bhreatain. Ná deoch pórtar nó uisce beatja. nó poitín, agus ná caith airgead ar na gcapaill. Tá mé cinnte go mbeidh sibh an-mhór, b'fhéidir níos mó ná Stepaside, nó na Buachaillí Bogey, nó na Poilíní, nó na Sex Gunnaí, nó na Bhráithre Everly."

Lean mé ar aghaidh: "Ná bí ag déanamh LSD, nó an 'phota', nó an 'tapaidh', mar bhí mé an-chion mé féin ar na rudaí seo, agus look what happened to me. Ach nuair a bheidh sibh an-mhóir sa Mheiriceá, ná déan dearmad ar Sam Mac an tSnort, nó bheidh ceann chapaill i do leaba."

Bhuel, bhí ceart agam. Ní raibh ach inne siad an rud mí-cheart. hain nuair a r'Sé sin an t-uair nuair a phléasc an ceirnín "Deireadh Fomhair" cosúil le buama. Ach, ag an t-am seo, leabhair An Tiarna do Bhono. Dúirt sé: "A Bhono, a mhic. Déan an rud seo i m'Aimn. Is tusa Mac An Tiarna. So for Christ's sake, write a few *tunes*."

Labhair Bono: "Buíochas mór le Dia, mo Mainman." Agus d'imigh sé go dtí an telefón, agus rinne sé clog ar Bhrian Eno. "Tar chúinn, a Bhrian," arsa Bono. "Táimíd ag lorg fuaim mór láidir cosúil le Boston agus Led Zeppelin le haghaidh na big stadiums. Cabhair linn, in ainm Dé."

Agus nuair a rinne siad an ceirnín "An Tine Gan Dearmad", bhí gach rud go deas réidh agus muggalee moocha.

Tar éis "An Crann Joshua", bhí céad milliún punts sa Bhanc ag gach éinne i U2, agus bhí Labhrás in ann dul isteach go dtí an Royal Howth Yacht Club. Tá sé i ngrá leis na mbáidí, go bhfóire Dia Orainn.

Not bad. Not bad at all.

• **Le Sam Mac an tSnort**